AF352591

English Composition
Teacher's Guidebook

Frameworks for Writing

Series Editor: Martha C. Pennington, School for Oriental and African Studies and Birkbeck University of London

The *Frameworks for Writing* series offers books focused on writing and the teaching and learning of writing in educational and real-life contexts. The hallmark of the series is the application of approaches and techniques to writing and the teaching of writing that go beyond those of English literature to draw on and integrate writing with other disciplines, areas of knowledge, and contexts of everyday life. The series entertains proposals for textbooks as well as books for teachers, teacher educators, parents, and the general public. The list includes teacher reference books and student textbooks focused on innovative pedagogy aiming to prepare teachers and students for the challenges of the 21st century.

Published:

Academic Writing Step by Step: A Research-based Approach
Christopher N Candlin, Peter Crompton, and Basil Hatim

Arting and Writing to Transform Education: An Integrated Approach for Culturally and Ecologically Responsive Pedagogy
Meleanna Aluli Meyer, Mikilani Hayes Maeshiro, and Anna Yoshie Sumida

Creativity and Discovery in the University Writing Class: A Teacher's Guide
Edited by Alice Chik, Tracey Costley, and Martha C. Pennington

Creativity and Writing Pedagogy: Linking Creative Writers, Researchers, and Teachers
Edited by Harriet Levin Millan and Martha C. Pennington

Exploring College Writing: Reading, Writing, and Researching across the Curriculum
Dan Melzer

Investigative Creative Writing: Teaching and Practice
Mark Spitzer

Reflective Writing for Language Teachers
Thomas S. C. Farrell

Tend Your Garden: Nurturing Motivation in Young Adolescent Writers
Mary Anna Kruch

The "Backwards" Research Guide for Writers: Using Your Life for Reflection, Connection, and Inspiration
Sonya Huber

The College Writing Toolkit: Tried and Tested Ideas for Teaching College Writing
Edited by Martha C. Pennington and Pauline Burton

Understanding the Paragraph and Paragraphing
Iain McGee

Writing Poetry through the Eyes of Science: A Teacher's Guide to Scientific Literacy and Poetic Response
Nancy S. Gorrell, with Erin Colfax

English Composition Teacher's Guidebook

*How to Survive (and Even Thrive)
as an Adjunct or Part-time Instructor*

Tom Mulder

SHEFFIELD UK   BRISTOL CT

Published by Equinox Publishing Ltd.

UK: Office 415, The Workstation, 15 Paternoster Row, Sheffield, South Yorkshire S1 2BX
USA: ISD, 70 Enterprise Drive, Bristol, CT 06010

www.equinoxpub.com

First published 2020

British Library Cataloguing-in-Publication Data

A catalogue record for this book is available from the British Library.

ISBN   978 1 78179 641 2 (hardback)
       978 1 78179 642 9 (paperback)
       978 1 78179 643 6 (ePDF)

Library of Congress Cataloging-in-Publication Data

Names: Mulder, Tom, author.
Title: English composition teacher's guidebook : how to survive (and even
   thrive) as an adjunct or part-time instructor / Tom Mulder.
Description: Bristol : Equinox Publishing Ltd, 2020. | Series: Frameworks
   for writing | Includes bibliographical references and index. | Summary:
   "This book packages together all the coursework required for one
   complete semester's materials in the introductory college composition
   course. It is concise but comprehensive, portable and accessible,
   pragmatic yet pedagogically and theoretically sound. And, it is filled
   with lessons and activities ready for any instructor to teach
   tomorrow-or even today, when necessary. This Guidebook is designed to
   help the part-time college writing instructor survive the first year of
   teaching an introductory college composition class. Written primarily
   for adjunct instructors, it could benefit any college professor,
   teaching assistant, or student taking or preparing to take the
   first-year writing course. Beyond survival, the Guidebook may even help
   you, too, to thrive"-- Provided by publisher.
Identifiers: LCCN 2019024077 (print) | LCCN 2019024078 (ebook) | ISBN
   9781781796412 (hardback) | ISBN 9781781796429 (paperback) | ISBN
   9781781796436 (ebook)
Subjects: LCSH: College teachers, Part-time. | Teacher effectiveness. |
   English language--Study and teaching (Higher) | English
   language--Composition and exercises.
Classification: LCC LB2844.1.P3 .M85 2020 (print) | LCC LB2844.1.P3
   (ebook) | DDC 378.1/25--dc23
LC record available at https://lccn.loc.gov/2019024077
LC ebook record available at https://lccn.loc.gov/2019024078

Typeset by S.J.I. Services, New Delhi, India

Contents

Classroom Illustrations

Hiking Illustrations

Tables

Series Editor's Preface

English Composition Teacher's Guidebook: How to Survive (and Even Thrive) as an Adjunct or Part-time Instructor represents the insights and experiences of a dedicated and creative teacher of college-level English composition who has developed a highly practical and motivational handbook for teachers like him. The author, Tom Mulder, is one of the multitudes of itinerant English adjunct and part-time instructors who travel between multiple colleges and universities teaching English composition to a wide array of students from different cultures and age groups. More than this, he is a keen observer and gifted writer who has been able to turn his observations over many years into lessons for teachers of college composition and their students. The book is unusual in speaking directly to the adjunct or part-time college composition teacher, providing advice and recommendations that are geared very specifically for this audience together with sufficient ready-to-use teaching material for a semester-long first-year composition course. It is highly original in its approach while offering a wealth of material that can fit well with the needs of first-year college composition teachers and students.

The lessons for teachers begin from vignettes based on Tom's experiences and reflections while hiking in many scenic locations across the United States. These evocative vignettes, which make for a pleasant and memorable opening to each chapter, are used metaphorically to highlight some aspect of teaching that will be presented as the chapter theme. In addition, each chapter includes a creative and light-hearted bit of conversation over coffee among colleagues as another sort of vignette which suggests the chapter's theme. Other features that provide lessons for teachers are Top 10 tips and some illustrative classroom language for implementing various aspects of Tom's recommendations. In these, the author speaks directly to teachers, where they live! About half the book is dedicated to materials for students in the form of highly accessible worksheets and forms that can be projected in the class or copied for the students, including work on sentence combining and analysis as well as topics, peer response forms, and assessment rubrics for a variety of essay assignments. Both the hiking vignettes and the classroom activities are illustrated by photographs which add to the interest and enjoyment of reading this book.

I recommend *English Composition Teacher's Guidebook* for its originality in addressing the majority of those who teach first-year composition as a distinct group of adjunct faculty and part-timers with unique needs. I predict that teachers in this group will find much to like and much to use in this book which is simply not available in any other teacher-reference book. I also predict that they will enjoy learning from Tom as a helpful teaching guide and companion who has very likely walked a mile (or more) in their shoes.

– Martha C. Pennington
Birkbeck University of London

Acknowledgements

First, I thank my students, who have taught me incredibly much – probably more than they know, and who graciously shared their ideas and lives through conversations and compositions. Their willingness and eagerness to try out the activities in this *Guide* humbles me and fills me with gratitude. Their practices and insights helped me refine and focus the activities making them more interactive, incremental, practical, and democratic.

Next, I want to thank many colleagues who live the collegiality that I advocate here. Linda Spoelman Kolk and Janice Balyeat reintroduced me to the value of sentence combining and student- and classroom-centered instruction. I am grateful to the RaiderCats – Lisa Palczewski, Susan Davis, Rachel Lutwick-Deaner, Michelle Allen, and Corinne Cozzaglio-Martinez – whose gatherings to blog, caffeinate, and plan are invaluable; to the Donut Gang – Linda Clay, Laura DeVries, Richard Garn, Mary Kenyon, Theresa Powers, Brandy Springstubbe, and Libby Turows – who kept the office atmosphere collegial and light; to the Lake Michigan Writing Project participants and directors, Lindsay Ellis, Susan Davis, and Kari Reynolds, for providing the impetus to gather my scattered lessons and ideas into this *Guide*; to the Integrated Tutors Seminar contributors, Shavval Fleming, Mursalata Muhammad, Jessalyn Richter, Kelly Roblin, and Beverly Shannon; to Roel Garcia, who is always good for good conversation but is never a food snob; and to so many colleagues who breaked for coffee and conversations around campus.

I am thankful to Editor Martha Pennington, who recommended the *Guidebook* for Equinox's *Frameworks for Writing* series and who reviewed these contents thoroughly, edited my drafts meticulously, and offered especially helpful and insightful suggestions. I would also like to acknowledge Reuben Israel for his skilled designing and typesetting of the book and Sarah Lee and Mark Lee at Equinox for their useful input on design.

Finally, I'm ever grateful to my family, Cathy Mulder, who has traipsed all about the country alongside me, Natalie and Neil Karsten, and Ethan and Sarah Mulder, who ever welcome new excursions, always ready to go roam some new trail; to Lois and Carl Mulder, Ann and Rich Bakker, and Philip, Megan, and David Mulder for their cheering curiosity.

– Tom Mulder
Hudsonville, Michigan

OVERVIEW

Section 1. Trailheads & Companions

Premises, Implications, and Applications for Teaching College English

Section 2. Paths & Maps

Praxis, Processes, Protocols, and Possibilities in the First-Year Writing Classroom

Section 3. Backpacks & Supplies

Essay Materials and Classroom Activities

Introduction

Learning is the lifelong expression of our wonder and worth.
– Roland S. Barth

Figure I.1. Hiking Colorado's Fourteeners.
Credit: David Badias at Pixabay (adapted)

Climbing Colorado's Fourteeners

"You look like you're in decent shape. How would you like to go hiking the backcountry with me this weekend?" Glen, my ruggedly outdoorsy teacher-friend cornered me in a hallway after classes.

"It's all coffee and caffeine-induced energy," I replied, holding up my mug as evidence.

He persisted, "Really, I have to log 200 hours before getting certified."

"Certified?"

"Mountain Search and Rescue. Hey, let's climb the fourteeners!" He made it sound like a pleasant prance through Denver's Wash Park, but because Colorado contains more than fifty mountains rising over 14,000 feet, so climbing those would prove no small feat. "I can log my hours, we'll catch some world-class scenery, and we'll get to sign the National Geological Survey registries, too! You know, the NGS papers stashed inside weatherproof tubes that were metal-gauge-stapled at the peaks of Colorado's tallest mountains," he continued, responding to my puzzled stare.

"No technical climbs? No ropes or crampons or axes?" I recalled his lounge talk of mountaineering exploits, particularly the time he'd kept himself from somersaulting off an ice floe by jabbing into it with an ice axe to check his descent, and then chopping niches step-by-step to ease his way off: "Man, no ice axe, and there wouldn't be no Glen here today. That's a fact!"

"*Any* Glen here," I righted his double-negative.

"Right, no technicals, only traipses," he promised.

"Cool, I've always wanted to go up Mt. Evans and Pike's Peak."

"Mt. Evans? Nah, that's all tourists and townies. We'll start up the Universities and then continue down in the Sawatch Range. We can hit the trailhead after sunrise if you pick me up at, let's see, 6:30 …, 5:30 …, 4:30 Saturday. That gets us off the peaks before any late afternoon mountain thunderbumpers spring up. Your wagon has at least a 12-inch ground clearance, no? It's a 5-speed stick, right? And take along your 3-man tent and sleeping bag, too, in case, OK? It is rated below freezing, isn't it?"

Not until we were well on our way west, passing through the Front Range toward the University Peaks of Colorado did I ferret out Glen's intentions to climb and camp the backcountry in a succession of overnight excursions. Although not a 4-wheel drive, my subcompact car stood high enough, and weighed little enough when the transmission was juggled from first gear to neutral, to reverse, and then hop-out and push to traverse the two-track Jeep route he'd chosen for our trip. He held all the maps and plans. Clearly, I was along for the ride. In fact, these rides with Glen invariably led to spectacular journeys, creating hiking memories of sloshing through mountain streams, crossing saddlebacks of snow between peaks, sighting vistas of snow-capped peaks extending to every horizon – even the pictures of Glen snooping around each peak for those ever-elusive NGS tubes that I've cherished ever since.

A Step Back – Seeking the Big Picture

Not unlike my own introduction to climbing the majestic fourteeners of Colorado, most college students appear ready for college composition class: they generally seem game for what may be termed a *moderate* workout, with maybe a few memorable writing experiences, as long as they require no attendant demands to train, condition, or plan. At one extreme, some arrive outfitted as if for an expedition with all the technological and academic paraphernalia they can possibly anticipate needing stuffed into an over-sized backpack, sometimes equipped with food enough to sustain a week's hike in the backcountry. Still others slip in presuming little more than a casual amble, slap slapping flip-flops and empty-handed except for a phone and maybe some sunglasses or a water bottle. And always there are some who arrive scared.

As their guide, I want to allay any fears and replace them with courage. I want to lead my students into a writing program which ensures that all of these students get introduced to and equipped for the rigors of college writing ahead. I hope to convince them of the necessity of writing well to acquiring a career and succeeding in the work-force. In addition, I want to acquaint them with the value of writing to communicating not only with peers and colleagues, but to wider and diverse audiences. I'd also like to familiarize them with the benefits and beauties of writing for themselves; of crafting expressions; of playing with words and ideas; and of thinking through processes, impli-cations, ramifications (Bean, 2011; Carroll, 2002; Graff & Birkenstein, 2012; Graves, 1984; Michigan State University School of Journalism, 2016). And I want to share the sometimes cathartic experiences of writing down items to get them out and let them go and so release those thoughts and feelings that can clog and drain psyches and spirits. Finally, I hope to inspire them to climb new heights, explore different paths, befriend new walking companions, risk new approaches, and see loftier and broader vistas.

I don't want to teach merely to disseminate data, simply to inculcate knowledge, only to instill fact. No, I want to inspire (Kezar & Maxey, 2016; Palmer & Zajonc, 2010). I want to share my love of learning, to walk alongside my students in every class meeting and see their dreams as well as obstacles, and maybe even assist through writing, thinking, and language in planning a pathway towards their overcoming and achieving their visions. More, I want the freedom to share my own convictions and interests – hiking naturally scenic and urban places, experiencing coffee shops and breweries, discovering and experimenting with creative approaches to teaching and writing. I hope to keep moving and never get stuck. This is my pursuit of happiness in writing and in the classroom.

What is yours? Do you want to share with students your love for learning? Your love for writing? And maybe your love for hiking and nature and the environment, too? Are you eager to connect beyond covering material and marking papers to genuinely attempting to make a difference in your students' thinking, language, and writing skills? Maybe as important, are you willing to share your own stories and experiences as well as listen to theirs – both good and bad – in other words, to walk alongside them as they work through the struggles and successes of college composition?

If so, I invite you along on this, my journey as an adjunct instructor.

Adjunction – Teaching English Composition on the Run

Adjuncts scramble. I like to call it *adjunction*, doing your best to cobble a career or add a class from the conjunction of all the commutes and schedules, colleges' policies and expectations, students' postures and stances, colleagues' conciliations and conten-tions, curricular shifts and standards, as well as the (occasionally comical) anomalies of the characters and situations that can and do accrue in English writing departments. *Adjunction* is the merger of all the pathways that intersect behind us and before us as we teachers guide our fledgling writers in the college composition classroom.

> ➤ **My adjunction story is also the origin story of this book.**

One semester, I found myself assigned to teach six writing courses for three different colleges on four separate campuses. I was commuting among three cities in West Michigan: Grand Rapids, Muskegon, and Holland. In the fall, I called it my Golden Triangle, as the beechwood and maples' greens began to glow red, red-orange, orange-red, and golden yellows. When the brilliant reds, red-browns, and finally the white oaks' rich browns all dropped, and nothing clung but clusters of white pine needles, clouds of snow began to float and blow. As every one of my six courses required a 30-minute or more commute on a clear day, the time could quickly triple when Lake Michigan's prevailing westerlies blew frozen precipitation sideways. Then my sometimes slippery, occasionally blinding, commutes could seem more like a northerly Bermuda Triangle.

Each of my six classes had between 22 and 34 students enrolled, and every one had a different textbook and set of student learning goals. As that semester progressed, I acquired a collection of different-colored canvas shoulder bags and open cartons to accumulate files and folders. This course-sorted gear commandeered my car's trunk and began making incursions onto the back seat, too, as I continued my campaign to keep all of those courses organized. Finally, however, the mass of papers – my shoulder bags stuffed with weeks' accumulations of assignments and the cartons of files crammed and overflowing – could no longer be contained. One evening I found myself out in a parking lot standing in a snowstorm digging in my trunk through drifts of loose papers, struggling to keep them from blowing out or getting wet.

> ➤ **I wanted a useful series of classroom writing assignments and activities that were contained and packaged.**

At one campus, the teachers' parking lot was the equivalent of two city blocks away from the office which housed the mailboxes, itself two lengthy hallways from my first class. Another parking ramp necessitated lowering a window in whatever weather, then swiping an access-badge to raise the yardarm before gaining access to the reserved, underground level for staff, who upon surfacing had to skip across a commons to enter the classroom building. A third had a serpentine layer of parking spots snaking alongside student commuters' parking, winding for miles along North Campus, South Campus, West and East Campus Drives, forming concaved and sometimes puddly foot-commutes from vehicle, to department, to office, to classroom, to computer lab, normally all in separate buildings. While logging so many distances, often in inclement weather, toting an ever-increasing pile of resources, I resolved to downsize my teaching gear.

> ➤ **I wanted a streamlined writing program, one that traveled light.**

From term to term, I am assigned different writing courses. It may be developmental or remedial writing, standard or traditional first-year college writing, or themed composition, such as Writing for Nursing Students or Writing for Business Majors. I might be asked to teach an integrated reading-and-writing course, fast-tracked high school with college merger, or combined developmental with first-year college piggybacked together.

> ➢ **I wanted a comprehensive college-level writing program that could be adapted reasonably within diverse writing courses.**

Once, I taught a class at a satellite campus located in the upstairs hallway of a city high school. While both the college and its site's support staff were especially accommodating and helpful, the classroom's technology glitched with gremlins. On top of that, the college's add-on program continually froze up or shut down. Another room where I was occasionally reassigned whenever the high school schedule fluxed had neither a classroom projector nor student computers. In fact, its instructor's desk computer wouldn't grant me access beyond the high school's log-in page. Not until I had passed the high school's succession of internal IT screenings was I granted access to the school's technology and log on – requiring three weeks to complete. In another of my classes, fewer than 30% of my students indicated on a beginning-of-term survey that they owned personal computers, and only 6% owned a printer. The rest were dependent on the availability of college PC's and printers, and the attendant log-in's and fees per page. At another of the colleges, students were required to take their own personal computing devices – purchased from a list of stipulated brands, models, capabilities, and software – to every class.

> ➢ **I wanted a user-friendly writing program that could be used with technology but wasn't dependent on it.**

Course textbooks also vary. One of mine included an ample appendix of readings to illustrate the various genres that students were asked to compose: narrative, a personal essay, a profile, a review, a research essay. Another made meticulous distinctions among reports, essays, and papers. Others focused on styles and patterns of writing to match the variations in different subjects areas. All of them accentuated writing as a process and suggested idea-generating activities. Most of them suggested a dialogical or dialectical approach, in other words, a conversational tone to writing style and peer review. Many were publisher-college collaborations containing a hodgepodge of chapter excerpts, topical essays, and departmental guidelines and policies. One was comprised solely of former students' sample essays. The differences, as it seemed to me in my attempts to distill them down to commonalities, lay mainly in the approaches they suggested to students: model your compositions upon some exemplary samples, build upon your own self-generated ideas, or ponder and respond to some others' claims.

> ➢ **I wanted a writing program that, without repeating any of the contents of writing texts, could supplement them all.**

While classes, campuses, colleges, and texts were diverse, the students themselves whom I encountered were probably more so, as many others have found (see, e.g., Delpit, 2006; Gamel, 2019; Inoue & Poe, 2012; Severino, Guerra, & Butler, 1997; Tatum, 2007). Students at the downtown campus of one college included significant numbers of African Americans (varying from 33%–50% of the classes during my five years teaching there); Hispanics (up to half a dozen from Mexico and any of the Central American countries); and one or two students each of Asian (usually Chinese, Korean, or Vietnamese), African (often Ethiopian, Eritrean, Sudanese, or Kenyan), or Eastern European (Bosnian, Albanian, Serbian) backgrounds. At the southern satellite campus, students were predominantly U.S.-born and white, with a handful of African American, Hispanic, Asian American, and Eastern European students. On the western campus, the class populations were largely U.S./white, with a Hispanic population (mostly Mexican American) approaching 50%, and one or two Asian Americans and African Americans.

> **I wanted a writing program that could meet the learning needs of all learners, often from diverse backgrounds.**

Alongside their ethnic diversity, I like others who have written about the college-student population, discovered other kinds of diversity. As much as 33% of my classes' membership was made up of "non-traditional" college students; in other words, as many as eight students in each class were older than age 24 (Drago-Severson, 2004). Up to two-thirds worked full-time hours or more (Carter & Thelin, 2017). One to four of the students were veterans or serving in the military (Doe & Langstraat, 2014). Up to three students had a diagnosed learning disability that required teaching accommodations (Gerstle & Walsh, 2011; Oslund, 2014). Between two and eight were retaking the course – a few for the third or fourth time – after dropping out or failing it before (Powell, 2013). Up to four students were second language learners (Ferris & Hedgecock, 2014). One or two were dually enrolled in both high school and college, and another one or two were dually enrolled in both a two-year community college and four-year college or university. As many as half of them had taken precollege, developmental, or remedial writing classes or were currently enrolled in one. Up to three drove farther than 35 miles to attend class. Up to two were taking it as a condition of parole or continued employment. On average, two-thirds of the students in any class were planning to complete a four-year degree, with one-third targeting an associate degree or trades certificate.

> **I wanted a writing program that fostered and motivated everyone's success.**

More than merely catering to their learning needs and career pursuits, I wanted a program that inspired students by sharing with them the joys and beauties of the English language. I wanted one that entertained with wordplay and humor. I wanted one that introduced them to some creative nuances and the dexterity of language, and that encouraged them to write experimentally and not fear trying some new approaches. I wanted one that caused them to think deeply and broadly, as well as converse openly and forthrightly. And I wanted one that involved them in writing regularly and frequently. In other words, I wanted a writing program that could do it all: if it were a multiple-choice test, it would include an Option D. *All of the Above*.

All of these features I wanted for my own course are those I have built into the *Guidebook*. In this guide, I aim to:

> **Offer reflections based on my varied experiences as a first-year writing instructor that together comprise a philosophy of teaching and offer guidance for effective practice in the college context;**
> **Present a sequential collection of ready-made, go-to lessons that can be adapted to any writing course's textbook and student learning goals;**
> **Suggest activities that allow for and dignify the diversity of every unique participant because so many of those that are otherwise available seem aimed at a rather specific, "standard" type of student;**
> **Unite the various approaches of effective English instruction into a compassionate, humane, and ethical praxis;**
> **Provide anecdotes from my experience as a way to entertain and hopefully also enlighten readers by making connections to a different context, that of hiking, and by relating stories about encounters with colleagues and students;**
> **Package everything into one appealing and convenient handbook-sized guide.**

The *Guidebook* is intended to be a field guide for first-year college English composition. It's a how-to book and in this sense a handbook. It's a full semester of incrementally and chronologically arranged course plans that I've evolved over many years of teaching writing and honed over many conversations with colleagues – over many mugs, cups, pints, and pitchers in coffee shops and other watering holes. It includes instant lessons ready to teach tomorrow. It contains a plethora of ideas and activities about college writing that are practical and applicable to teaching students, for conferring with colleagues, and for explicating to administrators. It is moreover a guide or handbook for first-year writing teachers in the sense of offering them a way to think about what they do, how they want to present themselves as teachers and professionals, and how they want to treat students.

Although primarily addressed to the beginning adjunct instructor of first-year college composition, any teacher of English writing may benefit from this backpack-, handbag-, or briefcase-ready field guide. First-year instructors as well as teaching assistants and teaching associates in colleges and universities could find particularly helpful the accessible, pre-packaged activities and assignments to launch and sustain a full 15-week semester, while a seasoned teacher might welcome the practical suggestions to bridge theories with classroom practices to ensure students' deeper learning and collaborative engagement. Some high school students and their teachers as well as college-bound homeschoolers may welcome these lessons to prepare for college-level writing. Finally, those who are looking for a fresh approach to teaching or taking the first-year college composition course could benefit from this guide as well.

Along for the Ride – Teaching English Composition on Demand

For years, I have met new composition instructors, graduate teaching assistants, and professors of English who are introduced to teaching their first college writing course by getting handed a textbook and told they are expected to cover its content. Or they are assigned a syllabus template and told to sequence together a 15-week semester, 10-week quarter, or 7-week half-semester term, and have a go at it. Unfortunately, course assignments and textbooks often arrive a mere week or weekend before the term begins. Have you experienced this scenario? Have you ever had a class that you had planned for weeks beforehand switched for another at seemingly the last minute, as I did when a full-time professor whose section didn't fill was bumped into teaching my class, which in turn bumped me into another? My most curtailed preparation was as a graduate teaching associate receiving a class assignment and textbook at the dismissal of a Saturday afternoon seminar before facing my first English composition class meeting the following Monday morning. I had one harried and abbreviated weekend in which to plan that course. Can you identify with that experience? If so, this book is for you.

Have you ever been hired to cover an unexpected, last minute surge of enrollees in English Composition 1, or as a temporary or tenured professor wrangled into adding the first-year writing course to your normal literature or creative writing assignment, but realize that you probably will never teach that new course again – once-and-done? How much planning time can you invest or spare for this added course? For the short-term composition teacher whose studies were literature, second language, or creative or business writing, maybe you have had no training in Education, pedagogy, or rhetoric – not to mention classroom management. This book is for you, too.

The *Guide* is written for a part-time college instructor, but it could be of value to an experienced professor who may seek some reassurance to attempt a new classroom practice or risk reconsidering a cherished tradition or assumption. An instructor untrained in composition or classroom teaching, a teacher of developmental or underprepared college students, a graduate teaching assistant, a high school college-preparatory writing teacher, or even a college student who seeks a writing prep or refresher could derive some benefit from this book. Primarily, I wrote this *Guide* for adjunct or part-time English composition instructors. You are my *compadres*. This is my humble attempt to help you survive (and possibly even thrive) in your own first-year college classrooms. Finally, it is my heartfelt thank-you to all my colleagues, mentors, and friends who have walked alongside me helping me advance my stride.

For you, this is a guide to college writing: a comprehensive collection of a full semester's worth of plans, lessons, classroom activities and writing assignments to copy, project, or upload for immediate use in a classroom, along with a concise rationale and undergirding theory. It is a ready-to-implement course package that can be taught as one complete semester's program of study. It is also readily adaptable to supplement or complement another first-year college composition course's design and materials. It can function as a stand-alone course, and it can be used alongside any number of other textbooks and established curricula. An incremental succession of lessons, which I have taught successfully in composition classes at a two-year college, a four-year college, and a liberal arts university, is included.

Whether you choose to implement its pre-packaged composition course ready to teach tomorrow, dip into its material to complement or supplement your course textbook, or consider its philosophy and practical ideas in reflecting on your own teaching and for potential future application, I hope you find the *Guide* helpful, challenging, and possibly even inspiring.

Topography – Teaching to Adjust

Teaching writing is like guiding a hike. We college composition teachers often blaze new trails as we seek to connect our students with their course contents. In every course, from class meeting to meeting, we encounter many surprising situations en route, as well as intriguing individuals who cross our paths. A student downloads a Hollywood movie on a tablet to stream beneath the desk during class. A small group decides during break to reconvene at a pizza parlor instead of returning for the second half of the class. A veteran asks for a permanent seat against the classroom's back wall to avoid triggering PTSD by any unexpected noises. Wheeling an oxygen tank as well as a medicinal drip bag still connected to an arm port, a student arrives late, explaining graphically an escape from the hospital ward. Dumping a mound of barbecue potato chips from an already opened bag onto the group's table upon arrival, a student announces, "Help yourselves: I'm already full." Another student arrives with two covered pans of steaming, homemade enchiladas, along with three two-liter bottles of soda pop, disposable plates, cups, utensils, and napkins, for the whole class to celebrate the passage of mid-semester. A final essay is turned in, printed all in purple ink. Another final essay is formatted impeccably in American Psychological Association (APA) style when the assignment called for Modern Language Association (MLA) format. These are but a few of the unanticipated surprises I've encountered in the last several years.

With all of their various backgrounds and differing predilections which students take to our college classrooms, we need to ask ourselves some questions before we set out to guide them: At what point do we intervene and redirect behaviors or speech? When is it better just to go along and get along? Situationally, is it fair to curtail an activity in one class but go along with it in another? Is it OK to allow in our class what other colleagues would not? When should we simply ignore a student's behavior and hope it goes away? Might disregard be misinterpreted as approval or equivocation, and if so, what might be any possible ramifications? All of the decisions we make – and choosing to do nothing is itself a choice – is like approaching a crossroads; and every path we select leads to new junctions that may branch out across all different terrains and new topography, like a walk in the park or maybe a climb up a ridgeline. All have their risks and advantages, from the leisurely strolls to climbs up mountain peaks of fourteeners. And all can lead to discoveries of grand new vistas – and the occasional saddleback connecting to yet another pinnacle beyond with its own glorious lookouts.

This *Guidebook's* Trailhead & Topography

Before setting off, you'll want to spend a little time at the book's trailhead, which gives an overview of its three main sections and a brief description of the *Guidebook's* topography, the terrain covered within each of these sections. Like a field guide or travel guide, the *Guidebook* is intended to be used as a reference, so each section is color-coded for convenience. In addition, *Signposts* in blue text, such as this one, indicate classroom applications of theories and explanations.

Signposts

Signposts connect you quickly to related class activities. Look for **Signposts** to point out where you can find more information about the topic.

Accentuated in blue boxes like this one, the signposts are directional signals to help direct you to related activities or examples in another section of the *Guidebook*.

Section 1. Trailheads & Companions
– Premises, Implications, and Applications for Teaching College English

Section 2. Paths & Maps
– Praxis, Processes, Protocols, and Possibilities in the First-Year Writing Classroom

Section 3. Backpacks & Supplies
– Essay Materials and Classroom Activities

In the first section, **Trailheads & Companions**, I introduce a few theorists and practitioners who have shaped the ideas that influence and shape my approaches to teaching college writing, and I look at many of the sometimes surprising and other times counterintuitive implications for writing instructors and our students. The second section, **Paths & Maps**, sets out the rationale for this *Guide* and the implications for teaching first-year writing. **Backpacks & Supplies**, the third section, is a semester's collection of lessons, activities, assignments, and forms ready to go in a first-year college composition class.

Distributed among these three main sections are seven chapters, each with its own separate focus. In **Section 1. Trailheads & Companions**, I compare teaching college writing to coaching a team and leading a hike, along with some seeming paradoxes that actually result in quality leadership and learning in *Chapter 1. Coach*. In *Chapter 2. Collude*, I indulge in a little purposeful fun stepping through 10 Commandments of Constructive Collusion (i.e., What Not to Do), or going against the grain to produce gains in students' writing and adjunct instructors' success. *Chapter 3. Construct*, is a more serious look at a few of the theorists whose ideas should inform the composition classroom's practices and their applications to writing classrooms and teaching.

Section 2. Paths & Maps, begins with *Chapter 4. Collaborate*, which points out the necessity of assigned small groups for students' planning, discussions, peer writing and review, and other in-class activities. *Chapter 5. Corroborate*, introduces the in-class activities of sentence combining and sentence surgery to target and strengthen composition skills, along with writing warm-ups and individual reflections on what has been learned in each class. The students' writing process and the teacher's evaluation of the product are the subjects of *Chapter 6. Compose*. *Chapter 7. Confab* takes a bit of a breather after all the classroom jaunts, meanderings, and traipses with students for a little mindful reflection on collegial interaction.

Section 3. Backpacks & Supplies, is a set of four Appendices that contains a collection of a 15-week semester's worth of essay assignments and forms, along with daily and weekly in-class activities that are ready to copy, hand out, project, or post – however they best meet your teaching needs. They can easily be adopted and adapted to fit your own composition classes.

Three sets of References are provided, one for the Epigraph Quotations for Chapters and Appendices, a second for the Motivational Quotations for Sentence Surgeries, and a Third set of General References for in-text sources referred to in discussion.

The *Guide's* chapters all follow the same basic format, with the following sections: *Coffee Klatsch Collegial Conversation, Chapter Trailhead, Top 10 List, Lingo, Q's, Chuckle, Quotation with Sentence Surgery, Closing Conversation*, and *Trail Marker*.

Coffee Klatsch Collegial Conversation

Every chapter begins with a brief **Coffee Klatsch Collegial Conversation**, marked by the silhouette of a steaming coffee cup.

It seems my teaching output is directly proportional to my caffeine input. Before leaving home, I fill a travel mug or two for the commute. Midmorning, I often duck out to one of the two on-campus or three off-campus coffee shops that lay within three city blocks of my current shared adjunct office. Usually, I am successful in cajoling a colleague to come along for the coffee and conversation. Admittedly, sometimes I have to prime the pump by promising to pay. Does coffee fuel your mornings, too? Does your coffee mug appear fused to your fingers whenever teaching those morning classes?

Besides reviewing professional titles on our English department blogsite, four friends and I take turns reviewing the coffee spots where we meet to plan, so with every new book review comes its attendant java shop, many of which are within walking distance

Table I.1. Coffee Klatsch Collegial Conversations

List of Coffee Klatsch Collegial Conversations	Page
Such Attitude: Jeers!	19
Developmental Syllabus	37
Hallway Hang Time	46
Writing Referees	54
Bonus Lecture	61
Call Out Cookie Cutters	73
Kidding	87
Sepulchral	105
Pepperoni Pinwheels	130
Scraped PBJ	146

of our downtown campus. Sometimes, I suspect that as many blog readers visit for the coffee shop reviews as for the book reviews. I know for myself – and I think I'm safe in making the same claim for my colleagues – that our caffeinated conversations seem many times more animated, nuanced, and insightful than the conversations we have when confined to a dry office or meeting room on campus.

You can eavesdrop on some excerpts of these collegial conversations liberally lubricated with all manner of roasts, perks, pour-overs, and refills. I imagine that you'll see yourself settling in beside us, mug in hand, ready to participate – at least, in your mind's eye.

Chapter Trailhead

The **Chapter Trailhead** provides a short list of each chapter's topics, as a sort of mapped outline to orient you beforehand. There are also Section Trailheads and Appendix Trailheads which map their topics. Like the map boxes posted near the entrances to hiking trails, these trailheads are included to provide a succinct overview of each chapter's contents.

Look for the hiker consulting a directional sign with the dotted directional arrow.

Top 10 List

Next comes a **Top 10 List** of related applications, suggestions for you to try with your own students in your college composition classroom. You'll find a list in every chapter beside this to-do checklist and pencil with the signifying "Top 10" at top.

Table I.2. Top 10 Lists

Top 10 Lists	Page
First Day	41–42
In-Class Small-Group Conferences	66–67
Theoretical Applications and Implications	81–82
Group On!	99–100
Sentence Surgery & Writing Warm-ups (Top 5 + 5)	124–126
Student Essay Revisions	141–142
Confabulate	152–153

Lingo

Then look for some **Lingo**, signified by a word bubble, with samples of classroom expressions, suggestions, icebreakers, and responses you may find helpful to initiate, continue, or conclude your own conversations and interactions with students.

Q's

Next, **Q's** indicate some thought-provoking questions – sometimes leading to higher-order reasoning and possibly meta-cognitive analyses or syntheses as well – to open or continue conversations, spur ponderings, or invite ruminations and reflections.

Chuckle

There's a brief **Chuckle**, too, mostly for fun. Often, it's good to lighten up the classroom atmosphere, and on occasion, humor can also be used to refocus or reboot the direction or tone of a discussion.

Quotation with Sentence Surgery

A motivational **Quotation with Sentence Surgery** follows. I collect quotations that relate to language, writing, thinking, and motivating college learners. I promise students to supply them one in every class meeting, and I encourage them to select one or two to post on their fridge, monitor, or dashboard to motivate them as the demands of a course increase or the semester's pathways grow more difficult. In addition, I ask students to help me spot suitable, robust and motivational quotations to add to my collection.

Typically, I begin by projecting one of these quotations to inspire, challenge, or simply open our studies with a motivator. Then I lead students through a step-by-step deconstruction of its components – which I call *Sentence Surgery*, to practice identifying the parts of speech and to assist in labeling clauses as well as types of sentences. As we practice sentence surgery on the quotations, I like to rearrange and replace some components to practice constructing several different sentence structures, in effect reconstructing the quotation. Before deconstructing and reconstructing a quotation, sometimes I quip, "With apologies to the author, let's have some fun playing with this quotation a little bit."

Signpost – Motivational Quotations

Thirty **Motivational Quotations** – enough for a 15-week semester if you use two each week – as well as suggested **Sentence Surgeries** for each one can be found on pages 194–208, ready to project in the classroom. Another page of the same dimensions immediately follows with the completed Sentence Surgery.

Besides the motivational quotations, Appendix 3, beginning on page 190, includes directions and an explanation of how I often use these quotations with my classes. You may prefer to demonstrate the Sentence Surgery yourself with the whole class, call on individuals or groups to respond to questions as you guide them through the Sentence Surgeries, or ask students to try Sentence Surgery on their own or in groups, checking themselves afterwards using the answers provided.

Closing Conversation

I offer a **Closing Conversation** to add a concluding point for reflection at each chapter's end.

Trail Marker

As an added feature, **Trail Marker** signals applications for you to try applying a chapter's topic to your thinking and planning about your own classes and teaching practices. Each Trail Marker section includes suggested reflective exercises, marked Easy, Moderate, and Difficult, for you to consider after reading about a topic in the *Guidebook*. You may select just one exercise or may want to do all three. In addition, you just might feel compelled to share your responses with those of your colleagues, comfortably cocooned in overstuffed chairs of the corner coffee shop with brimming cappuccinos.

I begin every chapter with a memorable hiking experience that I can recommend to any reader who may wish to take the *Guide's* extended metaphor a step further by discovering and exploring some memorably scenic hiking spots yourself.

The pictures scattered throughout the *Guidebook* are of my first-year college writing students, and all were snapped with their permissions.

Table I.3. Trail Markers – Chapter Application Exercises

Trail Markers – Chapter Application Exercises	**Page**
Team Coach or Hiking Guide	27
Take One … Take Two …	32
Call Me	35
Personal Connection and Academic Prowess	36
10 Commandments of Constructive Collusion	65
Dialogical Activity	79
Quartets	93
Group On!	96
Sentence Combining	117
Silent Socratic Dialogue (6) 5-4-3	121
Essay Assignments	134
Pick Your Poisons	150

Thank-You

Thank-you for joining me on this jaunt, traversing the field as we blaze a path together through a semester of teaching writing. I hope you find the conversations and suggestions cordial and beneficial. You're welcome to adopt the whole kit and caboodle, using the complete *Guidebook* program exactly as packaged, or you may prefer to scout out those portions of this field guide that support your own classroom practices or supplement your own writing syllabus. You shouldn't lose a thing by cherry-picking only those pieces that fit into your own kitbag.

Table I.4. Hiking Trails – Introductory Vignettes

Hiking Trails – Introductory Vignettes	Page
Introduction – Climbing Colorado's Fourteeners	2
1. See the Eagle – Michigan's Sleeping Bear Dunes National Lakeshore	20
2. Valley to Vista – Michigan's Deadman's Hill	47
3. Pragmatic Adaptation – Northern California's Point Reyes National Seashore	74
4. Capitalize on Diversity – New Jersey's High Point State Park	88
5. Scenic Detail – East Texas' Davey Dogwoods Park	106
6. Rugged Rambles – Southern Indiana's Clifty Falls State Park	131
7. The Extra Mile – Western Michigan's Ludington State Park	147

Ultimately, of course, this book reflects my explorations and discoveries of classroom practices and activities, all of which were tested and refined with students in my own first-year writing courses over more than a decade. Like me, you may want to test and tailor the fits of these activities for yourself. While I've tried and found them workable, on odd occasions they flail and founder as does any purported "best" or even "good" practice, so each may need to be adopted by you the practitioner and adapted to your own students, settings, and teaching styles in order to be successful. It is my hope that you find this field guide helpful and practical at this "adjunction" in your own English teaching and learning career.

Figure I.2. Welcome to College Composition

Figure I.3. Getting Started

OVERVIEW

Chapter 1. Coach – Team Coach and Hiking Guide

[S]uccessful teaching depends not simply on the implementation of fixed steps in an assignment, but on a deep knowledge of the needs and interests of one's own students. Such knowledge underlies the art, as well as the craft, of teaching, and accounts for something of the "magic" of the individual teacher….
– Pauline Burton and Martha C. Pennington

Figure 1.1. View of Lake Michigan and South Bar Lake from Empire Bluffs, Sleeping Bear Dunes National Lakeshore, Michigan. *Credit*: National Park Service

Coffee Klatsch Collegial Conversation – Such Attitude: Jeers!

Kara shook her head. "Did you ever have a student contradict you?"

"Is the moon bleu cheese?" quipped Jimmy.

"If I said it was blue, I swear she would declare, 'No, it's not. It's green.'"

"Why? Do you think she's just angling for a class reaction?" Patricia asked.

"I wonder if it's worse than that. She won't turn in writing, and she just sulks or hauls out her phone when the others are doing groupwork."

"So it's not just you? She's anti-everybody? Maybe she just doesn't like college or English?" Jackie wondered.

"… Or humanity?" Jimmy interjected, smiling.

"Maybe, but it all seems directed at me, like she's trying to become some classroom nemesis. I keep trying always to be smiley affirmative, but she's wearing me down."

"Have you sat down with her yet?"

"…or wrestled her to the mat, *mano a mano*?"

"No, I know I probably should, but she's an artful dodger, slipping in late most days and ducking out the split-second we're done."

"Maybe you could ask her during some groupwork or something if she'd stay after class to talk a minute or two?"

"Yeah, it's not like she's engaged in the group assignments anyway."

"Just one round after class!" Jimmy smacked a hand against the table and raised Kara's in victory. "And our champion is … Kara!"

"Jimmy, man, don't you have some papers to go grade – somewhere else?"

"Yeah, man, you're spilling my latte macchiato."

"Such attitude! Jeers to you-all; here's to mud in your mug!" He hefted his megamug in salute. "Cheers!"

All raised theirs and replied, "Cheers!"

Chapter Trailhead – Coach

- See the Eagle – Michigan's Sleeping Bear Dunes National Lakeshore
- Call Me Coach – Mantras and Metaphors
- Quarter-Court Sprints – Purposeful Works
- Fairplay, Please – People's Places
- Preamble to the Composition – The Syllabus and the First Class

See the Eagle – Michigan's Sleeping Bear Dunes National Lakeshore

Not long ago one summer, I walked the Pyramid Point Trail in Sleeping Bear Dunes National Lakeshore on the Leelanau Peninsula, roughly positioned at the upper knuckle on the pinky finger of Michigan's open palm. Nearly dog-tired from hiking excursions up, down, and across sunny shorelines, sandy open dunes, and shaded first- and second-growth dunes, while working my way among the knuckles and up to the fingertip, I debated saving the Pyramid Point for another visit. *No, I've already walked the Empire Bluffs Trail, and the Pyramid Point can't be any more than a couple of miles,* I rationalized, making up my mind to continue north until I found the trailhead. First crossing a grasslands meadow, then cresting two backforest dunes, I finally climbed the last ascent, trudging through deep white sands, out through a wooded aperture and onto a dune bluff, a clifftop eyrie perched more than 250 feet above Lake Michigan. The deepening blues of the lake curved, a layered navy topography convexed to meet the concaved horizon of equally deep cerulean sky. Out of sight below, voices rode the lake's updrafts from a handful of foolhardy tourists bemoaning their predicament through gasping breaths, as they realized the staggering effort required to climb a dune's cliff face of sand, every step a sinking, sliding, unsteady purchase. Whether all the way down to the water's edge or merely a couple of giant steps sunk under the cliff's edge, I couldn't fathom how far away they were. Northward were the two Manitou Islands: small, sandy cub islands just offshore from their mama bear, a huge dune shaped like a sleeping bear. In the Native American legend, while attempting to cross the Great Lake during a severe storm, the cubs perished, forming today's offshore islands. Mama, grief-stricken, collapsed into a perpetual sleep on the western shore of Lake Michigan. Today, visitors to Sleeping Bear National Lakeshore scamper up and down her steep, sandy eastward flank. From atop Pyramid Point, I could just discern her sandy snoot and bushy forehead and back, shoreside.

The crowning moment, the event that climaxed my whole day, arrived as a lucky happenstance: pushing back my cap to swipe away sweat, I was roused by the sight of a movement above that led me to glance upwards and spot a bald eagle riding updrafts, coursing directly above me. The same updrafts that raised the tourists' imprecations carried the eagle overhead. Had I quit after the Empire Bluff Trail and saved Pyramid Point for a later excursion, if I'd tilted down to look for the tourists, or even if I had merely left my billed-cap stuck sweatily to my head, I could have missed spotting my eagle. But I didn't. So I did.

In some ways, I expect that a hiker creates opportunities when remaining alert to the opportunities of passing circumstances, and those possibilities in turn affect all the others arriving in succession – just as writers make meanings, which draw forth others, as they craft their drafts. The trails for both hiker and writer continually open to myriads of networks, more and more trails.

Even before you pack your kit, before you plan the trip, you have to make up your mind to go. My buddy Glen, who so adroitly wrangled me into becoming his climbing companion of Colorado's nontechnical fourteeners peaks, chose our destinations, planned the driving routes as well as the hiking paths, and furnished the supplies – all but my sleeping bag, tent, car, and its fuel. Equally important, Glen set the pace and encouraged the tone for the journey. Never did he doubt my ability to summit the peaks or to keep up with his rapid ascent. When he sensed my flagging behind, he handed me a granola bar and paused long enough to munch one with me. Then when we had each taken a long draught of water, he grinned and then remarked something along the lines of, "Well, you catch that marmot? Think he's whistling at me? Must be a *she* if he is." And off we'd set. When I balked at forging a mountain stream, he'd quipped, "You watch, these elevated breezes will have our jeans dried in no time." (Actually, they didn't: my boots squished and legs chafed the rest of the way up.) "It's too early for clouds, but let's giddy up that ridge before any cumulous catch up with us, hey?"

As their guide, I lead my students to the summits. Like Glen, I plan the routes and provide the supports. Often, I have to cajole and encourage, distract and redirect to help them along. "Yes, that's the topic we're after, but imagine how clear it would sound if you slipped some illustrative dialogue between the barista and boss in here?" English composition is a mountaintop that looms over many of my college writers. As their teacher, I can choose the best routes, pack the appropriate equipment, and have at hand a ready assortment of encouragements and rejoinders to remark at apt circumstances along the way. "See this white house? What descriptive details do you have to add for your readers to view the complete setting on the movie screen in their mind?" A few only need me to point the direction, proffer some suggestions, and step out of the way. More require more of my presence and supports alongside. Most need my leading, supporting, and assisting throughout.

Before the students arrive at my classroom, I've developed three unrelenting attitudes that have helped me become a successful writing guide: achievement, purpose, and fair play. Relentlessly adopting these attitudes may help you to become such a guide to your students' success in college writing: Deeply believe that every student entrusted to your direction is going to achieve your course objectives. This requires your making an assertive assumption, believing that your students will succeed, and a firm confidence in their abilities to do so. As a sidebar, this necessitates an assured self-confidence on your part in your own capabilities as well. As often as you tell your students to believe in themselves, remind yourself to do the same. You are a great teacher. You are a fine writer. And you keep getting better. If you need an example, go no further than this book. You're the one reading it. You're taking the time, and you're making the effort to think about your field of college composition. You're bettering yourself, and because you're improving, you're likely helping your students grow as writers, too. Not only that, but as a representative English teacher, you're probably improving your department and your institution. Don't stop. You're improving the whole profession and vocation of teaching and writing – just by practicing your craft.

It's good to look up frequently to search the sky for eagles. Often, you may have to look up from the cluttered desk or glowing monitor, or out of the office and away from the naysayers' contraries to have a chance at spotting an eagle. You see eagles when you exult in your colleagues', your students', and your own successes. They are out there, waiting to be spotted – although they don't always ride updrafts and hover right over your head. So fire up that Elmo projector and share your student's especially poignant opener with the rest of the class, and ask, "May I show this to another class, too? I'd like them to read it!"

I like to begin a semester by asking my students to calculate how many English classes they've taken over the years. "Did anyone here go to preschool? Did yours have reading-readiness or prereading?" Then speculate why writing requires so much time and study and curriculum. "After all those years of English classes, why are you beginning college with another? Why do you or your department or the college think you should be sitting here for more?" I ask if they've written research papers, job applications, emails and text messages, poetry? "Are you any better at some than others?" Does the writing that requires more work offer more reward? I tell my students how much I love – and hate – writing myself.

Be a relentless and remorseless achiever. Share with your students the page lengths of your graduate-level essays and your thesis or dissertation and relish their collective gasps when you mention how often you had to rewrite that sticky second chapter. Tell them about your publications and attempts at publishing, the departmental committee reports, and the student recommendations you're asked to write, and enjoy their incredulity when you announce that you blog. Mention your prowess at War of 1812 historical-biographical fiction and your love for poetry that's dripping imagery. And decry the fiction editors who haven't yet caught on to the brilliant nuances of your 19th century revisionist historical fiction. It's OK to say that you write poetry so that you can purge it out of your head to allow you to sleep at nights. It's OK, too, to admit that your poetry sucks. But it's also cool to mention a colleague or two who writes amazing poems – stories, novels, or essays. You may even elicit a chuckle when you tell them that your department contains several essayists – but of course you're probably the best!

Be sure to spot the eagles in your students' writing, too. Self-fulfilling prophecies work on students, as on everyone. When you're convinced that they will succeed, guess what? Genuinely, forthrightly, believe-it-to-the-core-of-your-teacher-being. Know this: Your students will succeed and do better than just "OK." All of them are going to achieve the college-level writing skills required to do well not only in your English class, but on every single essay they write during their college careers and beyond. Don't only verbally compliment the excellent vignette or perfect metaphor they've written, then slam the essay with innumerable grammatical and mechanicals cuts and edits with a bloody red, royal purple, or gangrenous green ink thereafter. Aim to praise achievements and suggest changes in equal measure – in print that's preferably a civil blue or black. Or better yet, lavishly note the positives, and only suggest one or two revisions for the writer to address. Do allow for and encourage revisions. Always acknowledge and applaud hard work.

Signpost – Tom's Promise

At the beginning of each term, I often make ten promises to my writing students, assuring them that if they work hard and continue to rework their writings throughout the semester, I promise them success in our class. **Tom's Promise** can be found in Appendix 2, on pages 180–181.

Sure, some students are ready to scale the fourteeners. Others experience a workout merely ascending "the bunny trails and foothills." I try to take into consideration their different starting points and arrange for alternate, individualized routes to help everyone attain the course objectives (Tomlinson, 1999). After promising students' success, I go on to say, "Many may already be fine writers, so I'll try to help you become better. Even if you write well, I'll suggest some new approaches and angles to improve different writing skills." They'll do well, and after attempting some new risks in their writing, they'll do even better. "Others," I mention, "may struggle more with writing, so I'll try to help you become better, too. You may have to work harder at achieving the course's requirements, but all your extra efforts earn additional merits, besides helping you improve your college writing skills." So, I guarantee them that all can achieve the course's objectives, and with persistence will all summit safely and successfully.

That leads me to my second unrelenting attitude: every activity, every assignment, every portion of every class must be infused with purpose (Wiggins & McTighe, 1998). Make your course meaningful. Try to aim all activities and assignments – all writing warm-ups, sentence- combining exercises, and vocabulary-building activities – towards their production of required essays and assign essays that meet all the required departmental and institutional course outcomes. Your conversations and instructions, groupwork and peer reviews, idea generating and grammatical reviews – the whole instructional design – should all target purposeful writing skills that your students require to write the assigned essays. Besides choosing and arranging focused activities, call your students' attention to their alignment and point out their purposes. Demonstrate how different selections of words and variously arranged phrases can add nuances and alter meanings, and preferably show them using examples from their own writing. For example, I like to revise sentences by changing conjunctions in dependent clauses to form different sentence types, such as compound sentences. "With apologies to the author," I'll announce, "let's play with this complex sentence by replacing the subordinating conjunction here with a comma and coordinating conjunction over here. Look at the balance of these two independent clauses and how they set up two ideas or pieces of information as of equal importance. Listen to their evenness of cadence in contrast to the different rhythm and cadence of the two clauses of a complex sentence. If you want to sound balanced or if you want to give equal weight to two ideas or pieces of information, aa compound sentence will do the trick."

For some students, achieving the course's objectives by writing the assigned essays to an acceptable level may be enough of a purpose. They may experience enough challenge by following a trusted, tried-and-tested formula with step-by-step directions. Others may be willing to experiment with new ideas, such as trying to extend a metaphor throughout their memoir. They might want to branch out into a different technique by framing a third-person research essay inside a first-person vignette. Or they might like to try forging their own way through a writing assignment to identify an unsung hero by interviewing a second-shift barista working on campus, then exploring news articles in databases to research similar stories at other campuses for comparison. When assured of their success, many feel freed or possibly emboldened to take writing risks. With your encouragement, direction, and planning, today's flat paths can lead to tomorrow's foothills and possibly even to fourteeners someday.

Finally, relentlessly insist on fairplay by stating your expectations, grounding students with concrete examples, and clarifying with individual examples as necessary. "A cardinal sin against yourself," I declaim, "is declaring you can't write." One way I like to address such a declaration is with the rejoinder, "Stop! I don't like lying in my classroom. And I'm going to prove that you're a good writer. You watch!" Although I can put up with a lot from students, I don't allow personal put-downs. If a student criticizes another, I might shout out a drawn-out and sarcastic, "N-i-c-e!" Or hold up my palm to catch the student's eye and briefly state, "Let's talk up. We critique writing, never criticize writers – except maybe the ones who are too rich to care." I try to say just enough to ensure a cease and desist, but will also circle around to that student afterwards with a little non-condescending follow-up: "Did you see what I was saying? Do you see why?" And for good measure, repeat: "We need to keep positive in our critique, so we don't subside into negative criticism, OK?"

Relentlessly, I try to use my own communications to demonstrate encouraging yet purposeful critique. "I'm especially sensitive about my writing because my words reflect me, so when someone criticizes my writing, they ought to follow up with some good alternative suggestions." Where words equal power, I want to wield them for good. As their guide, I need to guard everyone's dignity and voice. You, too, might regularly practice slipping off your own shoes, tying on the laces of your students' boots, and traipsing around some in them; then, back in your own, lead with unswerving empathy. Be students' advocate. Graciously grant them uplifting loyalty – as you aspire for them to grant you theirs. Interrupt yourself whenever you're tempted to think ill of yourself: self-question, yes, but self-negate, never.

An unremitting mindset of guaranteed student achievement, purposeful selection and alignment of instruction, and insistent and positive fair play – even before you encounter a single student in a classroom – will help to ensure your success as an instructor of first-year college composition. You just watch!

Call Me Coach – Mantras and Metaphors

Besides a hiking guide, the comparison that I return to again and again in this *Guidebook*, several other metaphors are useful to elucidate the roles of a college writing instructor. In this section, I want to compare teaching writing to coaching, specifically coaching baseball. Of course, you're invited to select cricket, football – the American or the World rendition – or maybe you prefer softball, volleyball, yoga, track and field, or any of the wide variety of sports. I'm sure that you'll find the same principles apply.

The expression *covering all the bases* applies as readily to the instructor of writing as to the coaches of teams, and it may help to explain the patinas of sunflower seeds and chewing tobacco stains where baseball coaches direct their players from their dugouts alongside the first and third baselines. I imagine writing instructors have their own signature stains, too: coffee stain rings and spills leap to my mind, typically occurring on the days when I wear a white shirt and tie, unfortunately. Like a coach, the writing teacher is expected to do it all: make a game plan, train and motivate the players, speak back and forth from the management to the players to the fans, and always be the first to arrive and the last to leave.

Returning a moment to speaking of stains, indulge me by imagining yourself a long-suffering Chicago Cubs baseball fan before the World Series summer of 2016 dispelled the perennial gloom. For many years, I was another anxious Chicago Cubs baseball fan. Earlier and earlier every season, it seemed we would commiserate with one another, "Just wait until next year;" for we had already given up hope for the current season of our "loveable losers." Through it all, I came to appreciate the special skills that the Cubs' succession of team managers (for baseball coaches in the American major leagues are called *managers*) like Dusty Baker can use to cobble together team-achievement from a rabble of individual players, several with supposedly intractable egos. Or Lou Piniella's consummate abilities to deflect the press's scrutiny of an individual player's on-field flub by brushing it off as a necessary learning step, sometimes positioning himself in the glare of public vitriol to shield a rookie. Finally, finally, after the decades of watching the team's ballfield failures, I can laugh along when championship coach Joe Maddon introduces a mime, a magician, or a mariachi band at a game or practice. Besides loosening up his players with the levity, his antics entertain us lately entranced fans. Masterfully, we now ascertain, he juggles a gaggle of rookies with outsized talents across the Chicago Cub's historic Wrigley Field: the dugout and batter's box, infield and outfield, bullpen and pitcher's mound, guiding them to a top record and to the top position, a World Series championship, after a 102-year drought.

Likewise, as students' coaches, our success is defined by theirs. To lead students to achieve success in the composition course, like athletic coaches, writing instructors hold the unenviable position of revealing what's weak and demanding strengthening practices. I have often had to subsume exuberant egos to common civility in order to protect a collegial and productive learning environment for all my students in a class. "Although you scored all A's in high school, sometimes what succeeded then may have to be exceeded now. Have you thought about trying to add a backstory to this paragraph's claim?" Just as a baseball coach may arrange or rearrange the order of batters or instruct a player to practice swinging the bat to hit different pitches, writing teachers pencil comments, select specific topics to teach, schedule work groups or peer review partners, and assign tutorials to elicit the best from each of the disparate class members. "Switch rough drafts with your new partners and examine them for complex sentences. Highlight some subordinating conjunctions and be on the lookout for especially active verbs. Share your best samples with each other." Like a coach, I accentuate individuals' writing strengths, assist with groups' accomplishments, and suggest purposeful activities to evoke winning compositions. "May I share these highlighted sentences with the whole team?"

Good coaches instill success. The members of winning programs exude confidence, perseverance, pride, camaraderie, and esprit de corps that grow and self-replicate. First-year college writing instructors do, too. You have the ability to stand before a couple dozen college students and coach them into capable writers, helpful editors, and encouraging peers. You have the confidence to turn a classroom, your playing field, into a productive writing workshop where students embrace the freedom and discipline to practice writing. Communicate your aspirations and requirements and revisit them regularly with your own teams of rookie writers. Lead so that everyone succeeds. Take your best game to the classroom and insist they do, too, so all perform well and continue to improve. Treat each class of students as a team by assigning practice activities which require collaboration, such as in-class groupwork that is checked individually as well as collectively. For example, you might assign a group activity that requires all members to discuss, agree upon, and write down the answers, so no one can achieve completion of the assignment until everyone in the group has written the group's agreed answers and can demonstrate the soundness of those answers to the instructor's satisfaction. Take pleasure in their achievements, for your success as well as theirs is mostly measured through their accomplishments. As one student athlete liked to intone to her writing team, "Cover our back, all for the pack, no one can slack." Or, as Cubs' Manager Joe Madden entreated, "Just don't suck!"

Of course, unlike coaching baseball, it is not always the case that first-year writing students come to class longing to learn and eager to perform. You likely may have to do some initial convincing: One member in your class may be a tech genius who loves all of the technological affordances for writing. Another protests environmental waste and extolls reducing carbon footprints. Maybe someone has spent a lifetime filled with life-challenges. Somebody is a people-person, great at drawing folks together and putting them at ease. One's a gamer; another's a movie-buff; others like sports, animals, recipes, music, or superheroes. A prospective senator, one loves political science. A future reporter, another enjoys photojournalism classes. A business start-up owner, still another appreciates entrepreneurship and economics. One comes to class with street smarts, another with book smarts. When they share their different interests and ideas, strengths and aptitudes, in the classroom together, then we have a team. And when they improve their own and contribute toward one another's writing by offering suggestions and sharing examples, then we have a winning team. Finally, when diverse students willingly listen, speak, and write about their divergent opinions, experiences, and approaches, that's the kind of team with which we can develop greatness.

Since we teach the students before us, we tailor our course contents and our teaching delivery to the aptitudes, backgrounds, and interests of different learners and their specific writing abilities and levels. While I believe that we ought to adapt both up and down to our students' learning needs, I'll add that colleges, classes, and instructors have specific requirements that students must attend to. Insist on students' success, and don't settle. Require multiple revisions when necessary. Assign visits to the writing lab as needed. Be adaptable and flexible, ready to teach to the moment whenever you encounter teachable moments, and ready to respond whenever your students require or seek targeted teaching and reteaching. Likewise, be resilient and firm, intractable when it comes to ethics, standards, and process. Like the coach who has to communicate back and forth between players, management, and fans, you have obligations to all – and don't forget those obligations that you have to yourself as well.

Here are a couple of teaching mantras leading into one more metaphor, the educational truism, *I don't care how much you know until I know how much you care*: although usually applied to the teachers of younger learners, it fits college students, too. Watch how your adult, college-aged students respond when you make the extra efforts to initiate a personal conversation before class, or how animated they grow when talking about a promotion at work, a proposed school or community improvement, a financial aid resolution or scholarship award, or an essay topic that they are especially eager to explore. Of course, teach what you know they ought to know, but as often as you can, also flavor it with a dash of personal application, immediate value, fiduciary or career benefit, and even a little humor to heighten interest.

Another common expression was dropped on me at a fall orientation a few years ago when a dean entreated the adjuncts to teach less as proverbial *sages on the stages* and more as sympathetic *guides with the asides, alongside*. This expression also rings true to me, especially when instructors do skew away from what may be more valuable kinesthetic hands-on applications or interactive social learning activities to deliver classroom lectures alone. Still, sometimes we teachers appropriately function as onstage sages orating knowledge and direction, and a little theatrical, on-stage delivery can go a long way to making a lesson personable and memorable. Besides, as an English teacher, I – like many other literary types – love the stage.

From hiking guide to coaching, adding a little garnish and some acting – I'm going to tweet my whistle to stop the play and return to some more coaching. But first, I encourage you to take a few minutes to reflect about how teaching composition is like guiding hikers and coaching team players by comparing the two.

Trail Marker – Team Coach or Hiking Guide?

Easy – In this book, I liken adjunct instruction to hiking guides, and in this chapter, I compare teaching the first-year college writing class to coaching baseball. Choose one of the analogies, and list 3–5 ways that compare teaching writing to either coaching a team or guiding a hike.

Moderate – What do you see in your own mind when you compare yourself to a hiking guide? Briefly write a sketch of no more than a page describing yourself in the classroom guiding an individual or a group of college writers.

Difficult – Are both the hiking and the coaching metaphors equally worthy of comparison to the teaching of college writers, in your opinion, or do you prefer one over the other? Why? I've heard teaching writing compared to growing a garden, conducting an orchestra, starting a small business, running a soup kitchen, making a pizza, and attending a birth as a midwife. Choose one of these comparisons, or come up with one of your own, and develop your analogy in a page or two.

Quarter-Court Sprints – Purposeful Works

"When I coasted on my last leg, coach called me out, and he made the whole team run another three quarter-court sprints. Man, did I catch it from everybody afterwards." Brent, a back-up guard on the college's basketball team, was comparing his practice woes with those of Shari, a starter on the volleyball team.

"Yeah, we do those, too. Quarters have got to be every coach's curse upon athletes. Every practice, we stretch and run quarter-courts, and she makes us reach down and touch all five lines crossing the basketball court: both baselines, half-court, and both free throws. Only the top three finishers get to quit after the first five quarters."

Brent commiserated, "You have to touch the lines with your hands? Man, coach just makes us step on them."

Unlike student athletes like Brent and Shari, teachers neither have to touch down nor step on any lines. In fact, you don't have to run the quarter-court sprints at all. Teachers are like the coaches with the whistles. You get to tweet. However fine a writer you are yourself, you really do your class-team few favors if you monopolize practices by showing off your own exploits or pronouncing prolonged explanations. That would be akin to Shari's volleyball coach telling her players, "You watch, I'll run," then sprinting the quarter-courts herself. They do the practice running. You instruct practices and plan plays.

Another mantra, *never work harder than your students*, is a friendly reminder of the role of writing coaches. But it comes with a corollary: *Always work as hard as your students.* Although not running any sprints yourself, you do pick the plays, observe your players' performances, tweak their techniques, and prepare them for game days. You're out there on the classroom floor positioning the players and adjusting their approaches to help improve individual performances on successive drafts and essay assignments. Over the course of a season, you may work yourself into a mainly supporting role on the sidelines. Your target is self-directed writers, independent thinkers, focused learners, and strategic contributors who continue to develop facility in and appreciation of their writing craft. You succeed when they demonstrate their preparation for the world of college essay writing as well as career-related writing beyond it. You triumph if they evince broadening perspective, openness to diverse opinions, eagerness to experiment with writing, and an enthusiasm for the field of literacy.

What you don't want is to perpetuate dependence, students who only write to you and for their teachers. You don't want to foster a teacher codependency – you know, a student who blurts, "So what do I do?" immediately after you've explained the assignment. Such a student has become accustomed to private teacher tutorials, and so tunes out your instructions. You may have to help the student break that habit. To this end, you might ask one of the student's groupmates, "Could you answer that question while I begin with this (other) group?" Doing so acknowledges the question, implies the group members themselves have the wherewithal to solve it, and deflects the possibility of building an unhealthy dependence on you, the teacher. Furthermore, redirecting the question to a peer communicates the importance of student collaboration and problem-solving among themselves with their collective resources. You may reply, "Sorry, I'm not taking questions right now," or say nothing, and simply sit with another group to listen or participate in their discussions. Once, a student of mine followed me and tried to interrupt the group I sat with, but I merely held up a finger – my index finger – and said without turning my head, "Please wait until I can circle back to your group." Since I structure group assignments that require everyone's individual participation in writing the group's responses, peer pressure can come to bear positively on students who are trying to get a teacher's attention rather than interacting with groupmates. "He's not going to answer you, you know," I've overheard teammates redirect their peers, "so let's just get started ourselves." By structuring your class to take advantage of peer pressure, redirecting a teacher-directed question to the student's writing cohort, or sometimes merely applying some pointed ignoring skills, you can typically break a student's teacher-dependency to everyone's benefit, especially that student's own.

Whatever students may banter about wanting a "blow-off," "gut," or "crib" course, most truly do appreciate a demanding workout that requires them to demonstrate their mastery of skills through writing with clarity, purpose, and verve. They recognize that minimal effort on their part should result in poor performance. Without often expressing it, they appreciate the teacher who thoroughly prepares them with rigorous writing, challenging discussions, inspiring lessons, and purposeful practices. Besides, as fine a coach as you might be, it's their winning performances which, ultimately, indicate your success. Ideally, your students' memories of you and your class instill a commitment to write and to continually improve their writing. The hoped-for effect is that not only their performance in your composition class, but also their future course achievements and career accomplishments are advanced by your classroom guidance and their responsive preparations and performances.

I have two final thoughts to conclude this section: first, keep challenging yourself by writing (Farrell, 2013). As my cohorts and I try regularly to remind ourselves, "Guard time to further your own writing craft and your own written projects. All our bright ideas go nowhere until they're written, right?" Finally, unlike Brent's coach, don't penalize a whole team for one student's error. If only one or a few students require practice on pronoun agreement, it is not necessary to assign the whole class practice, as those who already have this skill mastered may resent the extra "busywork" and consider it a penalty. Peer pressure can be a powerful tool on sports teams and with classroom

Figure 1.2. Exploring Sources

expectations, but group animus can quickly turn against an instructor who is perceived not playing fair. Communicating softly and individually, adapting your intervention to suit each need, usually proves most effective, and so most appreciated (or at least the least resented). Fair may not always equal an equal treatment when different writers require the sharpening of different writing skills.

Fairplay, Please – People's Places

Most likely, as a teacher of composition, you studied English, and you probably teach writing within an English department or writing unit. Where else are your students going to experience the opportunity to explore the big ideas of the culture, examine the issues of our time, and express their common humanity? For some college students, the first-year composition class may be their only exposure to the big ideas. As an adjunct instructor, you may feel pressure to delimit the course contents merely to its instrumentation in other subject fields, or in assisting students to procure jobs and promotions. As important as these purposes are, you don't have to contribute to a reductionist tendency of turning a composition class into a grade-grab or a points tally. Instead, heighten its

Table 1.1. Team Coach and Hiking Guide – Roles and Implications

	Team Coach	**Hiking Guide**
Instructor's Role	Prepares individuals and class for plays and contests Chooses and calls plays Plans and directs contests	Selects paths to destination Suggests preparations Leads and supports Calls attention to highlights
Student's Role	Practices plays with team Conditions and trains Performs when assigned	May choose destinations Follows and leads Works individually and in groups
Purpose	Perform at peak on written compositions Score and win Relish personal successes and team's accolades	Accomplish learning goals Explore, meander, climb, assist, summit, finish, complete Enjoy walking trails as well as relishing completing them
Process	Teach toward a goal Plan with purpose Practice skills for mastery Seek to "win"	Discover new ideas Meander to explore Explore several approaches Seek to "arrive"
Limitations	Emphasis on winning (or losing may negate focus on learning Purpose and process can be overshadowed by skill-drills Fairplay sometimes crushed by overfocus on the coach or the team, or on rules and traditions Potential bias when coaches select players	Inflexible or overly flexible guidelines Always (or never) leading Doing everything (or nothing) Paying untoward attention to either the pathways and byways or the destination

intrinsic dignity by thinking, talking, and writing about some big ideas and attending to the words, the phrases and clauses, the actual practice of the craft itself. You may have to guarantee good grades and establish safety nets before your students will be willing to take any risks in their writing, but be assured that the purpose is worth any efforts.

Teaching in the humanities, I want to teach humanely. Unlike an "Ol' Yeller," the kind of coach who browbeats or ridicules players, who hollers corrections at individuals putting them to shame before their teammates, who will sacrifice any ethic to win at whatever cost, whatever import, I seek to limit individual directions to private conversations – as private as I am able to make them, given the constraints of a classroom environment. Sometimes I find it expedient to catch an early arrival before any teammates arrive. At other times, I try to keep someone after class, briefly, occasionally having to discreetly ask a student during class to remain. There are times when I think it appropriate to call out a student before his peers, such as if he were himself calling out a classmate, disparaging an instructor (mistakenly equating putting down another with puffing up himself), or consciously attempting to harm himself, a teammate, or the civil conduct of the class. On the other hand, when a student deserves public praise for a remarkable achievement, such as a spate of dogged, unrelenting focus on improving an introduction or crafting a meticulously fine-tuned thesis, I publicly remark on it, as I believe there is such a thing as positive public discomfiture also.

As with most classroom circumstances, I expect there is more than one good way to motivate and manage; moreover, I suspect there is at least one not-so-good way, and a better way to call on, call out, or praise students: it's situational, depending on audience, context, and setting. Still, I sometimes find myself after the fact thinking of another better response to a student's inquiry or in-class contingency, wishing I had had the luxury of more time to reflect beforehand. Even so, sometimes my best response is simply, "That's a good question. Let me think on it some more until next class, or may I email you an answer later today?" Another response that I have found useful is, "It depends." For example, "It depends: if introducing the other friend here leads to a more complete resolution of their dilemma, then I suggest you go with it. Otherwise, it could only replicate one side's opinion." My takeaway is to continue cultivating a propensity toward coaching with kind encouragement and calm support, consistently acknowledging attempts, arranging additional interactions, and assisting with improvements. Furthermore, if I can cast some noble goals, train for successful mindsets, and continue to practice the productive plays to generate growth, like some of the best coaches, I may succeed in teaching something of what it can mean to be a mentally active and engaged, contributing human being, in addition to the skills needed to be a proficient college writer. As coach, don't only call out directions from the baseball dugout, get in and among them, draw alongside your students to cheer and cajole, lead and nudge their progress, and you may just grant yourself an opportunity to inspire.

Fairplay is part of our humanity; it requires that instructors make classrooms welcoming places where all participate, and no players are left to sit out the game. You can make yours an inviting place that is conducive to learning and reflective of our collective humanity. Besides affirming students' work ethics and achievements, make a point of welcoming them to class, every class. Every day, greet them by name, and whenever you can, ask, "How are you doing?" Opening a cordial conversation can set a positive tone for the class as well as practice the niceties of casual interaction among some students who may not otherwise have the pleasure. Drawing in additional students as they arrive may multiply the joy, as well as initiate conversation among individuals who would never speak together if left to themselves. Besides, it sure beats the default of everybody silently and singly bowing down over their glowing phones or tech devices. Ask them to help out with arranging the desks, tables, and chairs into groups or seminar arrangements to encourage interactions among peers. As your schedule allows, arrive early for every class to mingle with your students and converse as they arrive, and to save them the discomfort of loitering around while awaiting your arrival. Choose affirmative and positive terms in your own conversations, commiserate with students' challenges and setbacks, and treat complaints as opportunities, using considerate questions and replies. Before a class begins, you can set an expectation for interaction and establish a tone that is inclusive and affirming.

Finally, fairplay inclines the instructor to communicate evaluations straightforwardly, instructively, person to person. No rubric or grading scale can exactly measure or perfectly communicate a student's accomplishments, particularly in the college composition class. Nevertheless, be as true as you can to your stated expectations, your evaluation rubric, or your grading standards (Huot & O'Neill, 2009; Lynne, 2004; Sommers, 2013; Suskie, 2009). If a student doesn't know why an essay received a B and not an A, begin by assuming that you may not have communicated your expectations well enough beforehand or afterward. To play fair, when I assign a paper, I try to describe what I seek in an essay, how I define what constitutes an A, B, or C, and what is necessary merely to pass. Sharing an example can be beneficial, too, but I have found that students most often do not transfer the expectations from a sample essay to their own writing. Or they try to pattern their own writing too closely, even to a point of mimicking the model essay.

Trail Marker – Take One … Take Two …

Easy – How many times do (or will) you allow your students to submit the

same essay? ____

Why? ____

Moderate – What are three criteria, components, or contents that every essay should contain?

1. ____

2. ____

3. ____

Difficult – What do (or will) you do to ensure that every student includes these three criteria, components, or contents in their essays?

1. ____

2. ____

3. ____

What is your yardstick? How many attempts do you allow? Which writing traits are primary, and which secondary? What are the criteria that cause you to spill your coffee while exulting with glee? Or that will make you spill your coffee when you flee? Without devolving into a landmine of points and petty quantifications, pointing out formative as well as evaluative criteria in relation to students' own writing drafts is helpful to playing fair. For example, requiring students to submit a rough draft of ideas and examples a week before a more organized draft with paragraphs and topic sentences may communicate the importance of taking the time to collect worthwhile contents for a written piece. What is required ought to be assessed. Not always formally with a letter grade, it may be checked or initialed as having been completed or evaluated for one or two specifically assigned components. I often simply initial the bottom of the first page of a rough draft when it fills two pages and contains at least three topics with examples. Before accepting the final draft of an essay, I usually require that students display my initials on the previous drafts, where I had designated my "seal of approval" by initialing and dating the bottom left corner on the first page.

Fairplay suggests students hear your evaluation criteria or see your assessment rubric before they submit an essay. I like to repeat five key criteria that I look for in an upcoming essay during every class meeting for a week or two – some classes meet more frequently than others –before the deadline. Sometimes, I point out two or three items to search and destroy as well, such as worn-out words like *good* and *bad*. Fairplay suggests you grant your students another opportunity (or more than one) to revise an essay after receiving your edit and feedback. After all, it's in the repeated practices that students often hone their skills – in writing as well as baseball. Fairplay suggests any summative, formal grade needs to take into account students' formative growth, efforts, and revisions, and not only the quality of the finished product. I like to offer my students another opportunity to rewrite every essay within a week after reading my comments and seeing its grade. "If you're happy, I'm happy," I like to announce, but then add, "Of course, the more you rework your essay, the better it may become and the better you may become, too. Practice makes … probably not perfect, but better and better." Sometimes I follow up with individuals, "You are planning to rewrite your introduction (or conclusion, format, active verbs…), right?"

As we continue along the fairplay pathway, two possible diversions may be worth wandering: First, even when introducing positive interactions by conversing before classes, it is as important for teachers to maintain those positive interactions throughout class time as well as between classes, particularly in electronic communications, such as email and the chat functions of educational software. Besides setting a positive tone and demonstrating civility in their own behavior, instructors need to assure it in small groups, partnered activities, online posts, and discussion threads. Sometimes, the higher the goal, the greater the risk. Encouraging mutual listening, understanding, and empathy among students can be especially challenging when encountering students who are unused to diversity, whether ethnic, age- or gender-related, and whether in ideas and opinions. Fairplay likewise demands instructors' attentive listening, understanding, and empathy for diverse students as well as their diverse ideas and opinions in the writing classroom.

Another important corollary is to decide how you choose to be addressed. I think it's important to tell my students this at the outset. One way I try to level the playing field is to interact with my students on a first-name basis. Being "of a rather mature vintage," a friend of mine likes to claim that our mutual age has attained, I typically introduce myself to students using my first and last names, and indicate that I prefer to be addressed simply by my first name. Although it risks disrespect and reduced stature in the eyes of some students, I think doing so actually (and maybe ironically) helps raise the students, lifting them and in a way according them welcome to the realm of adults, professionals, and academics. "Besides, you'll help me feel young," I assure them. My comfort with first-name address may be because I have taught adult learners for many years, including a retiree who was in her seventies, in addition to many who were nearly my own vintage, over the years. Two colleges where I have taught insisted on labeling adjuncts *Instructor* or gendered address terms (*Mr., Ms., Mrs.*) to distinguish between the full-time faculty, who were the *professors*, and the part-time, adjunct, or contingency instructors. A cohort of full professors, friends of mine who taught in one of those English departments, including my mentor, herself a professor and administrator of developmental adult learners, all insisted on being called simply by their first names, to demonstrate both solidarity with their adjunct colleagues and accessibility to their students. Besides, my single-syllable name *Tom* is quick and easy to pronounce, even for second language students.

Some students balk at using my given name and insist on calling me *Professor*. I've had several students, particularly veterans and members of the military, dub me *Sir*. One semester, a student who had been homeschooled called me *Mom,* once. I tell my students that I'll answer to it all (within reason) but would rather they simply use my first name. Now and again, one might chortle as though getting away with a peccadillo, but quickly they realize that they're in a tiny club of one and typically self-correct. Once, a student chose to intone a silly inflection when calling on me, so I simply replied in kind. There was no second occurrence. I expect if there were, I might sit down face-to-face to explain an appropriate mode for address, then ask if this would be an issue between us again. While I am comfortable with this means of address, I can see that not everyone would be, for example, a new adjunct instructor, a senior professor, or an instructor or professor teaching "shared-time" students from a high school class. Some teachers – particularly those who are close in age to their students – may feel the need to express this separation by requiring students to call them by title and last name. In addition, some teachers who are much older than students may feel it uncomfortable or artificial to be on a first-name basis with them. Different settings, such as teaching at a military or business-training institution could raise additional considerations. Given the automatic hierarchy displayed in being addressed by title plus last name, those who elect to require this form of address from students may need to redouble their efforts to demonstrate fairplay principles and practices in their class.

What about the professors who insist that students address them with the title, *Dr.*? When students ask me about it, and occasionally they do, I reply, "Did you know that to earn a doctorate, professors have to study four years of college for a Bachelor's degree, then two more of postgraduate studies for a Master's degree, plus at least another four more of postgraduate study, work, internship and residency to earn that Doctoral degree? If I had a doctorate, I might ask you to call me *Doctor*, too!"

One last point: even though I conduct the class on a friendly, first-name basis, and consciously work to establish and maintain an open rapport with my students, I don't "friend" any of them or add any to a social media account, which could allow them access to collegial, peer, and family interactions that are extraneous and may even be detrimental to our class focus on learning and writing. Our interactions with students, although always friendly, cordial, and especially humane, must remain professional, and although friendship may grow out of our relationships with students, the risk of

Trail Marker – Call Me

Easy – What do you ask your students to call you?

____

____

Moderate – What are three reasons why you prefer that they call you this?

1. ____

2. ____

3. ____

Difficult – What are three possible implications – for you, the students, your department, your colleagues, or the subject field, of their calling you this?

1. ____

2. ____

3. ____

Trail Marker – Personal Connection and Academic Prowess

Easy – Pause for a moment to recall one of your own professors who was especially memorable: Professor ____

1. Was the professor personable and approachable? Circle one: Yes   Undecided   No

2. Did the professor impress you with her/his smarts or academic credentials?   Yes   Undecided   No

3. Was either characteristic predominant?   Personal   Neither   Academic

Moderate – For numbers 4–6, choose two or three different professors whom you recall from your own undergraduate or graduate education. Then place a dot on the continuum to indicate the degree to which each professor tended more to exhibit personal connection or academic prowess in the classroom. (A dot in the middle would signify that the professor exhibited them both in equal amounts.)

4. Professor ____

Personal Connection ⟵————————————⟶ Academic Prowess

5. Professor ____

Personal Connection ⟵————————————⟶ Academic Prowess

6. Professor ____

Personal Connection ⟵————————————⟶ Academic Prowess

For number 7, reflect on your own view of your expression of Academic Prowess and Personal Connection in interactions with students whom you teach, as well as how you think your students see you on a scale of 1 (low) to 10 (high).

7.   Yourself   My View   My Student's View

   Personal Connection   _____   _____

   Academic Prowess   _____   _____

For number 7, are your rankings where you would ideally like them? Write down any changes you might like to make in either your Personal Connection with students or your Academic Prowess. Do you think there are differences between professors and adjuncts in the ideal combination of these? If possible, discuss your thoughts and ideas with a partner, colleague, or group.

Difficult – If you were to divide Personal Connection and Academic Prowess into percentages, totaling 100%, what do you think would be an ideal balance for the adjunct instructor of a first-year college composition class to exhibit to students?

8.   Do you think a 50%–50% equal balance in exhibiting Personal Connection and Academic Prowess would be optimal for your classes and students? Or do you expect that accentuating one over the other 25%–75% or 60%–40% or another ratio could be more effective?

9.   Thinking, instead, about the field of English composition as it relates to your own career, would this perspective change the equation? Does a 50%–50% equal balance most benefit you, your career, and your future? Would a different value better advance your own interests? The interests of your college? Our field?

its overshadowing or undermining a class's academic pursuits, or of dividing a class-room into those who are "in" with the teacher and those who are "out of step," may be too great to risk. Colleagues of mine have opened separate online accounts strictly for their communications with students. I tried it once myself but found my students' hours inconvenient so communiques sporadic, certainly not worth the efforts and time I invested. Now I limit my online communications to email and course announcements, which I find more direct and less time consuming. Perhaps I'm showing my vintage.

Coffee Klatsch Collegial Conversation – Developmental Syllabus

Patricia was perched at a table, frequently glancing out the coffee shop's plate glass window, awaiting the others, who had finally begun trickling into the water-ing hole, casually gathering and doctoring their pour-overs at a counter. She was rightfully proud of her ample syllabus, all stacked and smartly bound in bright black plastic binding-combs. "I try to anticipate practically every situation that might arise in my writing classes, so I have sections in here on plagiarism, MLA formatting, what to do if you're late on the day of peer reviews…," she announced pertly just as soon as Rob had settled into a seat.

"How can you predict what's going to happen in any class? I'm lucky if I can keep both my sections of Comp 101 on the same schedule from week to week. Honestly, I'm doubly lucky if I can just remember what I covered in my Monday class and try to replicate it in Tuesday's!" Rob replied. "Besides, the Monday students seem to start so slow, I wonder if they're all awake by the time they drag themselves to class. Tuesday's, on the other hand, threaten to sprint right past me if I don't keep up with their furious pace. They're my go-go group this semester."

"Covered, right here." Patricia smugly thumbed to page 13 and pointed at a subhead, "Keeping Up": "I don't pander to any slowdowns. They either keep up or they'll have to catch up afterwards on their own."

"Ouch!" Rob exclaimed appreciatively. "What happens with your develop-mental students?"

"Look, they're right here," Patricia thumbed back alphabetically and poked a page headed: "Developmental Learners." "Careful where you're slinging that topped up mug, Jimmy!" She hurriedly closed the binder, sliding the pile safely away from the brimming cups of coffee.

Jimmy hefted his megamug, then paused expectantly, "Now OK?"

"Yes, run your little ritual, you caffeine addicts."

"Here's mud in your mug, you-all," Jimmy tapped Patricia's, sending a wave of both splashing down onto the table. "Jeers!"

"Jeers!" all replied, Patricia, shaking her head and adding, "You're all incorrigible."

Preamble to the Composition – The Syllabus and the First Class

While I admire Patricia's comprehensiveness, I work at simplifying and shortening my own syllabus. Instead of elaborating for all possible contingencies, I am abbreviating, briefly listing expectations in terse bullet points in an attempt to make it more accessible to hurried students. It's difficult to shrink a syllabus. Still, the advantages of a condensed outline could be the difference between one that is referenced during a term and the one that stays snapped inside a binder or stacked on a pile at home because too heavy to carry or too wordy to be convenient. Every college or department that I have taught for has not only required a syllabus but stipulated that it be shared with students at the first class meeting. In fact, most specify mandated topics, and some even dictate the forms and wording, too – not all of which is very clearly stated, by the way. Of course, you have to do what you have to do.

Still, there often is leeway allowed – or simply overlooked. You don't have to read the syllabus to students (that is, unless you truly do). Instead, point out several highlights, like your attendance and grading policies, let them stow the rest, then start right into some learning application. At a college where I formerly taught, most students ditched the first class period because instructors were filling it with a reading of the course syllabus. The college retaliated by making attendance of the opening class compulsory for continued enrollment in the course itself – injury following insult. At the other extreme is a professor who wryly remarked, "Purportedly, they all can read, so I just hand out the syllabus on the first day to get it in their hands, and then I dive right into the curriculum, instead."

Between extremes, one colleague of mine hands out an admittedly lengthy syllabus with an assignment requiring students to search through it in small groups to locate the appropriate reply to ten quiz-style questions, such as "How many late arrivals may I have before they count against my grade?" Another includes electronic links to websites for the English department, the campus library, the writing center, Student Life events, on-campus eating spots and coffee shops, as well as a number of other sites to attract students' attention and (hopefully) frequent revisits.

Short, bulleted lists of fewer and broader rules or descriptive statements allow for and may even necessitate separate adaptations and interpretations. And, let's be honest, even the most lengthy and comprehensive syllabus will present at least one exception requiring clarification. Short lists of key topics help to make a syllabus appear accessible and inviting. Yes, its brevity may send students hurrying to you with a question, but that could turn out to be an additional advantage since instead of making an assumption that an answer is buried somewhere in the hills of text and preferring not to dig it out, students probably will ask you the question anyway or simply avoid it and you altogether. Instead of spending an inordinate amount of time to develop and syllabus, anticipating as many circumstances as possible, I suggest you make it as simple and straightforward as you can.

In class, point out only three or four highlights, and express them in positive terms if possible. Don't languish over plagiarism and penalties. I choose one "negative," my attendance policy, then launch into a series of three "positive" opportunities: how best to contact me between classes, where the nearest coffee shops and cafeterias are located, and a link to the Student Life video clip of clubs and organizations. These last few I borrowed from my friend who uploaded the electronic links into her syllabus.

In addition, a nice video clip of hiking the North Country Trail acquaints them with my interest; moreover, it serves as a metaphor for the efforts, stages, and progression of writing college-level essays for the course, an image that I can return to regularly over the term.

Before introducing the syllabus, I focus on personal introductions, preceding the *what* and the *how* of our class with the *who*. Instead of asking students to introduce themselves, I typically give them a list of ten interview questions and randomly assign them to pairs. I use the same questions to introduce myself and share some suitable answers to demonstrate solidarity and therefore some fairplay on my part before I ask them to interview each other and write down their partner's answers. Afterwards, I call them up by pairs in random order to introduce their partners to the class, using the same ten interview questions. I like to say, "Before the end of class today, you will get to know somebody new very well and another two rather well, and you will get introduced to everybody here. Not only that, but you will learn more about me than you ever thought you had any desire to know." Once all pairs have finished, they join with another couple to form a group of four, or as close to four as enrollment numbers allow.

Signpost – Who Are You? Partners' Interviews and Introductions Activity

A copy of the **Who Are You? Partners' Interviews and Introductions** activity that I often use as an icebreaker to begin a course can be found on page 182.

In every class thereafter I try to greet all of my students by name as they enter the room and encourage them to interact with one another as well using their names. This means that my homework after that initial class meeting is to study students' names, photos if available, and responses to their interview-and-introduction questions, so that besides including their names with a welcome, I can also ask a purposeful and relevant question to initiate a conversation. One of my adjunct colleagues snaps a photo of every student, one with current hairstyle and eyewear set in the classroom instead of having to manage with the college's furnished, assembly line "mug shots," which often do not yet include every class member and do not always show current distinguishing features of their appearance. I have asked groups of four to snap a group photo, complete with a suitable caption that includes their individual names, somewhere on campus with a sign, statue, or sculpture that iconically represents the university, which I upload into a PowerPoint file to stream as they arrive to the next class. Even when I inadvertently use the wrong one or mispronounce a name, they appreciate my genuine efforts, as I repeat names and note correct pronunciations. Also, I frequently sit down among their groups to join or begin conversations before class time.

As group members arrive, I try to move about the classroom, sitting with and kindling conversations with separate groups. I like to tell them, "You have succeeded as a group if I have to ask you to quiet down before I can begin teaching." In some classes, I have to add that they have botched the opening if they are all plugged into their electronics instead of genuine conversations. On occasion, I have assigned questions as conversation starters, requiring them to learn something salient about their group members before beginning class. Maybe cellphones have indeed made face-to-face conversation a dying art, or possibly sometime, somewhere they received a far too stringent training in Stranger Danger.

Although I roam about the classroom freely, I never allow students to select their own seats, partners, or groups. One of two things almost invariably happens if I do: either they choose a seat on their first day and stay put, not deviating from that same spot for the rest of a semester, or they cluster-and-huddle, cliquing with alikes, self-segregating by ethnicity, gender, or age. In either scenario, they become stuck, and so does the class. They write and talk – if they talk at all – with the same few neighbors who often have similar backgrounds, interests, and even writing abilities. Somebody invariably is neglected, gets left behind or left out, or is included only awkwardly as an afterthought or via the teacher's intervention. At best, it is awkward. At worst, it is exclusionary. On the other hand, assigning seats ensures a variety of writing and conversational partners, livelier conversations and interactions with oftentimes dissimilar opinions.

Seemingly ironic, if you are committed to making a classroom welcoming, inviting, and diversely democratic, you ought to assign seating. Assigning seats nudges students out of their usual cliques and comfort zones, giving them permission to cross artificial barriers. It frees them by forcing students to mix and interact, to converse and compose with classmates whom they probably would not, otherwise. Simply by assigning seats, you communicate an expectation for students' varied interactions (Bruffee, 1999; Gere, 1987; Hunzer, 2012; Scheuermann, 2018). If you don't arrange their seats, it is unlikely to happen naturally and typically becomes less and less likely as students settle into classroom routines. If you allow self-seating and merely hope they mix diversely, it's too late. They won't. Afterwards, when you attempt to rectify the problem by reassigning their seats, you look like you've retracted a privilege or removed a right; further, it could even be perceived as an untoward penalty, something some might even feel obligated to resist.

Finally, besides pairing individuals to interview and introduce each other, assigning seats, and distributing the syllabus, I usually briefly introduce a handful of writing skills that I expect the class members to aim for mastery throughout the semester. I cannot adequately cover everything in the composition text, much less teach it sufficiently to ensure students' ability to understand and apply it adequately. I select several that I think most salient for them to know and tell them, "These are the writing skills that I'm convinced have the most payoff for college, workplace, and life. We'll continue to revisit and practice them throughout the semester, so I can safely say that you should leave our class confidently able to use them." Starting with the English or Writing department's learning outcomes for a course, I generally distill them into bite-sized, bullet points and define them with appropriate writing activities. For every assigned essay, I try to target these same skills with a sequence of increasingly challenging applications. For example, with the personal essay (or memoir) assignment (see Appendix 1 for essay assignments), I ask students to try to locate or snap a photo of themselves in a defining place, whether it be a building on campus, a workplace, a favorite park or vacation setting, or some other place that they think represents them. Next, I ask them to position it with an appropriate caption beside the related text. In subsequent essays, I like to assign a graph, chart, or picture from a website in addition to another personal photo suited to that assignment's theme. Appropriately choosing, captioning, and citing illustrations is a skill that is worth revisiting, so students not only credit their sources, but also use them appropriately and effectively for other classes' projects and written assignments.

As I learn students' composing strengths and challenges, I try to adapt my teaching to use their strengths while targeting weaknesses for remediation. Addressing a limited and manageable number of skills to help students ensure their mastery is more beneficial than simply introducing many skills, hit-and-run fashion, without ensuring students practice and mastery of them. My merely addressing a skill or covering a writing topic does not necessarily result in students learning it or in their assured ability to apply it. What I aim and advocate for is their demonstrated understanding of composition skills through their writing. The purpose of my guiding them today is their finding, following, and possibly even leading another up these same – and indeed other – trails tomorrow.

Top 10 List – First Day

These are my suggestions to help make a first class meeting with your students memorable and productive. Like the guide who prepares instructions and outlines expectations for the hike and a description of the route before hitting the trail, these suggestions for your first day should set a positive and purposeful tone at the outset of the semester:

1. **Greeting Students.** Arrive 30 minutes early, if possible, to greet all students as they enter the classroom.
2. **Posting Introduction.** Write your name, contact information, course and section, and class time on the board or project it on the screen, so all see it as they arrive in the classroom.
3. **Outlining Daily Agenda.** Outline briefly the day's contents on the board: *Who*, *Why*, *How*, and *What* – in this order.
4. **Demonstrating Punctuality.** Announce a brief delay for anyone who may arrive late on the first day to show consideration, but begin very soon afterward to demonstrate punctuality (and begin every subsequent class on time, unless there is inclement weather or traffic, then announce a brief delay as on the first day).
5. **Getting Acquainted.** Introduce yourself and one another with a conversational ice-breaker that involves both collaboration and writing like the **Who Are You? Partners' Interviews and Introductions** on page 182.
6. **Purposing and Relating.** Introduce the purpose of the course, and relate it to their learning goals – I like to accomplish this with a brief *Why More Writing?* activity after the Introductions, following *Who?* with *Why?* I circle the word *Why?* on the whiteboard and draw several lines coming out like rays from the circle. Next, I ask "Why are you taking this class?" and write their responses in single words at the ends of the rays, normally including *required, job, communicate, improve*. After writing several of their responses, I add some of my own, such as *thinking, connecting, listening, believing*, and discuss an example of each.
7. **Introducing the Course.** Introduce the course, learning outcomes, syllabus, text, and schedule.
8. **Opening Writing.** Begin writing on the very first day by assigning a warm-up, introductory writing sample, or a list of course expectations.
9. **Closing the First Class.** Conclude with an **Exit Card** or **Ticket Out** like the one on page 188 to wrap up and preview a next-class attraction.

10. **Emailing a Follow-up Welcome.** Soon after class on the same day, send a brief, blanket email or announcement conveying your pleasure at meeting the students and your eager anticipation of learning together during the term.

Lingo – Introductions

These are some first-day statements that I have used in several different college writing courses at different colleges or universities. Not all of this lingo will fit as worded in every school with each class, but most, I think, can be readily adapted to different classes and settings. The key is to choose phrasing that is positive and that positions the course in the sequence of expectations for your students.

1. "Welcome to [Course Name]. I'm pleased to meet you, and I'm looking forward to working together this semester."
2. "This is the first in a sequence of two college composition classes. The first invites exploration and discovery. The second investigates and persuades."
3. "To move on to the next class, or to transfer this course out to another college, you have to score a 3.0 or grade of C. We'll do our best all semester to help make that happen."
4. "We mostly write, but of course we converse, compute, read, speak, listen, and think deeply, too. We look as well at how writing and English applies to every area of our lives: college, work, family, community, and even who we are. It's all English."
5. "This is going to be fun. Let's have a good time together this semester."

Q's – Introductions 2

Although sounding a lot like a continuation of the Lingo section above, the Q's are questions, chosen to initiate conversations and encourage discussions with your students as well as among them at the beginning of the class. So, in one sense, they're Introductions 2, and in another, Introductions, too!

1. What's your name? What are you studying? What degree are you pursuing? Is it a two, three, or four-year degree?
2. Have you bought the text? How much did it cost new? Is anyone renting the text? Did anyone locate a used copy? Was it available online?
3. Have you taken other college writing classes or English courses already?
4. What do you want to learn in here? What do you expect to learn?
5. Do you recognize anyone else in our class?

Chuckle – Savings

"After I finished my graduate degree, my professor, Dr. Jonstone, told me I could now call him by his first name, James. I'll save you all the expenses of the degree. You may call me Tom starting right now."

Quotation with Sentence Surgery –
Theodore Roosevelt

"When you are asked if you can do a job, tell them, "Certainly I can," and get busy and find out how to do it."

– Theodore Roosevelt

```
        dep    A        dep    A          ind A          dep      A
[When you are asked] [if you can do a job,] [(you) tell them,] ["Certainly I can,"]
      ind   A            A
[and (you) get busy and find out how to do it.]
```

3 dep's + 2 ind's = cd-cx

- 6 Verbs: are asked, can do, tell, can, get, and find
- 5 Subjects: you, you, (understood you), I, (understood you)
- 2 Dependent clauses (dep) beginning with subordinating conjunctions: When, if
- 1 Dependent clause embedded in quotation marks
- 2 Independent clauses (ind) connected with a comma and coordinating conjunction: and
- 3 dep's + 2 ind's = compound (cd)-complex (cx) sentence

Closing Conversation – Happy Class

After our first class meeting, a student asked me, "Are you always so happy?"

"Sure, life's good, English is great, and it looks like our writing class is going to be terrific. I think we can look forward to a good semester. Do you think so, too?" (Really, what could this student respond besides, "Yes, sure" – even if uncertainly or unconvincingly?)

Figure 1.3. *What are you writing about?*

Chapter 2. Collude – Adjunct Instructors: Paradox and Expediency

A hunger for coherence; yet a hunger also to be true to the natural incoherence of experience. This dilemma has led me more often than I realized to work things out in terms of contraries: to gravitate toward oppositions and even to exaggerate differences – while also tending to notice how both sides of the opposition must somehow be right. My instinct has thus made me seek ways to avoid the limitations of the single point of view. And it has led me to a commonsense view that surely there cannot be only one right way to learn and teach.
– Peter Elbow

Figure 2.1. Deadman's Hill Scenic Overlook, Michigan.
Credit: Antrim County, Michigan, website (adapted)

"How did you snag that Creative Writing class? You don't teach creative writing, do you?" Tara asked Michel, both adding caramel syrup to their lattes.

"The Creative Writing coordinator caught me in the hallway and asked if I'd ever taught it before."

"Did you?" Jacqui asked, tapping the spoon on her cup's rim as she joined Michel and sat across from Tara at the table where others had already gathered.

Jimmy interjected, "When you add your own caramel, you wreck that hearty-shaped thing the baristas form in the scum on top of the lattes, you-all know."

Tara replied, "It's cheaper if I do it myself."

"Plus, Allison behind the counter never adds enough caramel," added Michel. Then turning to Tara, Michel continued, "Well, not really, but I just said, 'Sure, I can do that.' And I guess that was that. She asked if I could be available to teach a creative writing class on Tuesdays and Thursdays next semester."

Jacqui shook her head, "So it's not what you know…,"

"…or even whom you know," Jorge interrupted. "It's which hallway you hang out in!" Jimmy raised both palms, turning one each to slap Jorge's and Tara's.

"It's your hallway hang time, too!" appended Tara, slapping Jimmy's hands.

Jimmy hefted his megamug. "Here's to mud in your mug. Jeers, you-all!"

"Cheers!"

"Cheers!" repeated the customers of adjacent tables who had raised their mugs to reply, too.

Grinning, the adjuncts turned and raised their mugs again.

- Valley to Vista – Lower Michigan's Deadman's Hill
- No Office Hours – Meet at the Classroom
- No Conferences – Use Class time to Confer
- No Extracurriculars – Play for Pay
- No Checks for Plagiarism – Assign Self-Checks
- No Weekend Wear – Dress Professionally
- No Tests – Give Essays Only
- No Paperless Classrooms – Photocopy Reams
- No Reteaching Lessons – Teach Understanding
- No Teaching Down – Stretch Understandings
- No Open Seating – Assign Seats

Valley to Vista – Lower Michigan's Deadman's Hill

Last Fall, I hiked down Deadman's Hill in the northern part of lower Michigan. It was called Deadman's Hill after a young lumberman lost his life when he lost control of a team of horses hauling a wagonload precariously over the steep grade and was crushed beneath the load of logs. Today, with its forest of hardwood trees restored and thriving across the Jordan Valley, the view from Deadman's Hill is reputedly one of the best in the state. Before cresting the hill, I looped down into the Jordan Valley below, following an intricate path along the Jordan River, winding along the river's twists, crossing tributary streams, and tramping on the roots of the reforested lowland. Rarely lifting my eyes, I had to focus on gingerly picking my way along the puddly, muddy trail, snaking through the woods beside the river. Finally, looping about the valley, the trail lifted and straightened, leading uphill. I rose up from the valley and emerged onto the well-traveled overview along the hilltop. The panorama from Deadman's Hill overlooks the broad Jordan Valley, with another dozen hills rising to form a backdrop of brilliant reds, oranges, and yellows of photosynthesis-spent maples glowing in the late afternoon October sunshine, and continuing to the horizon in all directions. Hike it on a sunny day in late autumn. Sometimes, to appreciate the highlights of a trail, it can be advantageous to take an approach that accentuates its contrasts.

The 10 Commandments of Constructive Collusion are my suggestions for working with the confines and constraints sometimes placed upon us adjuncts to ensure that our students learn, and we survive. To appreciate these 10 Commandments of Constructive Collusion, remain close beside me as we pick our way among their switchbacks, around the loops, and along the edges. I assure you that the destinations – and most of the traverses themselves, too – are well worth the results for both your students and yourself. It usually benefits scrambling adjuncts, who are perpetually on-the-go from class to class and sometimes also from college to college, to be expedient with time management. Without dissembling, you can collude constructively to avoid scheduling nonessential calendar commitments and adding unproductive items onto to-do's lists. Guarding your schedule and yourself through some creative collusion can help ensure success for you as well as your first-year writing students.

Although wishing to contribute as loyal comrades who stick to the designated, well-paved pathways, adjunct instructors normally wish to go along and get along with their employers' expectations. Sometimes, however, it's expedient to step off a worn trail in order to stay true to yourself and your own well-being, as well as your vocation and the higher purposes of higher learning, and to advocate for others – especially your students. Institutions have a propensity to regulate and standardize employees. Colleges and universities are no exception. Occasionally, a focus on finance, student-management, or a curricular intervention can monopolize an establishment. If a cloudburst of dictates and stipulations suddenly rains without consideration for compensation in time or treasure, adjuncts may have to shelter themselves – and sometimes look out for their charges, too.

I remember when a college where I taught a number of years ago launched a department-wide grade-norming initiative. It extolled the promised standardization in assessments as well as common language and objectives we could bring to professional meetings and conversations, which would purportedly result in measurable benefits to us teachers as well as to our Student Performance Outcomes, in their chosen businessy-behavioral parlance. The college, all on board, paid liberally for adjunct cohorts to train in aligning evaluations and led small groups of part-time instructors to practice the grade-norming model on sample essays. We enjoyed many good conversations about what comprises a strong student essay, and we appreciated the delicious buffets in a dining room situated in a historic house on campus. However, although we practiced scoring and aligning as many as a hundred sample essays, we were only able to achieve a semblance of agreement by the end of our norming sessions, and we never were able to sequence the Student Performance Outcomes incrementally among the three-course sequence of English 99, 100, and 101. Finally, we determined to agree: "These aren't real grades for actual students, so let's just settle on giving the same weight to three items, so we can finish up this task." In other words, we went along up to the point where we just couldn't. The next year, a new norming committee changed the evaluation template, and many of the adjuncts had moved on, anyway. Not long afterwards, a new department chair was elected (by the full-time faculty), who flew the banner of Academic Freedom and effectively killed grade-norming.

It may be helpful for adjunct instructors to see themselves not only as hiking guides without an obligation to their students, but also as the self-employed owners of a tour business. Adjuncts are subcontractors, and in that sense free agents. Simply from a financial perspective, adjuncts are invaluable members of colleges and departments, contributing individual skills and specialties. This has an advantage: adjuncts are generally not obligated to wholly commit to any department's or institution's agenda. You, in that respect, hold an enviable position. Independent, your allegiance is primarily to your students and yourself, and to a lesser extent to the institution, whether it be a university, college, or department. Committees, meetings, training sessions, and social events are usually optional for you. Of course, if you enjoy attending any of these events, you would often be welcomed to do so. Typically, you get to choose what is and what is not to your benefit.

The 10 Commandments of Constructive Collusion are a guide that may be helpful as you negotiate some of the unforeseen loops and switchbacks along the paths of part-time college writing instructors. Some may be more beneficial to you in your own circumstances than others. In fact, some of what follows may not apply to you at all in your particular teaching situation or career stage. Still, even for those points that may not be applicable to you, they should at least provoke some ideas and probably stimulate some good discussions in a coffee klatsch.

1. No Office Hours – Meet at the Classroom

If you're not required to keep office hours, don't. It's inconvenient for students, and it can be awkward for instructors, especially when meeting with students in offices that are shared with colleagues. As an adjunct, I have been assigned no office, I have shared offices of varied sizes with as few as one colleague and as many as hundreds of others. Once I was given an office all my own. (Maybe I should mention that it was a partial storage room that had been half converted into an office space for me.) At one school, I shared an office with two other adjuncts in the Geography Department, across campus from the university's Writing Department offices. At another, I shared a common adjunct office with five separate departments in two converted classrooms combined into one large room with the constant hubbub of a 70's era newsroom: desk phones ringing, doors opening and closing, instructors and students continually passing through. One of my offices, shared with English Department adjuncts, fills the fourth-floor corner of a former bank's suite of offices, with a floor-to-ceiling picture window overlooking a downtown central business district.

Even if you are required to keep office hours, it is worth your asking if you may substitute early arrivals or late departures from class, or limit the hours to appointments, instead. Every school where I have taught requires office hours, and every one also accepted my proposed alternative when I explained its rationale: it advantages students. Instead of asking students to seek and find me in my office, I try to convenience them by arriving at class early and remaining late to allow time for conversations and conferences, as my changing schedules allow. I schedule myself to arrive thirty minutes before class and to stay thirty minutes afterwards to answer any questions and conclude any student-initiated conversations, and I recommend the practice to you. If you can address students' questions when they're immediate, you may save both you and your students the extra time required to recall and revisit the context of something that came up in class or to go back over an explanation, which might be unnecessary if you met following right on the heels of the class time. Also, speaking on site at the classroom can save a student the consternation of both locating your office and then traversing campus to get there. Sometimes, it can save you both an additional hike.

Arriving before your students, in my view, dignifies them by making yourself conveniently available to them. In addition, your arriving early to unlock a closed classroom may grant them access to seats as well as to their groupmates, helpful when working on projects together. Especially for those with distant commutes who allow extra time to arrive early, your welcoming them to an open classroom demonstrates your consideration, and it acknowledges their scheduling ample time for their commute by having the classroom available, instead of requiring a discouraging wait. When they aren't compelled to wait for you outside, they don't crowd passageways or block doorways, which can show consideration for other students who are negotiating the hallways, as well as for neighboring classes and their instructors.

If another class meets in your classroom during the times immediately before or after yours, try to find an empty room nearby, or some other meeting place such as benches outside, or even an adjacent coffee shop, and you can announce that students are welcome to locate you there either before or after class times. Adjuncts scramble. If you teach classes that are scheduled in times that are near each other but physically meet in rooms that are distant, requiring your quick-march across campus or a speedy commute between campuses or colleges, choose to arrive early before the front end of the first, and resolve to remain after the back end of the second for some student-focused hallway hang time. Students, colleagues, supervisors, and chairs all recognize the challenges and constraints of adjuncts' scrambling. Invariably, they will appreciate your adapting your own schedule to accommodate your students.

On occasion, I have discovered students hovering outside my classroom, not wanting to interrupt my conversations, or suspecting that I may have begun class without them. Whenever I can, I prop the door open and invite anyone I spot waiting outside before the class is scheduled to begin to "Come on in, we're just talking while waiting for the hour to start." When students do arrive to class early or remain afterwards, I try to make a point of acknowledging them by sitting down and talking instead of requiring that they wait for me to prepare class materials – or to pack them up later. When I require time beforehand to set up for class, I invite early arrivals to come talk with me while I arrange to teach, usually adding this softening phrase, "if you don't mind." No one ever does mind (or at least no one has ever verbally expressed that they do). Always,

I plan to have the necessary time to arrange the classroom and materials so that all is readied for a timely start.

Occasionally, someone arrives in a rush just a minute or two before the class is scheduled to begin, wishing to ask me an individual question that could necessitate my delaying the start for the rest of the students. In that case, I will note that as it's almost time to begin, and maybe remaining after class could allow enough time to respond to a question, or possibly we'll have time to talk before the subsequent class session. This would not be the time to schedule an office appointment or negotiate calendars. Class time is sacrosanct. On rare occasions, a student may rush in to announce an emergency just before class. Once, a student raced in to my class announcing that he was driving a patient to the hospital but was instructed by his patient to stop en route to get his homework first. I assured him that I would email it, and urged him to finish his emergency run.

When no one arrives early to talk or ask a question, it may help to look upon your own early arrival as granting yourself additional time to arrange the classroom and your lesson, fire up technology, check any assignments and students' progress, or sit back to await and ease into the greetings and interactions as students arrive. As additional incentive, I like to hand out any material for class activities to early arrivals, so they can get a preview of class attractions or an early overview of what that day will involve. To those who come early to begin their classwork or just to get away from the hallway traffic, I converse: I ask them about their writing. Some students are hesitant, or don't know how or what to ask, but want or need to be asked about an essay or assignment. Even those who only want your individual attention appreciate and expect your inquiries into their course work and writing progress.

Now for a little collusion: Only once have I not been allowed to substitute a 30-minute early arrival to class for otherwise required office hours, even after I explained my convincing purposes. The office assistant persisted in insisting that I post and keep office hours, even though my office was far from the department itself as well as the classroom buildings in which I taught. Conveniently, that particular office was on a floor only accessed from an out-of-the way hall, no name or department or hours were ever posted at that office, and nobody ever checked my office attendance, at least as far as I know. In that case, as always, my students appreciated my meeting and greeting them at the classroom, and they didn't miss scheduling any office appointments. Also, the colleagues with whom I shared that office appreciated not having to share office space with me every week.

Back in the day when I did dutifully keep office hours, no students dropped in unannounced, or one student did if you count the times that student happened to see me or hear me while passing down that hallway. As an adjunct, my assigned offices are always in out-of-the way spaces. And I can always find ways to apply my time more productively than waiting around for visitors who never show up in an office that can be distant from departmental colleagues and students, not to mention distant from photocopiers, mailboxes, and coffee shops with donuts. Certainly, I can work more comfortably at a favorite coffee shop or at my home. I do admit that some colleagues of mine appreciate their office time, accomplishing a whole lot more than I would: marking papers, posting grades, planning lessons, uploading links for classroom instruction, or phoning family members. Some assign their students to locate and visit them during office hours, but this seems coercive to me. I'd rather collude with my students than coerce them.

If your college or department has a common office shared by the adjuncts, I suggest using it to socialize, converse, and experience some camaraderie among colleagues. An adjunct's can be a lonely profession. It can be weeks before engaging a cohort in good conversation if you don't initiate it. There is value in getting to know your compadres. Find out what they're doing and share ideas and resources. Since you're probably following similar pathways, it may be helpful to strike up a conversation. They may be as curious about you as you are them, so why not introduce yourself and get acquainted. You may gain a new friend, some new ideas, and possibly a little fun to break up your day. Granted, your new acquaintance may not return next term, or your future schedules may keep you from crossing paths for a whole year or more. Adjuncts scramble. Still, wouldn't you like to be seen as the one who dispels the sepulchral gloom hovering over so many shared adjunct offices? Many of those preoccupied-looking instructors hunched at their terminals are merely wiling the time before tripping off to a class. They are gratefully relieved to share their stories, converse with fellow professionals, or click off their crazy cat videos. I've witnessed a half dozen adjuncts push away from their computer monitors and close laptops, all sliding their chairs over to circle to introduce one another and join in a conversation that rose up seemingly spontaneously after an outbreak of laughter shared between two new friends.

Signpost – Gather for Blather

> For more ideas about using your common adjuncts office to promote collegiality, turn to **Chapter 7. Confab – Being Collegial**, beginning on page 145.

While collegial collaborating, camaraderie, and conversing are the most valuable uses of a common adjunct office, in my opinion, it is OK to slip on your headphones or earbuds and mark essays and plan lessons there. Certainly, it's beneficial to students that you be accessible to them. One instructor I know takes students on a fieldtrip from their classroom to the office, so they can locate her there. Another assigns her students to visit the school's library, writing and tutorial lab, as well as her office as a sort of scavenger hunt. Many adjuncts use their offices for scheduled student conferences, but that leads me to my second commandment of constructive collusion.

2. No Conferences – Use Class time to Confer

Don't cancel classes to meet with students individually for conferences, unless of course required to. They're a time-drain. They wreck schedules. Meeting everyone individually for even as little as 10 minutes outside of class results in a 250-minute time constraint for a class of 25, which is over 4 hours in total, and that's just one class. If, for example, you have 100 students in all of your classes combined, fitting in the time needed to hold even such brief individual meetings with all students could easily qualify for the equivalent of 4–6 weeks' worth of dedicated office hours. And of course, scheduling meetings at 10-minute intervals would allow for only a very minimal, hit-and-run style conference, possibly undermining part of its purpose.

It is not uncommon for students to miss a conference or arrive late for theirs, and then your time is wasted. A student's assigned time may spill into the next, bumping your whole itinerary off-schedule or into disarray. Your sign-ups may leave open gaps, marooning you in between times. Canceling a class meeting or two to help offset the time required in order to schedule individual conferences may be a disservice in that it withholds instructional, group workshop, or peer review activity that they could otherwise receive and benefit from – all time-on-task learning multiplied by the number of students attending the class. Moreover, requiring their attendance for extra time outside of the scheduled class period could cause an inconvenience or hardship for some students who have tight class schedules, who work, and who must arrange daycare or other family commitments, as well as for those who participate in student clubs, athletics, or other extracurricular activities. In addition, clearing a week for your classes at one school where you teach may influence your performance in an untoward manner at another place of employment.

An alternative that can multiply the benefit is to review students' performance in class in groups. Once you have established groups in your composition class, meeting with each group and progressing from group to group while the others continue working on an in-class activity honors both their and your schedules by concluding your conferences during one period. Purposely selecting review topics that affect the whole group, then applying them with examples in the members' essays would allow you to meet with several students simultaneously and have an extra advantage of leaving them with their group members to peer-edit in order to follow up with one another immediately afterwards. Peer teaching and reteaching one another as they review their work together in their groups has the added benefits of hearing multiple voices and seeing different ways of approaching and interpreting a writing assignment.

Signpost – Group On!

For more about the importance of teaching with groups, as well as setting them up and their purposes in the writing class, see Chapter 4, pages 90ff.

Further, when you conference from group to group within your classroom, you can confer another multiplied benefit when the members of other groups listen to what you've been telling a previous group or continue listening to what you say to a following group after you have left theirs. Along with the feedback they receive on their own essay, individual students may gain from what you have said to other students in their own and other groups as well – something that couldn't happen in an individual conference outside of class. For your students, the immediacy of working alongside peers who are attending to the same suggestions, then searching for and sharing examples in one another's essays can encourage and may demonstrate useful behaviors and skills. It is also the case that, for some students, the feedback from their peers can at times have a stronger influence or be perceived as more relevant than your own words or suggestions as their instructor.

Signpost – In-Class Small-Group Conferences Ideas

Turn to the **Top 10 Tips** at the end of this chapter on pages 66–67 for ideas to use with your own in-class small-group conferences. Normally, I conduct these in-class conferences on specific criteria of assigned drafts of essays while students are themselves peer reviewing one another's essay drafts in their small groups.

Of course, there are a few concomitant risks while you move around from group to group to confer. A student or group may misinterpret your unavailability as wait-time until your personal direct attention spotlights that student or group. A possible solution to this risk could be to assign group tasks such as a series of peer review questions that must be answered in the review process to train their focus while you meet with another group. Another risk is the chance that a student misleads a peer with misheard or faulty information, or strikes up an extraneous conversation that derails their group's peer review progress. Sometimes your making some pointed eye contact with a perpetrator, raising an eyebrow, or pausing to review one or more questions and posing the next from the review assignment can redirect off-track students and get them back on track. You know you're really doing a good job when groupmates begin to unobtrusively direct those students who have drifted off task to get them back on task with the group. An assuring wink, thumbs up, or affirmative cluck can communicate your commendation. Any of the risks you run in holding in-class group conferences, I believe, are counterbalanced by the greater prospective benefits of those in-class group conferences: potential for multiplied communication of messages, positive peer pressure, peer reviewing and reteaching, and collegiate camaraderie and bonhomie. So, don't schedule individual meetings with students, unless you prefer meeting one to one to one to ….

3. No Extracurriculars – Play for Pay

Departmental meetings and socials, professional development sessions and teacher orientations, student activity sponsorships, graduation and convocation ceremonies – all of the unpaid extras that full-time faculty are required to attend, but part-time instructors are usually not – my advice is: don't go. Of course, if you enjoy a gathering, benefit from a development opportunity or workshop, appreciate some pomp and circumstance, are assured that attending a certain event could heighten your chances for future positions or considerations, get compensated generously (or at least equitably) for participation, or merely have some extra time that you wish to fill, please please yourself. Otherwise, this may well be the primary institutional perk you earn as an adjunct instructor: you don't have to go to what you choose not to. If you're invited, cajoled, or even required to attend a supplementary event, you can still kindly decline. When needed, you can attribute an absence to overall time constraints or a competing demand from another institution where you teach or work. Many administrators and most colleagues understand, especially those who have themselves worked as adjunct instructors. I've missed opening term orientations because I taught at another college. And I've begged out of assigned professional development sessions when the times were scheduled to accommodate administrators' calendars and not those of adjuncts. When teaching at more than one institution, I normally limit my attendance to one orientation session, choosing either the one that appears to be most practical or one at a college or department where I haven't attended before or recently.

Do what best suits you. Go to the events you choose. You're the freelancer, subcontractor, free agent, so you get to pick your gigs. If those in control frown on your choices, weigh the relative merits of doing as you or they want. Two of the colleges where I have taught pay disproportionately different wages. The one that pays more has consistently granted me a maximum schedule according to its upper limit of classes per semester, and its English department welcomes adjunct instructors to faculty meetings and socials. However, it doesn't pay for attendance. A lower-paying one has accorded fewer hours, and it doesn't invite adjuncts to its functions. It does, however, pay adjuncts for attending orientations.

One college I have taught for used to assign courses to adjuncts according to their participation in departmental and college professional development activities. For a while, leaders dutifully passed around sign-up sheets to take attendance at all events, and presumably the results translated into a pecking order for hiring, semester by semester. A year or so later, however, the attendance sheets were no longer circulating, and adjunct attendance subsided into what it had been before the use of the sign-up sheets. Department chairs and deans must have come to realize, I suspect, that adjunct instructors had outside commitments which precluded their attending many programs. I know many adjuncts who are retirees, many others who have young children of preschool and school age, and not a few who work other jobs during the workday and teach college in the evenings or on weekends. And I know many who are angling themselves to be hired full-time. Each group has its own considerations.

I apply my loyalties selectively – and so should you.

Coffee Klatsch Collegial Conversation – Writing Referees

"I'm screwed!" Blaine joined our table late, not even stopping at the counter to order his light roast Colombia. "The dean wants to meet with the chair and me."

"Couldn't it be good news?" Tara queried.

"No, it's all about my student, the football player, who recycled his teammate's paper, right down to the misspellings and fragments. The online plagiarism program caught it all."

"I thought you'd covered it with the department chair and union rep already?"

"Yeah, I thought so, too, but now some coach has taken it up with the dean. Best case scenario: a third meeting and I'm clear. Worst case: I have to recant. Already I've lost a half-day to meetings, not to mention a week's sleep. My class is divided since the football player rallied allies among his classmates in my course, and they're up in arms because they're convinced he could lose some super athletic scholarship if he fails Comp 1. There's little open road left for yours truly."

"Ow. Well, let's see if we can't drum up something together," Tara pondered. "What do you think, Jorge?"

"What if you called the dean beforehand to try and run some interference?"

"You know, that might not be a half-bad idea," Patricia chimed in.

Chan added, "Really, I worked with her back when she taught in our department. She was pleasant, a team player – at least she was back then. You ought to try it, guy."

"You're the try it guy," Jorge tapped a fist to his shoulder.

"Here's to mud in your mugs, you writing referees! Blaine, go get you some java," Jimmy cajoled, hefting the megamug. "Jeers, you-all!"

"Cheers!"

4. No Checks for Plagiarism – Assign Self-Checks

For adjunct instructors like Blaine, there may be no open road to pursue a plagiarism charge through an institution. All English and Writing departments where I have worked have published plagiarism polices. One department requires each instructor to include its policy word for word in the syllabus for every course as well as commit one lesson to its study and demonstration. I agree we should forthrightly explain plagiarism and its pitfalls, and whenever we do encounter it, we should address it. But, if offered the option, I prefer to speak with offenders individually and grant them an opportunity to redo plagiarized work. Following a department's or institution's protocol regarding suspected plagiarism can be extremely time-consuming and can cause more damage than repair. Harried administrators do not tend to welcome the disruptions of investigating plagiarism and its time-consuming due process. Students who have inadvertently or ignorantly plagiarized feel alienated by such accusation, so explaining what they've done wrong and requiring its correction is usually the instructor's best practice. Those who plagiarize brazenly or surreptitiously will have little choice but to fall in line once they realize they're caught. While it can be argued that young people who deliberately plagiarize need to be punished as a deterrent, they can often be rehabilitated and will usually not take the risk of reoffending. Except in cases of clear intent to plagiarize, which in my experience is hard to discern, I find it is in everybody's best interests to assume students' innocence initially and then suggest ways they can redo their work to avoid plagiarism.

With the immediacy and ease of the internet and the temptation of copying and pasting, many students may succumb to plagiarism; but with the availability and universality of plagiarism detection programs, it's ever simpler to detect as well. The online submission program's plagiarism indicator included in your college's technology program can be a helpful deterrent. Often, I require students to submit essays electronically to a plagiarism detector and then to review its results before I accept it. This ounce of prevention may prevent a student's plagiarizing, either deliberately or not. Making the plagiarism detection program's percentiles available to students and allowing them multiple submissions can be a great deterrent. However, I caution that it can also raise some issues. Recently, a student arrived before class in a panic, "This report highlights all my sources and the quotations in my paper. It says I plagiarized 21%, so what do I do?" When I reviewed the report, I noticed a portion highlighted that indicated it had been copied from *Another Student's Paper*, but when I checked the source, the other student's paper turned out to be an earlier draft of the very same essay diligently uploaded by that very student two days before.

Your effort at preventing plagiarism can save a student a punitive mark on an essay, a besmirched academic reputation, or expulsion from a class, degree program, or possibly the university. It could save you the griefs of getting forced into the roles of investigator, prosecutor, and judge – then possibly find yourself investigated, prosecuted, and judged as well. Please don't get me wrong. I'm not in any way conceding or sanctioning plagiarism or turning a blind eye. Instead, I'm recommending turning it into a valuable learning experience whenever possible, one that can both redeem and restore a student who has fallen from grace either intentionally or unintentionally. More than once, I have worked with students who, comprehending a definition of plagiarism and recognizing it in examples, were nonetheless unable to avoid it to their own writing. More than once, when pointing out the copied elements in these students' own work, I was met with incredulity, "Really, that is plagiarism?" Until taught to recognize it in their own writing, they truly hadn't understood. I advocate comparing the potentially damaging consequences of plagiarism with the compensating merit of their truly learning how to fix it and of you having the opportunity to help your students learn this important lesson for all their future written work.

Besides using an online plagiarism detection program and granting your students opportunities to review and revise any suspicious text, you can take a few more preliminary steps for prevention as well. Work with your students in class to generate ideas and begin writing drafts of essays, and regularly check their work in progress to help head off any temptations to copy. Accentuate authenticity and fairplay. Your own honest interactions and ethical expectations can assist with prompting their own authenticity in writing, as they want to meet your standards and not disrespect you, an instructor whom they come to admire. I often share, "When I have poured my heart and soul into writing something that I think is worthwhile reading, I feel cheated if someone steals my good words or my good ideas to pass them off as their own. Plagiarism is basically theft, stealing what really belongs to the author. Can you tell that I take this personally?" A good guide points out a trail's perils, directs hikers away from threats, and warns and restrains those who take risks. You can also spend time showing them how to properly reference, summarize, and paraphrase other people's work within their own. You may save yourself the trials of search and rescue with one or more of these strategies for rectifying and avoiding plagiarism.

5. No Weekend Wear – Dress Professionally

A former colleague of mine invariably wore a dark suit, white shirt, and tie to class. Not a traditional podium lecturer, he favored project-based instruction, preferring to lead his classes in local explorations of community issues involving plenty of interviews and research in community centers and historic halls. In fact, it was these field trips – some of which involved service learning activities – that convinced him to don this teaching uniform. "You know, whenever I wore my suit and tie in the city, I found that I could gain extra admittance for my classes," he claimed. "We were welcomed into back doors of foundations, theater stages, and even restaurants, all because I showed up wearing a suit. Also, my students act different, prouder and more self-assured, I think, when I appear more professional. And I think that I act just a little more confident when I dress the part."

I suggest that our vocation, as well as our classrooms, subject, and students, merit the honor that dressing up can bestow. I therefore recommend that as your budget and the sales racks allow, dress up for your classes. You may well discover yourself performing better or more professionally, but more importantly, you may find your students responding more respectfully and acting more professionally themselves. This behavior could even influence their achievement. Just like the students who, in deference to you would not cheat by plagiarizing, some may improve their attention and attitude, rising to the level that they perceive you to project and expect. Suiting up may support your unspoken call to quality in the classroom.

No, clothes don't "make the man," but they do make an impression. Their effects are clear in interview rooms and meeting rooms, and they may make a similar impression in the classroom. Of course, this may not play the same way in every situation. One of the business colleges where I taught has a stated "business casual" dress code for students and a strict "business professional" one for instructors. Another school has a dress code for students but none stated for faculty (some of whom took perverse pleasure in appearing more slovenly than the students). Most of the colleges where I have taught reveal a wide range of garb among faculty, from tees and tattered jeans to suits like my former colleague, leaving it up to each individual. Since many students, and not a few colleagues, pay attention to your wardrobe, choose what works for you – both now and possibly for your future – with your students and maybe with your colleagues, to distinguish yourself or maybe to blend in if hoping to enlist in the full-time ranks.

Different departments can project individual images, too: business professors in suits, science instructors in white lab coats, and writing instructors looking like Jack Kerouac, on the road. Once, I encountered an English department without a stated dress code, yet the men all seemed to sport a subdued ensemble of sweaters and slacks, and the women wore flamboyant scarves with pantsuits. If a beginning instructor, your dressing more professionally may gain a proportionate measure of respect from students and possibly colleagues, too. Conversely, standing out may be perceived as aloofness, contrariness, or even breaking ranks. Even if your department happens to have a stringent, lock-step dress code, as did a couple of schools where I have taught, you could consider tweaking your wardrobe with some striking colors and patterns or maybe accessorize just to break up a "monotony monopoly." I have taught with several colleagues who sport striking bowties, scarves, socks and other footwear, or eyeglasses. Do collude. But you may have to fit your costume to the characters and play you're performing.

While it could be of benefit to you to distinguish yourself by dressing at least as professionally as your students and as your departmental colleagues, dressing well can also improve the image of our field – unless perhaps your specialty happens to be the poets of the beatnik generation. At many of my schools, students have participated in frequent professional internships, job fairs, and practice teaching from which they often raced to classes looking like they were prepared to interview, as in fact several were. Merely dressing to maintain the level of many of the students necessitated my own professional attire. Thanks to thrift stores, outlets, discount chains, and sales, dressing up shouldn't result in busting the budget.

Dressing more professionally for the classroom may appear contradictory to introducing yourself using your first name, instead of using a title of Doctor or Professor, as I recommended in Chapter 1. This is, in a way, embracing what seem to be opposites, but that is OK. As I like to tell my students, readers appreciate a nimble turn of phrase, an unexpectedly novel supporting example, or an adroit juxtaposition of otherwise unrelated topics or ideas, which is the case here. Like a hiking guide, I undertake both the excursion with a one-of-a-kind destination, stunning overview, or challenging terrain, and my easy-access, paved, everyday rail-to-trail pathway. Adjuncts can contemplate some overtly creative, professional individualization to cleverly embrace such seeming contradictions, especially when both can be of benefit to oneself and one's students.

Signpost – First Name Basis

To review my rationale for using your first name with students, turn back to pages 33–34 in the **Fairplay, Please** section.

Finally, if you dress casually simply to go along and get along, or merely have never thought much about your wardrobe, you might consider that, like a guide, your apparent preparedness may signal competence to your followers. Like a climbing guide who shows up in a ball cap, tropical shirt, and sandals, the image you project may not match the capability to which you aspire. Try an experimental dress-up test adding or substituting just one item in your wardrobe – or performing a complete makeover, if you wish – for a set amount of time, and attune regularly to how you're received – and how you yourself react. You may be distanced, perceived as putting on airs, or you may feel too self-conscious to continue. Of course, some tweaking up or down in the level of formality can typically appease these concerns. Probably, your dressing more professionally will result in your students, your department, your field, and yourself all benefitting.

6. No Tests – Give Essays Only

Writing a college essay, like hiking, requires planning a destination and route, gathering equipment, training and practice, then pacing and adjusting for the season, terrain, and partners. The processes of selecting a relevant theme and appropriate supporting topics and examples, drafting and revising for consistency and audience, revising and editing for correctness and clarity, and formatting for readability and style require nimble applications of several kinds of mental skills, involving evaluation, analysis, and synthesis of information. Further, the advanced skills required of students to craft a satisfactory essay involve regular metacognitive reflection on language and rhetoric as they weigh alternate mechanics, vocabulary, syntax, and organization. What better way for students to demonstrate their mastery of our subject than writing extensively?

Since you teach writing, you can also test with writing. Your assigned essays carry an abundance of higher order processing skills, cognition and metacognition, applications of organization, style, word-choice, grammar, editing, and typing to demonstrate students' learning with markedly more breadth and depth than any fact-check, multiple-choice, true-false, short-answer, or recall-definition type of test could attempt. Even the midterm or final that is composed of essay questions cannot compare to the comprehensive nature of producing a multi-page essay. In a way, particularly in an English composition class, any time taken away from writing and its processes and toward taking tests is a poor investment; in fact, it is time squandered. Testing about writing is not the same as testing writing. Writing is itself a test, one that amply demonstrates students' understanding of multiple skills, such as choosing a strong theme, organizing with direction and clarity, phrasing with dexterity and creativity, formatting correctly, and proofreading accurately.

Written revisions and formal drafts of essays are more appropriate than any other kinds of tests of achievement, and early drafts of papers may be better substitutes for pretests or quizzes. Writing assignments require that students apply course contents, and they involve their internalizing the skills as they work with them, practicing writing processes with every successive revision. Examining students' multiple writings, therefore, is a superior method of assessing students' writing. In fact, if you teach English composition but test your students' mastery of it by using some mode of assessment other than writing, you are in effect not playing fair with your students by not testing what you teach. Of course, if your department or college requires you to give a midterm and/or a final examination in composition, as some do for all courses, you will want to structure this to directly test the writing skills you have been teaching.

7. No Paperless Classrooms – Photocopy Reams

Buck the paperless classroom trend. With many institutions promoting online courses, substituting electronic course packets for textbooks, and exhorting instructors to limit their use of student handouts, I advise giving paper and books a central place in your classes. Handing out a paper syllabus ensures that everyone has a copy. Asking students to download their own or reference it online may or may not accomplish its purpose. Besides, I like to ask students to highlight items or underline or mark them with a star, sometimes having them number their top three topics to reference them again later. Handouts, such as the sentence combining activities that I assign in groups, work best when all have a copy of the directions and assignment as they mark, revise, and compare their constructed sentences with those of their groupmates.

Signpost – Sentence-Combining Activities

Fifteen **Sentence-Combining Activities**, one to use every week during the semester, can be found on pages 214–228 in Appendix 4. Each has a separate theme to relate to the first-year college student's experiences.

You teach college composition, certainly an in-depth and rigorous course. Requiring pen and paper as well as computer and printer reinforces its complexity and range. Besides the sentence combining group exercises, I suggest that students take notes on paper, printed articles, and in their textbooks. To generate ideas for new essays, I often have them list their ideas on a piece of paper or a blank page in a word processor, or jot them down on a brainstorming template or other idea-generation or composition planning schema. Frequently, they sketch warm-up responses to writing prompts or draft their dialogical written conversations with partners within student groups using pen and paper or one student's laptop. Peer reviews, self-reflections, and proofreadings of essay drafts typically are written by hand in my classes, though many students nowadays like to use a computer for much of writing activity and may be accustomed to bringing their laptop to class. I like to initial and date individual drafts of students' essays as I review them to further reinforce the importance of planning, pondering, and practicing valuable stages in the writing process before polishing and producing a finished copy. Normally, I accept either a handwritten or a printed typewritten draft, as long as they have a paper copy for my initials. For some students, a paper copy with suggestions and comments may encourage their making substantial, topical changes in a subsequent revision; whereas typing onto an earlier typed-and-saved draft can result in their making simple, surficial, mechanical changes. For some, it may elicit more thoughtfulness to produce a handwritten, roughly sketched draft before revising by typing a word-processed document. Others, accustomed to the keyboard, readily draft, rework, and revise all drafts of their essays using this mode alone. (I'm not convinced yet of the efficacy of the few who have tried convincing me of the convenience of thumbs-only typing on their miniscule phone screens.)

One college I know required all students to purchase a laptop preloaded with software applications from an approved list, but few students complied – probably because most already owned a laptop. Instructors at that college didn't enforce the dictate out of respect for their students' budgets and because they didn't want to make the required purchases, either, as the college didn't provide hardware or software to its teachers. Each of the colleges where I have taught has an online learning system that it stipulates faculty must use to varying degrees. Typically, when I collect students' essays to mark, I ask them to produce all of their drafts that I have initialed and dated with my quality control check to ascertain that they have met the writing skills and any other requirements for that essay, then I have them electronically upload their latest, formatted and edited copy. Not only does this allow them the opportunity to check for plagiarism beforehand, it saves me the burden of toting all of their printed essays and preliminary drafts back and forth from class. Since I review each of their preceding drafts for separate writing skills, I can typically limit my comments on their electronic version to feedback on mechanics and MLA or APA formatting, acknowledgements of their changes from earlier copies, and a final assessment of the work.

Other than for producing and reading students' final drafts, I often use the electronic learning programs for other features, too. For the most part, my students appreciate it when I post their grades individually as well as announcements to all students weekly. I upload most of my in-class activities and materials, so that all students can access these online even when absent. This enables students who miss class to keep up with the workload, occasionally the rationale I need to convince a student to return home when too ill to attend class – which students and instructor alike appreciate. While most of my students purchase printed textbooks, a number buy the electronic, or ebook version of their texts when available, for convenience and also to save money. This has had mixed results because, although some are proficient at logging on, locating pages and chapters, reading, and taking notes on their electronic devices, a few of them have encountered numerous difficulties, such as trying to upload onto incompatible devices, negotiate the electronic book's unfamiliar format, read from a small (laptop) or miniscule (smartphone) screen for lengthy periods, or highlight or mark notes.

Here, I wish to take a brief sidetrack regarding custom-published compilations in lieu of the more traditional text. The cost advantage can be significant to students. However, an abbreviated packet of three-hole punched pages seems to cheapen the class, devaluing it by association. Replacing a professionally produced and bound, appealingly illustrated textbook with a plastic shrink-wrapped packet of perforated or three-hole punched pages, which substitutes a single-use throwaway for a durable investment, concomitantly can shrink the course's importance in the eyes of the students. These shrunken course packs can also add to your workload, if you end up having to supplement them with additional materials. Not to say that we shouldn't rein in the exorbitant costs of college textbooks, but books, especially those that look and feel like what is expected of a college text-book, do equate to learning value. The size and heft of a book, moreover, may carry a metaphorical weight, too. Reselling a text, as most do after finishing a course, confers an added value. College teachers of other subjects assign respected textbooks in their fields. Why shouldn't college composition?

Another practice that can cheapen a course or subject by association is linking to internet sites for sample essays, grammar exercises, and videoclips, as academically advanced as they may be. Since such sites are associated with purveyors of cheap entertainment and instantaneous social media and often use some of the same "quick and dirty" and "cheap and cheerful" methods of presentation, this can limit their effectiveness in a college classroom. It may therefore be wise to relegate their use in class as only supplemental. That said, I enjoy projecting a news brief or videoclip to spur a writing warm-up, class discussion, or written dialogue with partners, and these online video resources can serve appropriately as attention-drawing transitions between course topics as well. In addition, I link several websites as references for citation formats or grammar checks for times when the internet is more accessible than an index in the text or an English handbook. A college library's electronic databases, subject guides, and ebooks collection can be quite useful to advance research skills and acquaint students with the range and convenience of electronic sources. At the same time, a handy printed reference guide can prove useful to consult while writing, as questions arise about citation and referencing.

Coffee Klatsch Collegial Conversation – Bonus Lecture

"I couldn't believe it," Patricia complained. "Seven students walked into my class late today."

Jacqui commiserated, "No kidding, four of mine drifted in late, too. What's gotten into them anyway? Are we competing with springtime already?"

"Well, I fixed them," Patricia continued with a conspiratorial smirk. "I kept them all until the last minute of class as I retaught what they missed from the beginning of class. But I let all the rest of them out 30 minutes early."

"You did *what*?" Jacqui, Kara, and Jimmy exclaimed all together.

"Look, Patricia," Kara drew her aside, "let's see if I can explain. Rewarding your students with time off sort of undermines the importance of class time and what we teach. Plus, it kind of accepts the late arrivals by telling them, 'It's OK to blow-off my class since whatever you missed I'll just go over again later whenever you get here.' So there's no penalty for arriving late. In one way, it penalizes the ones who did get there early because they either have to sit through your replay of what they already heard, or they lose out on the teaching that you canceled because you decided to replay it for your late arrivers. And, worst case, that could even make you look like you hadn't planned the whole class time so coasted by just rewinding and pressing replay. You don't want to equate coming to class or sitting through a whole class with some kind of punishment, do you?" Kara concluded, waving off the others. "Oh, shut up with your stares!"

"Bonus, an after-class lecture!" Jimmy declared. "Kara, your next coffee is on me."

"You know I don't drink caffeine. This is herbal tea, cheapskate!"

"Geesh, now what do I do?" asked Patricia.

"Just carry on, same as always," suggested Jacqui, "since nothing happened."

"But don't do it again, OK?" Kara added.

"No call, no foul, eh?" Jimmy hoisted his megamug. "Here's to mud in your mugs. Jeers, you-all!"

"Cheers!"

A healthy familiarity with both print materials and electronic technologies is an important outcome of the first-year English composition class. When arranging both, your job is to determine and maintain a proportionate balance as well as to decide which of the technologies will have the staying power to remain applicable beyond your class, possibly throughout your students' college careers, and hopefully beyond.

8. No Reteaching Lessons – Teach Understanding

Class time is sacrosanct. More than any other factor, time spent writing and practicing writing skills both individually and in writing workshop activities with groups is the most beneficial to students' growth as writers. Classwork is rewarding, whether they realize it or not. Besides the facts that the students have paid for it and instructors are contractually obliged to fill it, students' sustained writing practice with peers and our direction and guidance develops them and grows composing, thinking, interpersonal, and learning skills. As much as teachers are able to, guarding class time for sustained writing practice produces better essays as well as gains in thinking, speaking, reading, writing, listening, and researching – all of which have applications to most other academic subjects and professions, not to mention their application to life skills.

Likewise, repeating a lesson could be considered an affront to those who attended its first release. It may have an unintentionally detrimental effect of snubbing those who truly deserve commendation instead. Essentially, it can be construed as condoning lateness and punishing timeliness. When you find that students haven't understood or are unable to apply something you've taught, there are two recourses if you choose to review a point already made. You may offer to reteach an individual student or a small cohort of students who would benefit from the repetition, at an opportune time when others are working independently. Or, if most students in the class did not understand the first time around, you might have to reteach a concept to everyone, but using a different angle or approach, or a new delivery or modality. Simply repeating a lesson does the students who did not understand it the first time the disservice of doubling their failure, since merely repeating it could compound the students' failure to understand it the first time, and possibly multiply any attendant frustration.

Sometimes it can be advantageous to ask an individual or two who do understand a new concept to assist their peers in applying it within a class activity, since some additional examples, particularly when supplied by classmates, often alleviate misunderstandings. In either a whole-class or small-group format, it can be helpful to revisit a topic with those who require reteaching by connecting it with a related concept that they have already mastered. Another possibility is simply to continue on, but loop back to revisit the topic periodically both to assist those who haven't yet learned it thoroughly and to deepen its understanding among those who have already learned it but who can still learn more and deepen their understanding with another application.

9. No Teaching Down – Stretch Understandings

Target your teaching somewhat above the median. Assume that your students, like the residents of the fictional Lake Wobegone of *Prairie Home Companion,* are all above-average learners, and when you teach accordingly, they will achieve to your expectations. The bar you set becomes the goal they aim for. You can scaffold assignments with several different components adjusted to different students' learning approaches, so everyone is appropriately challenged while assuring they all accomplish the required learning outcomes. Higher performers can be encouraged to take on more intricate and demanding essays, or be required to write additional pages to achieve a top grade. For those who struggle to meet the requirements – whether they self-sabotage, are underprepared, or haven't the stamina or confidence to perform well – you can assist by defining exactly how many pages they must write or what criteria they have to meet to earn a passing score. Always encourage, assist, or adjust as befits their learning needs. Fairplay doesn't mean you have to treat every student exactly alike. In fact, since students in your class likely begin with very different abilities, to be truly fair, you probably should adjust the destinations chosen and paths taken – while ascertaining that all achieve the course requirements. Overall, target the goals of your course just a bit high to stretch and challenge all.

As a way to stretch students, I encourage them from the beginning of the semester to read and write daily and to be on the lookout for interesting sentences and quotations that they can learn from and bring to class to share. I also encourage them to build their vocabulary by being on the lookout for college-level, academic words – what I call "$10 words" – that they might be able to use in their own writing. I ask them to find 3–5 $10 words every week and to complete a S-A-G-E-S index card that gives a **S**ynonym, an **A**ntonym, the **G**eneral context (definition, source sentence, part of speech), an original **E**xample, and a **S**ketch (representative drawing) for the word. I further encourage them to review their S-A-G-E-S words for possible inclusion in their writing, and I consider use of appropriate $10 words in evaluating their assigned essays.

Signpost – S-A-G-E-S Vocabulary Cards 5-4-3

A format and instructions for the S-A-G-E-S Vocabulary cards is given in Appendix 2, page 186.

Additionally, show your students how your class fits in the college's course sequence and where it's positioned among other requirements and subject strands. Try to mention a benefit and application for the majors, certificates, and degrees that your students are pursuing. Note the importance of college-level research and essay writing to those who will likely be required to write the average number of seven research papers – or more in some majors – during their college careers. To build your case, you may give previews of writing assignments in upper division courses across a variety of disciplines to give your students an idea of what they need to learn. You may even want to adapt such assignments for your course, to help your students get a leg up in preparation and confidence when they matriculate on to their next courses. You can also bring up the value of developing their vocabulary and argumentation skills for other classes.

Teaching down drags the pacing of a class, sometimes to a crawl. Doing so can discourage those who want a challenge, and it can demoralize those targeted for the slower pace. Although many students speak positively about an easy course, no one really appreciates a course in which the time goes slowly and the level of the work, and of learning, is low. Students want rigor and challenge, as well as the supports, scaffolds, encouragements, and acknowledgements their teachers proffer to ensure that all accomplish the promised learning outcomes of the course and that all receive fair play en route.

10. No Open Seating – Assign Seats

I've been over this point before, but it bears repeating: Always assign seats. When left to their own devices, likes gravitate to likes. Either that, or in an application of the bus seat principle, students individually sit apart from one another, waiting until every one of the seats or groups has someone in it before filling the gaps. Often, students of different races and ethnicities cluster separately, that is, they self-segregate. Later arrivals look and probably feel a little like the kids on neighborhood playgrounds who get picked last when choosing players for teams.

Diversity is a cultural strength of any nation, so schools and colleges, and especially individual classrooms, ought to reflect it and nurture it. Too often, although schools recruit for diversity and trumpet it, they do little to purposely promote, engage in, or actually teach it. On campus and in classes, students continue unconsciously self-segregating until instructors intervene to mix them up. Of course, classroom arrangements can inflict their own wounds if all the teacher does is assign students to a diversity group. For not a few students, face-to-face social interactions with classmates from different backgrounds may require some guidance or assistance to initiate a conversation, sustain civility in their discourse, and accept full participation by all their classmates. Practicing interracial, cross-cultural, multi-gender, and interfaith courtesy and conversation is not a skill that all students have acquired before arriving at college. Yet it is well worth our while as instructors of their first-year college composition classes to work on this, since we probably have the best opportunity to reach the broadest population of the college, given that nearly everyone must take our writing classes. We likely get the widest diversity representative of the college's student population before groups and cohorts break off to study in their chosen fields. Therefore, our classes are an opportunity to broaden their ideas and experiences.

Trail Marker – 10 Commandments of Constructive Collusion

Easy – Select one of the ten collusion commandments that you want to question or think more about. On a scale of 1 (low) to 10 (high), to what extent do you agree with this commandment? How would you rewrite it to match your own teaching practices? How might you try adapting your current teaching to align more closely to this collusion command?

Moderate – Rank order the 10 Commandments from the most important (#1) to the least (#10), in your opinion. Choose any three to explain why you positioned them where you did.

__ No Office Hours
__ No Conferences
__ No Extracurriculars
__ No Checks for Plagiarism
__ No Weekend Wear
__ No Tests
__ No Paperless Classrooms
__ No Reteaching Lessons
__ No Teaching Down
__ No Open Seating

Difficult – Choose one of these 10 Commandments to replace with your own. Which one would you replace? What would you select as your own Commandment of Collusion, instead? Briefly write your own rationale and explanation for your new commandment.

Top 10 List – In-Class Small-Group Conferences

In the second commandment of collusion, I recommended replacing out-of-class, individual, student conferences with in-class, small-group ones. Here, I make ten suggestions for you to consider as you conduct your own in-class conferences, group-to-group. To enhance their success, I encourage all group members to listen while I review only two or three writing criteria in everyone's essay – skip ahead if you wish and look at the next section, Lingo, for some suggested conversation starters and phraseology I often use in class conferences.

1. **Encouraging Idea Generation.** When I move about the class to visit each group, I usually begin in-class conferences by checking students' idea-generating efforts for their first assigned essay. Typically, I ask them to produce their list of starting ideas, questions, proposal, bubble or spider chart, brainstorm, or free-write – whatever I assigned them to prewrite in preparation for the essay – and to have it ready for me when I arrive at their group. Often, I ask them to share their topics with one another within their groups before I arrive to look them over. After skimming each list, I write my initials and the date in the bottom left corner – this is what I call my Quality Control. When I collect final drafts, I ask them to produce all of the preparatory drafts, including this prewriting to generate ideas, which have my initials and the date noted on them. I attempt to move quickly from individual to individual as well as from group to group, asking, "Do you have enough topics?" "Are your topics college-level worthy without being too lofty or too elementary?" and "Are you interested enough to write about this for the next couple of weeks?" I stipulate a length, such as a half or a full page of listed ideas, or a minimum number of topics and subtopics – something I can measure or count before initialing and dating. As you practice in-class, small-group conferences in classes of different sizes, lengths, and participants, you will determine appropriate amounts of work to measure within the class time.

2. **Working with Multiple Drafts.** One benefit of the in-class, small-group conferences is that they allow you to check multiple drafts of a single paper. In an initial draft, you might tell students to include three ingredients, such as a poignant story, a vivid description, and a detailed explanation with examples to illustrate each. So you can quickly check their work, ask students to highlight an example or two. Again, before you come around, suggest they read their group members' drafts and help them elaborate or clarify their text by asking a question or two they may have about some aspect of the writing. Usually, I conduct my in-class conferencing at the same time as the small groups are reviewing one another's drafts. Often, I conference about the very same writing points that they are reviewing. Doing so both reinforces concepts and demonstrates processes with their small groups. As with the prewriting example in Top 10 List number 1 above, initial and date the drafts in the same spot on the first page for quality control, so you can easily tally all of their drafts of an essay.

3. **Refining Paragraphs.** For an in-class, small-group, one class-period conference session with a revised draft, suggest that students number their paragraphs for easy reference. Recommend that they combine some simple sentences, or if many of the sentences within their paragraphs are very lengthy, advise instead that they deconstruct one or two down to simpler, shorter sentences. In a rudimentary way,

given the time limits of a class period, doing this will stimulate/encourage some initial thinking about organizing paragraphs and varying sentence structures. As your students become more adept at these tasks, you can adapt your suggestions and questions in the small-group conferencing sessions, by asking them to label sentence types and include appropriately punctuated dialogue, flashbacks, frame stories, or foreshadowing techniques. Remember, afterwards, to initial and date the bottom left corners – or another spot – after they have finished.

4. **Focusing on Introductions.** If you conference for another revision, focus on their introductions, checking for an opening statement, or hook, and a thesis statement to summarize or overview the theme or purpose of the essay. You might also try adding a couple of stipulations, like, "Try to make your introductory statement a question [or a quotation, conversation with quotation marks, personal story, or another appropriate opener] this time, and rewrite your thesis as one compound-complex sentence for me to check." Then circle back later to check it.

5. **Identifying Best Paragraphs.** Another idea is to ask students to identify the best paragraph in the body of their essay, the one with the best illustration, sentence variety, or optimal length, and announce that you plan to read only that paragraph this time – or only that paragraph and the introductory paragraph, as you have time. As always, initial and date it when up to your specifications, or, if not, return to review it and initial and date it as you have time.

6. **Creating a Title and a Subtitle.** As you near the turn in date, a possibility is to assign a two-part title: a snappy, attention-grabbing phrase, and an explanatory overview as a subtitle, connected to the main title with a colon (:). For example, if a student is exploring the nursing profession and course work required for the degree, a sample, two-part title could be "Healing Hands: Becoming a Degreed Registered Nurse."

7. **Considering Reader Response.** Inquire how students anticipate that their readers would respond, and ask, "What do you intend for your reader to think or do when reading your essay? Mark three places in your essay where it most effectively communicates this, and read the selected passages to your groupmates."

8. **Checking Referencing and Format.** Instruct students to "review one another's Works Cited or References pages, in-text citations, and picture captions for proper MLA or APA format. Compare them to the samples in the text [or handbook, website, or another source]."

9. **Improving Wording.** Suggest they select and highlight key words and weed out any repetitions or replace them with synonyms, identify verbs and aim to make more of them active verbs, search for worn out or flat adjectives to replace with fresh and innovative descriptives. Have them spell-check and grammar-check their work.

10. **Reviewing Other Students' Work.** Besides your initialing and dating their several drafts of an essay, you may ask them to peer review by initialing some key criteria that you stipulate they identify in one another's drafts.

Lingo – In-Class Conferences

1. "Curiosity may kill cats, but it enlivens writers, so all eavesdropping is encouraged during in-class conferences."
2. "From our conference and everything you overhear in your own and others' peer reviews, make a list of 3–5 Notes to Self, things that you plan to improve in your next draft."
3. "Someone once said that imitation is the sincerest form of flattery. Find something in your partner's essay that you'd like to try in your own."
4. "In this activity, it's called collaborating, not cheating. Share your answers in your group. Share what you learn."
5. "When everyone in your group has reviewed one another's drafts and finished a Notes to Self list, get my initials on each as I circle back to your group. That's my quality control."

Q's – In-Class Small-Group Conference Starters

1. "How did you arrange your story, description, and explanation parts? Why did you organize it this way? What is another arrangement that you could try?"
2. "How would your introduction sound if you rewrote it with your own backstory or personal reflections in a first-person narrative?"
3. "What is one topic that you could still add to the body paragraphs of your essay? Where would it fit best with the others? Why?"
4. "What did you change in this draft of your essay? Why?"
5. "What is something you plan to try that you saw in a group member's writing? How could this look in your essay?"

Chuckle – Overtime

"As much as I'd love to keep you all after class to go on writing and revising, I'd have to charge you more for overtime."

Quotation with Sentence Surgery – Mark Twain

"Whenever you find that you are on the side of the majority, it is time to reform."

– Mark Twain

```
      dep      A         B         dep              B       ind
[Whenever you find] [that you are on the side of the majority,] [it is time to reform.]
                                                     dep + dep + ind = cx
```

- 3 Verbs: 1 Action and 2 Being Verbs: find, are, and is
- 3 Subjects: you, you, and it

- 2 dependent clauses beginning with subordinating conjunctions: <u>whenever</u>, <u>that</u>
- 1 Independent clause
- 2 dep + 1 ind = Complex sentence

Closing Conversation – Float Your Boat

Adrian wondered, "What if I didn't have my draft ready to review today or get your initials on my Notes to Self list at the end?"

"Good question. I imagine it wouldn't sink your ship, but I do count them all as drafts when I mark your essays. When you turn in all your drafts, so I can study your writing processes, I don't expect it would necessarily float your boat, either. Does that begin to answer?"

Figure 2.2. Gathering Ideas

Figure 2.3. Curiosity Enlivens Writers

Chapter 3. Construct – Democracy, Development, Dialogue, and Design

Deweyan learning communities found in a thriving democracy would be well prepared to identify and confront student marginalization. These communities would practice the kind of communication and sharing that has the power to illuminate the behaviors, policies, and beliefs that marginalize individuals. They would practice the kind of close communication and experiential learning that promotes individual growth.
– Clifford P. Harbour and Gwyn Ebie

Figure 3.1. Point Reyes Lighthouse, Point Reyes National Seashore, California.
Credit: Emily A. Matthews file, Bay Area (adapted)

Coffee Klatsch Collegial Conversation – Call Out Cookie Cutters

"Nah, I'm not into all that social constructionist, deconstruction, post-apocalyptic mumbo jumbo," Michel slouched in the booth, cradling his glass with both hands. "I just want to try to meet my students where they are."

"But you have to have a theory," Rondela reasoned. "Whether or not you acknowledge it, you must operate from some underlying premises."

"Yeah," smiled Patricia, "so, let's have it, are you a breaker-downer or a builder-upper, a constructionist or deconstructionist?"

"Postapocalypse or predispensensationalist," added Jimmy, "or is this all just purgatory – or worse?"

"Or," Tara replied, "he could be none of the above."

"Maybe," added Mehdi, "plus he can be all of the above, too. It's OK to cherry-pick bits and pieces from separate sources when they work in different situations."

"How about if they contradict?" Rondela posed.

"Especially if they contradict, I say," Mehdi interjected. "That's a whole lot more like real life than those prepackaged, everything-in-alignment, one-size-fits-all, cookie-cutter curricula!"

"Hear-hear, let's call out those cookie cutters!" Jimmy called out, raising the megamug. "Jeers, you-all; here's to mud in your mug!"

"Cheers!"

Chapter Trailhead – Construct

- Pragmatic Adaptation – Northern California's Point Reyes National Seashore
- Course Creation – Dewey's Pragmatic Democracy
- A Couple of Russians – Vygotsky's Development Zone and Bakhtin's Dialogism
- Course Design – Build It, Bridge It, Brand It

Pragmatic Adaptation – Northern California's Point Reyes National Seashore

On the day I visited Point Reyes National Seashore in Northern California, a rolling fog and persistent rains limited my hiking to short loops of the Earthquake Trail and a bit of the Rift Trail, both inland. As long as I could, I tarried at the Ranger Station and museum hoping the weather would improve, but it steadily declined, so I drove out the Sir Francis Drake Road, a narrow lane (certainly by California freeway standards) of broken pavement traversing a succession of muddy ranches and cattle grates, out to the lighthouse on the Point, out across the tectonic faultline, out to the edge of the North American continent. Cold and damp, with my visibility limited by splattering rain showers, I hurried from the car, hearing more than I could see: a fog horn rose up from the lighthouse, positioned out on the Point. When I encountered a gate blocking access to the stairs that led down to the lighthouse, I halted to soak in the view, mostly of the lighthouse's roof, and some of seething surf snaking white along the cliff lined coastline northward. I felt and heard surges surf beneath me, but I couldn't see any of the waves break. Then a fog enveloped it all. When there was little left to view, I felt the rains perceptibly chill. Disappointed, I squelched back to the car and slowly traced the winding route back across the peninsula, back to the mainland. Not what I had anticipated, weather made the day memorable.

In teaching as in hiking, so often it is necessary to adapt to the circumstances. Instead of the weather and terrain, the class atmosphere and makeup can change. It is prudent to have a Plan B ready, and it is wise to adapt your teaching to a class's unique circumstances. I remember the final examination for a college Education course many years ago – it is that memorable, in which I was asked whether I adhered to either B. F. Skinner's behavioral modification theory (e.g., Skinner, 1953) or Jean Piaget's model of stages of cognitive development (e.g., Piaget, 1977). I had no idea. Although I wasn't too enamored of the concept of conditioning children to learn by manipulating them through the dispensing and withholding of rewards like the bell used with a Pavlovian dog or the birdseed used with Skinnerian pigeons, still I used rewards and praise to motivate students' achievement and shape their behavior. Piaget I liked because he studied mental cognition, something that seemed appropriate for an answer on an Education test. I chose him.

The good news for teachers is that you don't have to choose between theories. Like Mehdi, you may cherry-pick among them. Choose the approaches that match your classroom experiences, your own predilections, and your students' learning needs. It's OK – even advisable – to apply what appear to be paradoxical methodologies since different students and situations may require alternate approaches, and mixing them together in a complementary teaching method is entirely appropriate – as long as it is effective. Skinner and Piaget are not mutually exclusive, and neither are other Education or English theorists. I wonder if we expect different schemas to be contradictory because they are frequently introduced in reaction to a predecessor. This means that an appropriate response to be up-to-date is to throw yourself all in with the latest program, and then throw out the others that it discounted. Today, if I had to label my teaching approach, I think I'd call myself a pragmatist, someone who cherry picks from any and all theories. If required to choose among different models for my own teaching methodology, I would today require an Option D. *All of the Above.*

Course Creation – Dewey's Pragmatic Democracy

Like John Dewey, the eminent philosopher of Education, I lean toward democracy and pragmatism. I embrace what I understand as John Dewey's call to start with the resources and with the people we have in the classroom, then work together on project-based activities, and in so doing to form a democratic community (Dewey, 1967; Harbour & Ebie, 2011; Pappas, 2008). More situation-guided than philosophy-driven, his theory, or praxis, emphasizes that learning arises through collaborative practice (Dewey, 1963; Fesmire, 2003; Fishman & McCarthy, 1998). It seems to me that the writing classroom is perfectly suited for such activities involving student interactions: discussing ideas, peer reviewing essays, constructing sentence combinations, and revising drafts of essays. When run as a writing workshop in which students and instructor continually draft and review written work, and discuss and critique one another's ideas, the first-year college composition class is the ideal setting to practice the process of give and take that is constantly undergirded by mutual dignity of the democratic society. In such a place, students freely speak and respectfully listen to one another's differing opinions and are introduced to others' divergent perspectives and experiences.

I aim to form a microcosmic democracy of my classroom, and I encourage you to also. As a teacher of first-year composition, you have an unparalleled opportunity to facilitate the interactions of diverse students, and there may be no better place to coordinate their engagement with democratic practice than your first-year college composition classroom. There, students from every background gather to write, review, think about, discuss, and analyze their varied ideas and ideals with their peers – and you. They bring to bear all their multifarious beliefs, biases, and backgrounds to the writings and discussions that you prompt and guide.

Sometimes, I wonder, with all the separate public school districts – not to mention the magnet, charter, private, parochial, and home-schools feeding into the university – whether our students have ever before experienced the great diversity of which our writing classroom communities are comprised. Many, I suspect, have never formerly been exposed to the vibrant variety available to them on our campuses. Possibly, many have been self-segregated, and not only themselves but their ideas and attitudes, too. Further, I wonder if our classes may be the last and best chance for many students to experience and appreciate testing ideas and thoughts in this richly diverse, democratic microcosm of society before they step out into it as fully fledged participants.

Dewey (1963, 1967) maintained that students ought to be taught technical skills, life skills, and vocational skills, interacting with these projects and tasks along with their fellows. He seemed to suggest that clear and immediate application adds value to learning. To my thinking, guiding students to select topics that interest them and pertain to their studies, careers, home lives, and communities, and to relate their writing explorations to themselves both individually and together with their classmates, befittingly meets the criteria. As well as nurturing students' thinking, communication, and social learning, composition classes can benefit job skills, too. As part of composition classwork, students can draft cover letters and resumes, email responses to career postings, and reply to interview questions. Exploring a career, they may investigate where new jobs are listed, how much an entry-level salary pays, which colleges offer appropriate training programs, and how many openings may be anticipated in their chosen careers when they graduate. They may shadow or interview a practitioner of the trade, and report their encounters, or reflect upon and analyze their experience. They can explain, as writing assignments, how to design a website, post a blog, update an email inbox or online calendar, or organize a picture repository. Additionally, students can review articles on topics in their prospective fields, thereby practicing the genres that will likely be assigned them in specialized courses and perhaps also on the job later on.

Arranging students in heterogeneous groups encourages their interaction, bringing their diverse ideas and perspectives to bear on one another's topics through assigned collaborative writing as well as peer review activities. Paradoxically, it is through their differences that they best help one another address a college-level, diverse audience, by conversational give-and-take, questioning and answering, both responding to and anticipating one another's different perspectives and experiences. From these interactions, they may recognize and add, examine, or compare various dimensions of their writing topics as they shape them into stimulating themes to engage more informed and pluralistic audiences. While working at crafting their writing and honing their ideas within such a democratic classroom community, they can learn to attend to and appreciate others' ideas and examples, and thereby broaden their abilities to observe and respect, address and accept, different perspectives and peoples – the underpinnings of a democratic community.

A Couple of Russians – Vygotsky's Development Zone and Bakhtin's Dialogism

In addition to the prototypically American educator, theorist, and philosopher John Dewey's pragmatic democracy, I'd like to review the theories of two seminal Russians as well. Lev Vygotsky and Mikhail Bakhtin were Soviet Russians who taught, thought, and wrote about the interplay of language and learning during the first half of the 20th century (e.g., Bakhtin, 2002/1934; Vygotsky, 2012/1934). Both examined the social and dialogical character of language, its acquisition and application, and its moral implications and ramifications. I think their ideas contain several vital applications for the teaching of writing to first-year college students.

Vygotsky examined the interplay of students' social interactions and how this prompted their learning. His theory of the Zone of Proximal Development (ZPD) posits that students achieve better when presented learning activities that exceed their abilities yet lie within reach when they stretch themselves with suitable effort and purposeful guidance (Zebroski, 1994). This is the "zone" of their "proximal development." Since college students come to first-year writing with a wide range of composing abilities, discovering their zones is of great benefit for an instructor to tailor instruction to students' and classes' learning needs, but doing so can present its own challenge with such diverse writers. Still, there are a number of approaches to uncovering their ZPD's.

To discover what first-year college students already know, and then arrange learning to match these ZPD's, the instructor could simply begin by asking them. A one-page survey at the beginning of a course can provide a preliminary snapshot of students' past accomplishments, including whether or not they have taken other college English classes, how long it has been since their last English class, what genres they prefer to read and write, how they feel about writing and their own writing ability, how proficient they are at researching, and how computer-savvy they are. In addition, surveying a class at other points, such as when introducing a new concept to a class, can be helpful. A teacher can ask for a show of hands: "How many of you have written a memoir or a personal essay before?" "Who's familiar with compound and complex sentences?" "Has anyone ever written an APA-formatted essay?" Asking questions about their experiences and knowledge after introducing the concept and providing an example allows students an opportunity to refresh their memories and collect their thoughts before committing themselves to a response. In this way, they don't overcommit to a concept that they may misremember, and they can avoid replying if uncertain whether or not they do remember. Asking students to write a brief, introductory sample can also furnish a quick indicator of their writing aptitude.

Another way to check students' knowledge is to circle the room and eavesdrop when groups converse while collaborating on an in-class activity like sentence combining, or read over students' shoulders as they craft their own ideas into drafts of essays. (When they do work together in pairs or groups, their sharing answers and copying from one another is not cheating; in fact, it's collaborating, cooperating to craft their own best practices by drawing on each other's strengths.) Besides, the more they converse, the better an instructor listens to learn what skills may need targeting or reteaching and which have already been mastered. Targeted listening and over-the-shoulder readings can help a professor purposefully plan activities to best benefit individuals, groups, or classes. Sometimes, with a few timely suggestions, the teacher can guide them along a fruitful path, and spare them unproductive wandering in a bewildering wilderness.

When students sit together in groups, even when working individually, everyone can hear your directions and may apply them independently. If occupied with groupwork, they can turn towards one another with immediate questions, especially when you are attending to another group. This collective peer pressure can be a positive step towards their becoming independent learners who adroitly seek guidance as needed. Even puzzling with their peers over different ideas or activities may draw groupmates collectively into addressing one another's Zones of Proximal Development while helping each other. Now and again, especially when group members' ZPD's do not closely align, so they scatter at their own paces, you may have to refocus a group's attention to encompass their trekking all together and not simply accomplishing a task singly. Groups, usually encouraging and industrious, may discourage or mislead members, especially when ZPD's diverge. When that occurs, your simply stepping up to a strayer or pulling up a chair to join a group that is drifting or backtracking might itself redirect them. Since their conversational cooperation is often important to your monitoring for their zones of proximal development, as well as maintaining a pragmatic, democratic classroom, your regularly circling and listening, and sometimes intervening and redirecting, may well be necessary.

Reading students' choices of words and expressions, sentence structures, and paragraph logic and organization in their writings may readily tell you if they're over their heads, too easily skipping through the activities, or are appropriately challenged at an attainable level just beyond their present aptitudes. Discerning how they vary phrases and sentences, arrange paragraphs and ideas, and select words and mechanics, you gain evidence of their writing strengths and limitations that suggest direction for future teaching topics and focuses. Their interactions with a writing assignment itself – the planning, drafting, revising, rethinking, polishing, and formatting of an essay, for instance – quite naturally addresses most students' own ZPD's while expressing and exploring their ideas through the craft of writing. Essay drafts and revisions, together with peer and instructor's reviews, can help construct helpful scaffolding for students to achieve their writing goals. As Vygotsky (2012/1934) suggested, choose challenging assignments that stretch students' abilities and periodically ratchet the difficulty upward, so they may continue practicing, reinforcing, and refining skills they've already learned, then attempt more advanced challenges.

One more application of Vygotsky's ZPD might be in the region of ideas. As an example, if you deem it valuable that students learn to practice a Deweyan pragmatic democracy to appreciate diversity and respect their fellows, then assigning varied groups, requiring civil discourse, and developing collaborative class activities may themselves comprise a suitable zone in which to challenge without overwhelming them. With students whose previous schooling might have been made up of simplistic worksheets of fill in the blanks and copying notes from a blackboard, merely coping with great ideas could be less a proximal zone and more a continental leap. If the sole -ism they appear comfortable discussing is consumerism – or a subset of consumerism such as electronics or entertainment – another -ism, such as feminism, may require additional bridges to bring into range. Still, especially with those whose learning was limited, a big idea or two, along with the wherewithal to draw it into their ZPD's, could be like discovering a life-giving oasis after having crawled across a barren desert.

Another helpful theory is Vygotsky's (2012/1934) inner speech hypothesis, which claims that language is social and dialogical, even when internally considering responses and conversations, or, generally, in thinking. Thoughts and written compositions as well as verbal interactions are all social formations that reflect and initiate the interplay and reflexivity of dialogue. Therefore, it is through an internal dialogic interplay that ideas and images are formed to allow the making of meanings, development of thoughts, and assimilation of cultural conventions. As James Zebroski has interpreted these notions, "Writing . . . from a Vygotskian perspective . . . is a *relation*, specifically a *social* relation shared by a community with its own history, traditions, and motives, and individuated by each new student in her or his own unique way" (Zebroski, 1989, p. 196; original emphasis). Instructors enhance students' learning and literacy, it seems to me, by making their writing classrooms places for interaction, where students converse socially, compare thoughts and texts, and consider ideas and texts, all in the context of dialogue with others. It's good for them to talk and also to think, ponder, and reflect; that is, the classroom is a place for both external and internal dialogue. I suggest that we arrange class times to allow for both in approximately equal measure.

Like Vygotsky, Mikhail Bakhtin's (2002/1934) theory of dialogism accentuates all the varieties of voices and genres within the interplay between conversation and composition (Fecho, 2011; Halasek, 1999; Ward, 1994). He, too, encouraged social interactions in learning. Frank Farmer notes Bakhtin's claim that we gather meanings through our conversations, and our understandings come together somewhere in between speakers and listeners or readers and writers, both "created and sustained through dialogue" (Farmer, 2001, pp. 16–17). Making meaning and reaching understanding, therefore, require dialogue, whether it be external with somebody else or internal within oneself. Besides writing and speaking, our thinking, too, is a theoretical, internal, conversant consultant, one's own imaginary writer–reader–critic–friend residing in the mind, and whom everyone reads into every interaction. Bakhtin calls this a *superaddressee* (Farmer 2001, p. 23; original emphasis), an internal editor through whom we negotiate our lives, interactions, and relations.

Bakhtin's (2002/1934) dialogism seems to suggest that students should be allowed multiple opportunities to practice language with as many and various interactions as the instructor can make possible – writing and speaking with classmates and instructor,

Trail Marker – Dialogical Activity

Easy – Write an example of a discussion question or class conversation that you could use to initiate dialogue among the students in your classroom. Better yet, craft this question in dialogue together with a colleague.

Moderate – Design three dialogical classroom activities that you could use to promote pragmatic democracy among the diverse students within your own classroom. Again, consider crafting this in conversation with a fellow instructor.

Difficult – In one of your dialogical classroom activities from the Moderate Trail Marker activity above, write a sample script including the supposed dialogue among three or four diverse students who are grouped together in one of your classes. After crafting a page of their possible dialogue, what do you predict is a strength of your activity? What may be a weakness? What might you change before applying it in your own class? If possible, work on this activity together with someone else.

with other written texts, and with diverse audiences – along with regular opportunities to ponder and reflect. Arranging the classroom as a writing workshop with abundant opportunities for interplay among its various participants may be well-suited for inspiring many students' dialogic interaction, and allowing retreats for their individual, interior reflection and cognition can stimulate their thinking and construction of text. Alternating the order in which students perform meaning-making activity – from groups to individuals, or conversely from solo to ensemble – could assist different students with the prompting of both their external and internal dialogical processes. Dialogism, the Zone of Proximal Development, and Pragmatic Democracy – use these three notions, I suggest, to underlay your own college writing classrooms and courses. In a democratic, dialogical classroom, you will keep calibrating and recalibrating activities to ensure that they challenge learners and connect them with the requirements of that specific class, the course, and the college.

Course Design – Build It, Bridge It, Brand It

Sometimes teachers consciously operate from an internal philosophy or a driving theory, designing essays and crafting activities sure to connect students with Aristotle's rhetorical triangle (i.e., logos, ethos, and pathos),[1] to trek with them across Berlin's (1987) three categories (i.e., objective, subjective, and transactional rhetorics), or to bring them to feminism or Marxism, to semiotics or structuralism, to deconstructionism or dialogism, or to pragmatic democracy. Teachers may lean on textbooks or institutions' expectations for their grounding theories, supplementing them with personal perspectives. Other times, instructors might plan their own maps in the way of assignments and activities that do not follow a textbook or course package: they may lead along their own favorite pathways with their own tried and true lessons, or they may prefer to discover new trails or blaze their own. You may, too. Scholars ranging from Bizzell (1992) and Flower (1994) to Bartholomae (2005), Christensen and Christensen (2007), and those writing in the Villanueva and Arola (2011) collection have reflected on the many and varied factors motivating composition teachers and the design of their courses.

Much of my joy in teaching derives from the exploring of new ideas, making forays beyond standard texts and learning outcomes, and adding my own insights and excursions to the common curriculum. There often is more than one route leading toward your goal, and you may not realize which you prefer or which works better with each class until you have attempted a few. After you have had an opportunity to teach several different course philosophies, textbooks, or packages – including what you decide to use from this *Guidebook* – try to merge several elements of each. Continue to tweak and adjust your curriculum to fit your own theories, practices, contexts, and students. The classes that you specially design and guide yourself may be some of your students' more memorable college experiences, as well as your own. You will find that the same course never takes the same path. Students change, as do classrooms and circumstances. So does writing theory. And you do, too.

Have you ever experienced that an activity which succeeded remarkably well with your morning class fell flat in the afternoon? Its failure could have been due to the

---

[1] For a brief overview, see Lutzke and Henggeler (2009).

groups' arrangement or to the students' aptitudes or behaviors, homework preparation, or out-of-class circumstances; or possibly it was an even more random thing, such as a change in the weather. It could have been caused by a multitude of unrelated influences or even a one-time confluence of several factors occurring all at once. Regardless, it is vital to your own as well as your students' well-being to acknowledge and appreciate the differences in your classes, and then teach to each one accordingly. As much as you may be tempted to ensure standardization of your course contents and delivery across different classes, writing and its instruction is never a one-size-fits-all proposition. Choose the trails that appropriately challenge the learners in the classrooms you're leading and practice the skills and activities to best prepare them for the terrain they will encounter. It is important to bridge your course to your students' learning needs. Classes, like individual learners, seem to have characters of their own.

As guide, you keep recalibrating and reconstructing the delivery of the course's contents to meet your students' learning needs, by adapting the pace. When some have to slow down, it may be helpful to surround them with others to motivate and reteach. This can benefit both groups. If others require greater challenges, send them ahead, let them take some more difficult excursions, or assign them separate challenges. Your task is to elicit their best performance and keep prompting them to become even better. Your classroom is filled with students who are in many ways one another's best resources, so encourage them to look out for group members' and the entire class's commonweal. Encourage them to ask a classmate for assistance – even assign them to do so when a class is characteristically too hesitant or self-conscious to talk amidst peers. Since your students are either full-grown adults or on-the-cusp of being grown-ups, tap into their accumulated experiences and ideas by having them read one another's drafts, contribute to collective writings, and discuss all that they are thinking and doing.

Finally, besides building course contents and bridging them to students, brand your classes. Freely be yourself. Just as students and classes have their individual peculiarities, you, too, are allowed your own idiosyncrasies. Exult in your individual quirks. No one is just like you. No one can take to the trail exactly what you do. You don't have to clone someone else; instead, be true to yourself and make your class your own. Let it reflect your character and your style. Trying to replicate somebody else's purported best practice can be frustratingly unproductive. If you can't take it and make it work for you, cast it aside to keep working at your own best practices. Smudge your fingerprints stickily all over whatever you're doing, and stamp your footprints muddily wherever you're teaching. Consider sharing your own stuff – writings, drafts, assignments, and ideas, along with your adaptations and adoptions of what you find practical and workable – with your students.

Top 10 List – Theoretical Applications and Implications

1. Structure classroom time around workshop, group, and hands-on writing, so students learn primarily through interactive, hands-on practice.
2. Arrange classroom chairs or desks and tables if available in groups rather than rows. Sets of four position students to interact readily in duets and quartets.
3. Align classroom activities towards written essays, and frequently explain their connections and purposes.

4. Anticipate and invite the student question, "Why?" They deserve to know the course's direction and that of all assignments and activities, too.
5. Assign ample classwork as cooperative, exploratory practice with plenty of challenging team exercises requiring sustained interactions.
6. Involve students in writing for the majority of class time.
7. Engage students in dialogical interactions among peers to practice verbal as well as written communications.
8. Begin every draft of an essay during class time, and check a portion of it to ensure that students are challenged yet working within range of their Zones of Proximal Development.
9. Acknowledge all hard work and persistence towards a writing assignment to motivate students to continue addressing their challenges.
10. Continue to encourage students to tackle new challenges by allowing them abundant opportunities to draft and revise their work.

Lingo – Encouragements for Challenges

1. "You've certainly made substantial changes between your rough draft and revision. Way to go!"
2. "When your thesis is packaged into one focused, robust sentence, call me over to initial and date it for quality control."
3. "How can you rearrange the explanations and examples to best communicate your topic in these three paragraphs?"
4. "Where could you look for articles from newspapers, magazines, and journals that relate to this theme?"
5. "After you've read my comments on your essay, please resubmit it at the start of our next class once you've had a chance to rearrange the organization of your body paragraphs."

Q's – Dialogical Democracy

1. "After you have had an opportunity to greet all your group members today, ask each one, 'How was your weekend? What did you do for fun?'"
2. "What did each of your groupmates decide to write their essays about?"
3. "Of the three readings, which one did your group choose to read and analyze?"
4. "What is something your partner did in this essay that you would like to try yourself in the next draft of your own?"
5. "Could you add a description to communicate a cross-cultural exchange, such as dialogue in another language, a holiday custom, or an interaction that leads to a better understanding of yourself or another character in your essay?"

Chuckle – Senescence

"I've always said that a loss of memory is the second indicator of senescence, the encroachment of old age, and … I forgot what the first thing was."

Quotation with Sentence Surgery – Milton Gregory

"True teaching, then, is not that which gives knowledge, but that which stimulates pupils to gain it."

– Milton Gregory

<pre>
        ind   B   A   dep   A
[True teaching, then, is not that] [which gives knowledge,] [but that which stimulates
      dep
pupils to gain it.]
</pre>

ind + dep + dep = cx

- 1 Being verb: is
- 2 Action verbs: gives, stimulates
- 3 Subjects: teaching, which, which (double-duty as subordinating conjunctions – see below)
- 1 Independent clause
- 2 Dependent clauses with subordinating conjunctions: which, that which
- 1 ind + 2 dep's = Complex sentence

Closing Conversation – What to Write

"Why don't you just tell us what to write?" Ron complained. "I preferred it when my teachers used to tell me exactly what I had to write about."

"Did you really? I imagine that could work in some instances, but I usually find real-world writing like ours to be more wide-open and wide-ranging. What are you finding in your other classes and on the job? What would you expect to encounter as you continue in your field and in your life?"

Figure 3.2. Beginning Drafts

OVERVIEW

Section 2. Paths & Maps
   Praxis, Processes, Protocols, and
   Possibilities in the First-Year Writing Classroom

Chapter 4. Collaborate – Working Groupwork

Writing fits comfortably in the domain of collaborative learning because writing demands dialogue between writer and context. Writing can succeed only when it adheres to the conventions of "normal discourse" for a given community, and writers can learn this discourse through using it in the kinds of conversations that occur in collaborative learning.
– Anne Ruggles Gere

Figure 4.1. High Point Monument with Lake Marcia, High Point State Park, New Jersey.
Credit: Beyond My Ken

Coffee Klatsch Collegial Conversation – Kidding

Jacqui was steaming and sputtering to herself, not participating in any of the conversations percolating around the table.

"You look like something's brewing, Jacqui!" Rob jibed.

"That kid uses a tone like that with me again, I don't care if we're in front of the whole class. I'm showing him the door," Jacqui fumed, half-standing to slap her palms together.

She sat back down to take a sip of her drink, then smiled around at all of the hushed faces staring back. "What? Kids like that need direction, and I'm the one to point the right way! You'd do the same, right?"

"Kids today!" Tara chuckled. "Back when I was in college, I walked across the state, uphill and upwind both ways, through snow and sleet."

"And that was just for summer semester," added Patricia. "Don't get me started on winter."

"Besides, they don't need any directions," Jorge chimed. "They have GPS."

Jimmy hoisted his megamug. "You're driving me to drink! Jeers, you-all!"

"Adolescents!" Jacqui slapped at Jimmy, smiling. "Cheers!"

"Cheers!"

Chapter Trailhead – Collaborate

- Capitalize on Diversity – New Jersey's High Point State Park
- Group On! – Advantages and Assumptions
- Who's on First? – Assigning Groups
- Friendly Confines – Growing Loyalties

Capitalize on Diversity – New Jersey's High Point State Park

Circling the summit, the *high point* in New Jersey's High Point State Park, located at the northwest corner of the state, my family, in-laws, and I admired alternately the broad, placid Delaware River and Pennsylvania Poconos Mountains across it, New York's city of Port Jervis tucked in the river valley on the north corner of the tri-states' confluence, and the Catskills peaking up north. The northeastern view reminded me of the Appalachians' Blue Ridge region, with heights and hollows extending in rows as far as I could see. The southwestern centered on the wide Delaware valley edging around mountain slopes until coursing through the Water Gap out of sight southward. Having climbed the monument, my kids went with the nieces and nephews, aunts and uncles, to swim or boat in Lake Marcia, so I had the afternoon to traipse about the trails. While the monument and picnic area were mobbed with tourists from New York and beyond, the lakeshore's beach was blanketed by families with grade school and preschool children. The middle and high schoolers threw frisbees and footballs, lounged in hammocks, or explored inlets and crossed the lake in kayaks and canoes.

Climbing from the lakeshore, bustling with families, I strode back uphill toward the monument. I skirted the parking lot, where a group of Albanian twentysomethings had popped their hoods to rev and compare their car engines, alternately migrating from the autos' exteriors to interiors to test their sound systems, with doors opened wide. A Puerto Rican family reunion, gathered at the picnic area along the ridge, was barbecuing, a number of the party attending to an impressively high-flying Chinese dragon kite with streamers buzzing aloft, having rigged an ingenious weights-and-pulleys system attached to a car's back bumper. When the winds shifted, I watched several carefully maneuver the car across the parking lot to take advantage of the winds rising from the opposite ridge, after first riotously swooping their dragon back and forth over the crowded picnic tables. On that sunny Sunday afternoon, I heard Japanese, Korean, Spanish, as well as English spoken with pronounced Texas, Chicago, New York, and plenty of New Jersey accents.

Returning to the trail, which narrowed suddenly, I continued along the ridge and sloped downhill. Two turns, and the tourists were remotely distant, only the dragon kite sailing now and again into view high above. Besides the wind, I could hear nothing. I crossed through a hiking shelter made of stone and cross timbers, watching for the blue A's which marked the Appalachian Trail. Rounding a corner, I encountered a hiker. By no means Bill Bryson just starting out, the grizzled sight, scent, and sounds of this hardened specimen accosted me all together. Stepping off the trail to allow him free passage, I can't say he slowed his determined pace or acknowledged my presence at all, except that he pulled his floppy hat lower down while bursting past me, perhaps eager to get into town with its little laundromat, pizza parlor, and post office. From tourists to young people, from families to solo adventurers, I encountered such a great diversity of travelers and trekkers during that one afternoon vacationing in New Jersey. Who could have imagined that just one ridge over from that teeming recreation spot are vast miles of mountainous wilderness?

Like the variety inherent in a random set of day trippers, afternoon strollers, and Appalachian Trail backpackers all negotiating the same space, the students who all end up taking the same writing class negotiate it differently. Some come to stroll, others ramble along, and a few march through, and they all have different tastes as regards writing genres, activities, assignments, and instructors. Some students prefer learning to be like straight-ahead hikes along the paved or improved roadbeds of former railroad tracks, their writing tasks clearly defined through teacher-led instruction and concrete directions as to when, what, and how to write their notes, their assignments, and their essays. Others would rather ramble among an assortment of options, lingering at the trailhead to consider the available options, preferring customized writing topics that free them to explore their own interests at their own pace. And now and again, a rugged individual appears who wants immersion, hoping to comprehensively explore one topic from beginning to end. The writing assignment and approach that guides one student to success might trip or possibly even exhaust another.

Students of diverse backgrounds and experiences can be expected to respond differently to writing classrooms, especially since they are placed in what for many are unfamiliar situations. How they respond should not always be taken at face value. A silence may signal tacit comprehension, or it might indicate a fear to speak before peers, an aversion to admit they don't understand or aren't keeping up, or possibly even a disinclination to participate. It's helpful to an instructor to figure out students' underlying motivations before guiding their learning. Whenever unsure, give students the benefit of the doubt by assuming good intentions on their part. Even if incorrect, your treating them positively may prompt their best efforts.

Nowadays, technology plays a heightened role in students' college learning and writing, but not all use it with the same dexterity. Some students arrive with all the latest electronic accoutrements. To many of them, an electronic device is like a third hand – remove it, and they feel wounded, shorted. They favor using a laptop or tablet to communicate, research, take notes, and write essays. Others (e.g., older adults returning to school after a long absence) may be uncomfortable placing fingers upon a keyboard. Unlike the tech-savvy student, who might benefit from just a short-and-swift cursory review of formatting an essay on the computer, the latter may want considerably more practice and direction. Seating technophiles alongside technophobes whenever in a computer lab or typing at laptops may be an answer: the self-styled geeks can benefit by having to explain verbally to a writing partner, who in turn can profit by having to ask their assistance and review the explanations.

Moreover, students' pre-college writing experiences and preparations can affect their college expectations and self-perceptions, affecting their successes in the first-year college composition class. They may come from sprawling high schools in urban, suburban, or rural settings. They may have been taught individually at home. Some have achieved their high school diplomas or GED's in a community center, magnet school, military base, or prison. Classes may have a student or two beginning college while completing high school. Some may have published essays, poems, raps, or blogs, or they may have edited the school newspaper or magazine. Others may not have entered a classroom, opened a book, or written more than a two-thumbs text message in over a decade. College classes get them all: overachievers, unrelenting workers, underachievers, and those who invest minimal effort into their classwork and compositions. Some have been thoroughly or even over-prepared, while others arrive noticeably under- or unprepared. Some come confident, yet others are downright fearful. They want motivation, challenge, hope, realism, interventions, assistance, listening, guidance, interest – and, every one of them, fairplay.

Like my sunny summer's afternoon at High Point, you may encounter students from different ethnicities, nationalities, and a wide variety of cultures with as many customs. They are invaluable resources of fascinating experiences and perspectives that may require your extra interest and attention to elicit from them. While some students may require a friendly interruption to slow or stop their incessant personal monologues, others could require a starter question and a sympathetic setting to start them talking. Not a few may need a series of prompts en route, too, to assist them in continuing or completing a thought, an example, or a story. Some merely want your permission to respond. For them and for the rest of your students' benefit, make an effort to call on everyone with a greeting, question, or acknowledgement, and not always to default to those who raise hands or continually demand your attention. Without making the process too intrusive or complicated, I typically direct a first question to the student who is sitting farthest away from me. Then I call on the individual in every group who is sitting the farthest from me, usually working my way from group to group clockwise around the classroom. After calling on one person from every group, I cycle around the classroom, asking a question to a second person from each group, normally calling on the one seated to the left of the first respondent – in other words, working clockwise around the class and each group. This way, I try to ensure everyone's participation. To help students prepare for their turns, I often ask the groups to discuss their responses beforehand or together arrive at a consensus, before calling on individuals for answers.

Diversity adds little value to classes if left alone, if you do little to capitalize on it. The advantages of arranging and rearranging students to ensure that they interact with seeming unalikes helps them help one another, not only just getting along, but also producing assignments collaboratively and contributing to a group collectively to ensure everyone's achievement. The trick, then, is to recognize students' differences as varied classroom resources, all of them necessary for constructing community and building bridges, instead of obstacles to understanding dialogue. In both Chapters 1 and 2, I examined the importance of assigning seats to students as forming and practicing a pragmatic democracy. In this chapter, I begin by introducing some ways to implement this practice in your classroom.

Group On! – Advantages and Assumptions

Assigning groups is necessary to ensure that the diversity of our students is spread effectively about the classroom, so they can reap the benefits of talking, writing, and thinking with others who may have dissimilar ideas, approaches, and skills. Working in a diverse group of others accords students and classes many advantages. At the macro level, it helps them participate in a vibrant democratic model in which all participate actively, learning not only English skills, but also how to interrelate and dignify one another as well. Working together on a common assignment leads students into forming relationships of cooperation and solidarity, drawing upon their disparate talents and backgrounds to contribute towards a group's common purpose. As with many worth-while objectives, arranging students to accentuate diversity has some risks. For example, arranging students to accentuate ethnic diversity among groups in a classroom can cause the untoward effect of students' feeling singled out to be scattered among a dominant ethnic group. It may be difficult for a minority group of students to be parsed apart for distribution among a larger cohort. This may lead them to conceal their differences from the other students – in effect, pretending to be other than they are as a way to easily get along – or to resent the attention and so withdraw from full participation. To offset this risk, I typically assign small groups randomly.

Here, it may be advantageous to revisit some assumptions. First, learning to write can be better when vocal and interactive – *dialogical*. Students in the composition classroom don't have to sit singly in rows, silently copying notes. Although it can provide time for quietly composing and individually reflecting, class time is an opportunity for students to interact and participate collectively in writing workshops. Dynamic conversations about common group tasks result in stronger, more memorable learning and a more democratic community. Classes where many conversations are going on at the same time may sound and appear chaotic, but this is the look of a pragmatic democracy in action. Asking students to read their writing aloud or express their thoughts orally before writing them down can help them to speak and listen more effectively, maybe also help them develop a "taste" and "feel" for words and syntax as they craft different combinations, and it adds a dialogical component as they hear and contribute to other group members' verbalized constructions. When they try out their ideas by speaking them aloud, the instructor can eavesdrop on their productions and conversations, and so assess their group's interactions and individual understandings.

Further, as your students engage in groupwork, you may cast yourself in a facilitative, supporting role, stepping from the front of the classroom to move among the groups, listening and affirming as well as leading and directing. When you move into such a supporting role and out of the center of attention, you empower students to lead conversations, working with the words and ideas that they supply, rather than waiting for you to furnish them. Your allowing them to lead can free them to explore ideas and to experiment with sentences and paragraph constructions that your presence or directions might have suppressed. Even if your leading would have resulted in a better end product, when students take the initiative to collaborate among themselves, their own approaches, processes, and leadership can engender deeper learning. Occasionally, their work may even overtake what you had anticipated. Their chosen pathways can also help you plan for their future activities as you circulate, watching and listening for skills to target, suggestions or redirections to intercede, and accomplishments to call attention to and celebrate.

Frequently, observing students' progress may require your standing or sitting apart, circulating outside the student groups, like a baseball team manager who studies the game play from the dugout; at times, you may have to refrain from intervening inopportunely and allow a group of students to work out a problem themselves. It may be helpful to keep reminding yourself that your goal is to promote democratic interaction and invite individuals' independence. Keeping this in mind might mean that you experience fewer temptations to interrupt students' changes in pacing, their explorations down what initially appear to be less productive paths, and their sometimes seemingly extraneous conversations. Group time can sometimes be as valuable when spent discussing how to enroll online for the next semester's classes or where to find financial aid on campus as when spent working on an assigned writing activity. Your steering them back toward the lesson task afterwards may be necessary, but it may not be if the group itself does so of its own accord. Not only can this be a powerful lesson in independence, it exemplifies democratic self-governance – thus, well worth some additional class time.

Regarding groupwork, *share and share alike* is a refrain worth emphasizing. All students share their answers and ideas within their groups. Even if they choose to jot down prospective answers as trial runs before committing to them or pausing for some silent or whispered internal dialogue before sharing their ideas aloud with the others, students can be encouraged to discuss answers and share writings.

Figure 4.2. Group-on Quartet

In addition, when working together on class activities, require group members to agree upon their responses, and ask them all to write the same answers on activity sheets or in their writing notebooks. Doing so has some benefits to each group: every member has written down what is collectively deemed to be their best work; they have confidence knowing that their answers and writings have the approval of the others; they all contribute; and they usually accrue over the course of a semester a notebook filled with good and varied writing samples.

Who's on First? – Grouping Students

You may select from many different techniques to ensure that student groups are diverse, but you need to be the one doing the grouping. Possibly as important as any other direction you give in class, your assigning of students into groups can acknowledge and honor students' diversity and help to shape your class's democracy. Left to their own devices, even if only once, likes flock with alikes, and unalikes get picked up last or left behind, as castoffs. While never your purpose, by not carefully grouping students for diversity, or worse, allowing students to choose their own groupmates, you ultimately sanction

Trail Marker – Quartets

Easy – List and explain 3–5 reasons why students in your first-year college composition classroom should be seated in assigned groups as their "default" classroom seating arrangement.

Moderate – Normally, I assign my classes into quartets, groups of four, but they may as readily be grouped into duets, trios, quintets, sextets, septets, or even larger groups. What advantages can you think of for one group size over the others? Select a couple of group sizes as headings for columns, then list the relative advantages and disadvantages for each. Write a paragraph giving your rationale for one group size over the others when forming groups in your own classroom.

Difficult – Think of two or three different collaborative activities to assign in your classroom, such as peer reviewing an essay, then explore how the number of students in each group could affect it. For example, might it be more beneficial for pairs of students rather than larger groups to conduct a peer review? How could peer reviews be assigned to trios or quartets instead? Write a page to explore your ideas, comparisons, and implications.

a classroom division. Like the chosen and the castoffs when children choose up teams on the playgrounds in grade school, a pecking order is established: fittest, fit, unfit or least fit. Undemocratic, the classroom has been turned into a sanctioned oligarchy, and its instructor unwittingly endorsed students' self-segregation.

You want your students to collaborate with as many of their classmates as you can arrange, yet you want to guarantee them a welcoming and comfortable classroom. Some may be working alongside peers from other ethnicities, cultures, politics, or communities for the first time. College may present their first experience outside of a nurtured subcultural enclave, whether ethnic, racial, or another identifier. Their comfort zone may be stretched as far as it ever has before simply by sitting in their teacher-selected small groups. Your best approach, it seems to me, is to design activities that get them to work together; in other words, give them a common cause. Spend no time dwelling on any initial differences or discomforts if you can help it. If you introduce a task that requires their interaction to achieve together, students often demonstrate an admirable democratic diversity as its (maybe unwitting) practitioners.

In Chapter 1, I talked about establishing partners, randomly assigning a number to form pairs who interview each other, then introduce themselves to the class during the first class meeting. Next, I usually pair partners together into groups of four, my default classroom arrangement when feasible. Usually, I rearrange groups at the beginning of each new writing project.

This is a good time to consider the individual needs of those who have special accommodations requirements such as assigning a partner to assist with note-taking, sitting near a board or screen to see, or allowing additional room for a wheelchair or service dog. In addition, you may experience a situation in which some students are best kept apart. It occasionally happens that students who are unfriendly to each other find themselves in the same class. In such cases, it may be desirable to make sure those students are not in the same group. On the other hand, you cannot automatically assume that separating students based on your own sense of its necessity is in fact necessary. I once discovered that two of my students had immigrated from opposite sides of what was then a civil war in their home country, and so I was careful not to put them together in the same group. As the class progressed, and I'd repeatedly assigned them to separate groups, they together assured me, smiling, "We are in America now where people need to get along. You don't have to keep us apart anymore." On the other hand, I've also experienced a situation in which I'd assigned members of rival gangs into the same group and then wondered why they skipped alternate classes until reassigned into new groups weeks later to begin another writing project. Sometimes it may be beneficial to ensure that someone has a similar partner assigned to the same group. I recall an ESL student who struggled to ask "the Americans" questions but opened right up when placed in a group that included another ESL student – it didn't matter that the second student had immigrated from a different continent. At any rate, it is a good policy to attune to and adapt as circumstances arise.

Randomly assigning groups can present many playful, positive possibilities. It can be as simple as announcing, "Gather all your possessions, it's time to group on!" Then number off individuals within each group to coincide with the number of groups we're forming: "Ronald, start us off, OK? 1 … Kaitlyn … 2 … Minghan … 3 … Jose … 4…." Normally, I take this path of least resistance and most diversity: randomly numbering, that is, "counting off," individuals within groups up to the number of groups I wish to form, such as 1–5 or 1–6. I try to remember to start in different places and count in different directions from group to group, so as to maximize the differentiation among group assignments, causing different student arrangements every time I reassign them.

Different colleagues of mine prefer to seat students as they arrive, greeting them at the door and adding individuals to groups as they step into the room. Others have had each student draw a playing card from a deck – using, say, only the Aces, Twos, Threes, Fours, and Fives to assign students to five groups of four – all those with the same number (or Ace) card going to the same group. You can get creative and ask them to line up by height, birthday, or commute time to class (if you teach on a commuter campus) as criteria for forming groups. While this can get them physically moving up and out of their seats for a refreshing, brief break and prompt some cheerful conversations, it may not always assure that students work with different and diverse group members. Sometimes, to achieve your desired results, it's important to stack the deck or prearrange your assigned numbers beforehand.

The main goal is to form groups of diverse members to reflect and practice pragmatic democracy and so gain from and contribute to a diversity of perspectives and ideas while collaborating on common class activities. Arranging groups of students who are studying in the same program while the class is working on an essay researching careers can meet the goal. Assigning students with similar interests to groups may be appropriate to explore similar themes – or separate topics about the same theme. Use your discretion, sometimes playfully positive and light, at other times purposefully direct and task-oriented, as best befits your classes.

Figure 4.3. *New groups already?*

Trail Marker – Group On!

Easy – Which one of the suggested techniques for grouping your students heterogeneously would you like to try? Can you think of a different approach that may present an advantage?

Moderate – How frequently should you rearrange the groups in your classroom? Why? How would you balance the comfort that students gain by remaining in a group for a lengthier period with the diversity attained by exchanging groups more often causing students to group with a greater variety? Compare your response with a colleague, if possible.

Difficult – In the last paragraph, I gave an example of assigning groups of students with similar interests or who share a program of study together. What are some other circumstances when grouping students with similar interests could be advantageous over heterogeneous groupings? What disadvantages might homogeneous grouping present? Share your ideas with a cohort.

Friendly Confines – Growing Loyalties

"We still get together every week at the coffee shop," Lori greeted me when we crossed paths on campus, one term after she had participated in a student study group with three classmates in English 100. "Some of us are taking the next English course and studying together, but we mostly just compare our classes and schedules. Ariel and I are signing up for the same Government class in the spring."

For many students, the personal connections that they make at school influence whether or not they return for subsequent semesters. While some come to college with a whole coterie of already established friendships or some acquaintances from their hometowns or high schools, many arrive at our classroom doors without any compatriots. If left alone, they may easily make new friends, or not; they may sit apart, work separately, and study solo. When instructors make optimal use of the diversity in classes by arranging students into groups, they help to alleviate students' tendencies to feel alone or unsupported. In addition, making the effort to greet every student at the start of each class period, and encouraging them to greet one another by name as well, turns classrooms into inviting places to come and study. A formulaic routine of cordially greeting each other may instill the genuine habit thereafter. And it may be just the impetus necessary to keep a student returning to class – and to college. Adding a professional handshake and focused eye contact in addition to the daily positive greeting could prove a useful career or interview skill as well.

Once you've established diverse groups, optimize their functioning with regular group activities. Remind your students periodically that their goal is to make sure every groupmate understands the assignments, fully participates in the activities, and aims to be able to explain them to a class visitor or new student. Sometimes a group or group member races to finish or competes with others to finish first. When that happens, it's good to remind them of the goals. In some cases, you might have to step back a bit to adapt your purposes to your students. I'm reminded of a student who was fluent in three languages, but struggled with the prepositions, conjunctions, and articles of the English language. Requiring him to finish a common class activity at the same pace as other group members served only to slow the others and led to their resenting his participation. I made an exception for him, allowing the others to furnish him their answers and allowing him to not complete every group activity when doing so dragged the whole group behind. This worked out better to everyone's satisfaction, and it safeguarded his dignity. That student unfailingly took his lessons home and meticulously completed them all – initially with a tutor – reinforcing the importance of adjusting the activity's demands for his group's and his own well-being. Everyone appreciated the consideration. No one cried foul.

Now and again, you may encounter a group or an individual who wants to dominate discussions. Or on the flipside, you might come across individuals who resist working in groups. Instead of undermining our democratic intentions by succumbing to these students' wishes, you may attempt to avoid the problem with a few well-directed instructions beforehand. Asking the groups not to turn in and not to ask you to check any completed assignments until everyone has finished, announcing that you'll initial everyone's completed work only after you have checked everyone's responses or listened to them all reading aloud from their finished work, could refocus them to collaborate together.

Another approach is to assign a different daily spokesperson for each group, announcing, for example, "Together agree on your group's responses, and when everyone is in accord, practice the answer with your spokespersons to prepare them to represent your group accurately." Sometimes I delay assigning the spokespersons until after the group's assignment has been completed, so everybody has to prepare thoroughly should they be called upon to speak for their group. Then I may state, "Today's group spokesperson is the person sitting closest to the door / sitting farthest from the clock / the youngest." Switch spokespersons daily or weekly until everyone in a group has served. Typically, I call on every group's spokesperson, moving in clockwise order around the classroom so as not to overlook anyone.

On occasion, I make use of the spokesperson arrangement, too, to ascertain that a group has discussed an issue together before anyone may ask me. In this case, I attend to questions only when a group's spokesperson raises a hand, even if the question didn't originate with the spokesperson. Usually, when I arrive at a group, I ask that spokesperson what the group thought before responding myself. If they haven't addressed it as a group beforehand, I simply reply, "That's OK, just get back to me after you're ready." If the spokesperson simply points to another groupmate with, "They have a question," I lock eyes with the spokesperson and respond, "What is it?" then, "Let me know when you're ready." If another group member asks the question when I arrive, I simply say, "Sorry, I only reply to the group spokesperson now. Can you discuss it in your group?"

Another technique can be to ask everyone in the group to raise hands when there's a question, and not entertain any individual questions when doing groupwork. Instead of using a spokesperson for this technique, it can be important to call on someone randomly when you respond. This can circumvent an instance in which one person with a question tells everyone in the group to raise hands, calling you over merely to attend to that individual's question without discussing it in the group beforehand. If that occurs, ask, "Have you had a chance to discuss this all together? So I can ask anyone about your group's ideas first?" If it's clear that they haven't, just say, "OK, I'll get back to you once you've had a chance to talk together."

Usually, to allow groups the time to discuss ideas and answers, and to ensure that they do so before seeking my input, I often announce after giving directions for a group assignment, "While you're working on that activity in your groups, I'm coming around to check the homework assignment that you completed for today, so please set it out for me while you're working together." If someone stops groupwork to ask me something when I arrive to check, I may give a brief response, but I probably will redirect back to the groupwork by saying, "I'll circle back after I've had a chance to check everyone's assignment first." Sometimes, I add, "Keep working ahead until then."

By the way, this approach of delaying your response to students' questions can work well if you happen to have any narcissistic pupils who choose not to listen to initial instructions and expect you to repeat them individually just to them afterwards. Requiring them to wait until after you have finished checking everyone's assignments or making them turn to groupmates to glean what they should have noted before can prove to be an effective deterrent. If they don't catch on themselves, the peer pressure from groupmates who rapidly tire of regularly repeating directions to those who are clearly capable of understanding the first time ought to curtail such a self-centered exercise.

At the beginning of this chapter, you were introduced to Lori and Ariel, two participants in a voluntary student study group. During the first third of a semester, I usually look for potential student study group leaders who are faithful attendees, hard workers, creative revisers, and collaborative team members whom I will invite to lead optional student study groups. Student study groups are made up of 3–5 participants who want to meet together for an optional additional hour outside of class, in which they continue reviewing one another's essays, working together on classwork, or reading and discussing a book together. Student study groups encourage collaboration beyond the class period as well as offer extra work on assignments and papers among students. Identifying prospective group leaders, as I get to know them and watch through their interactions with others how they're perceived by their peers, then asking them to serve as the prospective leaders of a study groups of 3–5 classmates can be rewarding in itself. I sweeten the deal by promising them a grade-gain of 5%, so they do not experience any penalty for diverting time and attention from their own writing work to plan and assist with the work of others. Besides, the students who lead deeply internalize the writing skills for themselves.

Participants in student study groups, besides gaining from an additional hour of study, revision, or practice outside of the class time, benefit from the interaction and guided review with their classroom peers. And they make two, three, or four more social connections to help cement their commitment to continue college towards their own matriculation. I check in with the group leaders to ascertain participation and study topics, and sometimes I provide them supplemental materials. On the whole, I keep my distance. They decide whether their time together is best spent completing assignments, reviewing lessons, or revising essays. Allowing them to decide how they spend their time increases the value of participating in these outside, student-run study groups for their collaborative independence and practice of lifelong learning. Such groups extend students' supportive networks and learning environments beyond our classrooms to the coffee shops, cafeterias, and study rooms of the college campus and community as well.

As necessary as the assigning and arranging of student groups may be, it is of at least equal importance to plan purposeful and challenging learning activities. In the next chapter, I suggest some appropriate in-class activities to suitably utilize pragmatic democratic groupwork in a first-year composition class.

Top 10 List – Group On!

1. **Grouping Regularly.** Try to divide the class into new groups regularly. You don't have to get very creative or fancy. Merely count off to assign or reassign groups, and then you can get right back to the real work: writing, reading, conversing….
2. **Pairing within Groups.** Within each group, ask members to partner up with someone different from before whenever doing a paired activity in class.
3. **Calling for Responses.** When calling on responses from groups, allow time for members to discuss and agree upon an answer before you select a student to reply instead of always calling on those with hands raised. Try not to allow anyone to hog the spotlight or cower silently in the shadows.
4. **Asking All.** To vary the respondents when you pose a problem to the whole class, and to avoid only calling on those who raise their hands, you might begin by calling on the person sitting farthest from you, then the one nearest, the person farthest to your left, and the one farthest right – like superimposing the cardinal points of the compass on your classroom with North farthest and South nearest. Then I usually work my way clockwise, calling on the next person Northeast, then Southwest, and so on to include everyone in class. Another approach is

to select the one who's the oldest or the youngest in each group. Others could include asking for the person who has visited the most countries or the most states or provinces, who has traveled farthest, who is wearing the oldest pair of shoes, who most recently saw a movie in a theater.

5. **Checking for Understanding.** When you wish to check students' understanding of a concept, try this: pull up a chair to sit with a group, and at random choose an individual to reply to your question or to show you an example of this concept in a written draft. Then visit the next group to check for the same concept, and the next, and the next, until a random student from each group has responded.

6. **Selecting Representative Assignments.** If in a time crunch for checking in-class groupwork, randomly select one or two individuals' assignments to check, alternating between them to read several representative responses. (It is unnecessary to read all; in fact, it defeats your purpose of finishing on time.) If the one or two representatives' groupwork is acceptable, I normally initial and date all the group members' work to indicate my approval. When the work for whatever reason is not satisfactory, in the interest of time, I normally suggest they all make one – and only one – significant change while I check the other groups' work. Then I return to confirm their having made this singular change, and I initial it, even if overall at a substandard level.

7. **Offering a Bonus.** Sometimes, your providing a bonus question or task can stretch students' engagement with an assignment. Especially when a group completes its in-class work before other groups, an extra cooperative activity for them to aspire higher as well as to further apply or challenge their thinking about a class concept can be rewarding – and it can forswear their retreating from classwork via cellphone.

8. **Prowling About.** Prowl, circle, eavesdrop, and lean in to scan their work, going from group to group but sitting with each group for no more than a few minutes to check an item, ask a question, or initial and date a completed activity.

9. **Acknowledging Effort.** Besides the quality of a group's work, acknowledge good collective effort, especially when everyone is wholly engaged, or all members strive to contribute to the group's tasks.

10. **Flying Solo.** Individual students may run out of steam and require some separate time out to recharge. Groupwork can be extra demanding and especially draining for some students. Allow for regular opportunities to retreat in class from groupwork as you observe the need. Interspersing opportune times for such solo tasks as writing drafts or reflective thinking can offer a welcome break from group activities.

Lingo – Shake and Share: New Groups/Spokespersons

1. "OK, it's time for another Group On! I'm taking away your name and assigning you a number to randomly rearrange our groups."

2. "Gather your belongings and prepare to migrate. This week, let's count off clockwise, beginning with Fiona, 1; Richard, 2; …. [when a quarter of the way through the roster, to form quads, or when midway through the roster, to form pairs:] Nate, 1; Jamie, 2; …. Gather your belongings and sit someplace new,

beside your new partner [or group members]. Take a minute to get acquainted or reacquainted, then settle in."

3. "As you arrive in class, greet everyone in your group by name, and shake one another's hands. In addition today, share together …[your essay's theme, what changes you made in the revision for today's class, what you did for fun this weekend, the last movie you saw, or another conversation prompt]."

4. "This week, the group spokespersons are the youngest members of each group. Who is the youngest in your group? Discuss what responses [to assigned group questions] your group's spokesperson should share with the class.

5. "Sorry, you're not the group's spokesperson, are you? Who is? Take a few more minutes to communicate all together in your group, and if your question still hasn't been answered internally, have your spokesperson get back to me again."

Q's – Who's Number 1? Group Placement and Protocols

1. "Who is in Group 1? Let's place your group over here by the windows. Group 2 – Let's sit back center. Group 3 …?"

2. "After everyone in your group has finished the assignment together, go ahead and try the bonus application questions. I'll pull up a chair and check the answers to a few key questions from somebody in every group and then initial and date everyone's to signify their completion. Who has a question about the group protocol?

3. "Does everyone in the group have the same responses? OK if I check numbers 3, 5, and 8 for your group?"

4. "Does everybody in your group have the same answers written? Does anyone want some additional time before I check your work?"

5. "Who would like to participate in an optional student study group to review classwork, essays, or a book from the reading list [of titles provided] with 3–5 classmates for an hour once a week during the rest of the semester?"

Chuckle – Lovable Losers

"For all you baseball fans, I have two favorite teams: My favorites, those lovable losers, the Chicago Cubs … and whoever happens to be playing against the St. Louis Cardinals." (Of course, this chuckle works equally well for any other two rival teams, and it's worth repeating whenever a student sports a jersey or cap from one or the other – or even another team in the same league. Some, occasionally, will choose to do so just to provoke my response. Here are a couple of my standards: "Uh, Rachel, about that [Cardinals baseball] cap…," and "Go, Anthony, [sporting a Chicago Cubs baseball team jersey] we're going to get along well today.")

Quotation with Sentence Surgery – Walt Disney

"We need to be life-enhancers, people who reach out to enrich the lives of others, to lift them up and inspire them, and we need to surround ourselves with life-enhancers."

– Walt Disney

        A   ind   A   dep
[We need to be life-enhancers,] [people who reach out to enrich the lives of others, to

                                    A   ind
lift them up and inspire them,] [and we need to surround ourselves with life-enhancers.]

ind + dep + ind = cd-cx

Closing Conversation – Picking Teams

"Are we ever going to pick our own seats?" Sheila asked after class.

"What, and revoke all my vast power?" I retorted, chuckling.

"Really," she persisted, "why can't we just sit with our friends during the last month of the semester?"

"Yes, honestly, that is a good question, but think a minute about everybody else, those who aren't your friends, who don't get to sit in your group. Where do they end up?"

Sheila shrugged, not wanting to concern herself, "I don't care. They can go sit wherever."

"See, that's really the issue. I do care, so that's why I try to make sure that everyone gets to sit with and work with and maybe even befriend everybody else in here."

Figure 4.4. Peer Reviewing

Chapter 5. Corroborate – Tackling Class Activities

[S]entence combining is really about building relationships among ideas and showing them in clear and interesting ways. Sentence combining shows ... writers options for creating effective writing that sings while they gain experience and stamina for relentless revision .... Sentence combining is about playing with ideas and shaping them into effective syntactical patterns that make sense for individual writing situations .... Sentence combining gives students the flexibility of options, revision fluency, and confidence.
– Jeff Anderson and Deborah Dean

Figure 5.1. Dogwood Blossoms at Davey Dogwoods Park, Texas.
Credit: Roy Luck at Flickr, Creative Commons

Coffee Klatsch Collegial Conversation – Sepulchral

"When I start class, it's like I'm unearthing a tomb. Can't anybody carry on a face-to-face conversation anymore?" Patricia bemoaned.

"You're not kidding. Yesterday I told my students that they were playing alone together – like preschoolers sitting in a sandbox. They're sitting with each other, but nobody was interacting with anybody else," Tara added.

"College students, thumbs tapping phones, all playing alone together – now that's a picture!" Mehdi agreed.

"Yes, maybe we should start calling it 'unsocial media.' So what can we do about it?" Tara asked.

"More than that, how can we get them to talk together in class?" Patricia continued. "Some days I'll toss a discussion question onto the floor, and all it does is writhe and die. Oh, is that ever painful to watch!"

"No hands!" Jimmy called out, raising his like goalposts.

"What? Like 'No hands on deck'?" Mehdi retorted.

"I call it 'No hands.' Don't raise a hand because I'll call on a few folks at random, so you all have to have your answers ready."

"What if they don't have an answer? Then what? Sucks to be you?" Tara grinned.

"Sometimes, but usually I tell them to talk it out in their groups beforehand to agree on an answer, so if they do hang, at least they all hang together."

"Cool idea, man! But I want to go back to that quiet-before-class thing," Jacqui interjected. "My afternoon class was so bad, it seemed like they were incapable of conversing face-to-face. I started giving them a daily greeting protocol just to break the icy silence. Let's see, today's was, 'How was your commute to class?' OK, I know, it sounds kind of lame, but some days I have a hard time getting them to shut up before I can start class. Today, when I called on Pedro, he said his group got talking so much about their bikes that he forgot about what the greeting question was."

"Shut up and commute on over to our table, already!" Jimmy raised his megamug. "Jeers, you-all; here's to mud in your mug!"

"Cheers!"

Chapter Trailhead – Challenging Tasks to Tackle Together

- Scenic Detail – East Texas' Davey Dogwoods Park
- Sentence Surgery – Parsing Passages of Motivational Quotations
- Sentence Combining – Strong Sentences and Paragraphs Weekly
- Silent Socratic Dialogue (6) 5-4-3 – Paired Writing Warm-ups
- Exit Card – Ticket Out Reflective Survey

Scenic Detail – East Texas' Davey Dogwoods Park

Although it's designed as a drive-through scenic park, I suggest driving only as far as is necessary to find a place to park, preferably nearby the picnic area in the center of the park's hundreds of acres, then get out of the vehicle to really appreciate this city park just north of the city of Palestine in east-central Texas. Stretch your legs by meandering along and over the creek, through this beautifully wooded valley, looping one, two, then all three of the nearly concentric loop trails. All together you might total a couple or a few miles. Try if possible to visit on a sunny day in mid or late March when the namesake dogwood trees are blossoming. Before any first canopy filter of leaves has budded to block it, the sun alights, making luminous this middle canopy of the dogwoods' white petals, which glow in layered tiers. Hiking amidst this glorious early burst of spring sun, I marveled at the innumerable drops of sunlight bobbing and blinking from this valley of flowering trees. You won't come close to this experience, though, if you sit stuck in your car on the scenic drive-through amid a jam of tour buses and petal peepers, backing up bumper to bumper during the peak blossom season.

Students don't want a drive-through writing experience, either. What they really want are rigorous, college-level challenges to accomplish: tasks to tackle and attain (Eodice, Geller, & Lerner, 2016). Probably as important as establishing groups to foster a pragmatic democratic classroom, planning purposefully challenging activities is necessary to engage students with writing. I suggest establishing a series of valuable activities for every class period that follow a common general outline each week, in other words, an interest-generating variety of learning experiences within an assuring classroom routine. Typically, students want the comfort of coming to classes knowing what to expect: they thrive on routines. Yet, in what may seem like a paradox, they also relish novelty and variety: pleasant surprise is usually a welcome diversion (Elbow, 1986). One effective way to address the paradox is the periodic reassigning of students to work with diverse groups. Within the familiar routine and expectations of groupwork always lies the diversion of collaborating with different individuals, all with their distinct ideas, styles, and suggestions. Another way to keep class both comfortable and motivating is to assign a customary work schedule of similar assignments with regular expectations and then, within such a common class time agenda, introduce incrementally challenging activities to keep the learning threshold rising as well as interesting. Like Vygotsky's (2012/1934) Zone of Proximal Development, these scheduled class activities stretch students' writing and thinking skills, but they do so with an accessible and achievable process. Students are continually nudged into and become absorbed with novelty, variety, and surprise inside the classroom's comforting customs. The theme of this chapter is the first-year college writing classroom's daily procedures and weekly routines.

Typically, I begin classes with a motivational quotation to discuss and deconstruct both its import and application as well as its parts of speech, clauses, and sentence pattern. Beginning with a lighthearted and lively tone, I usually call on individuals to identify the verbs and subjects, conjunctions and clauses, in a quotation that I supply. Once a week, I assign as in-class groupwork a collaborative sentence-combining activity in which students work together to construct more robust sentences of clusters of simple sentences to form into a paragraph. Often, I ask them to deconstruct the sentences into constituent clauses with conjunctions to reconstruct novel sentence combinations, too. Generally, I end the week with an Exit Card, which I call students' *ticket out*, made up of three brief questions to reflect about the week's learning topics and their achievement.

Figure 5.2. Motivational Quotation with Sentence Surgery

Within this common weekly agenda, I arrange activities to target students' writing skills and planning and preparing their drafts of essays.

Sentence Surgery – Parsing Passages of Motivational Quotations

Every class, I typically begin with a motivational quotation that we parse all together. I like to think of myself as coming from the school of Learn Fewer Things Better. So, instead of racing through a textbook or course syllabus to be certain to cover everything, I seek instead to choose what's most worth learning, then continually practice the points I have selected to ensure that students understand them well. One skill that I want to teach is how to construct sentences. At the start of the semester, I promise students a daily quotation to add to their writing notebook, so that by the end of the term, they will have amassed a library of nearly thirty inspirational sayings. In addition, we perform sentence surgery on each to identify its verbs and subjects, conjunctions and clauses, and sentence pattern. So besides a collection of quotations, they accumulate a variety of deconstructed and identified sentence patterns to refer to as they operate on other sentences and to emulate while crafting their own.

Signpost – Motivational Quotations for Use with Sentence Surgery

Thirty **Motivational Quotations**, enough for a 15-week semester, along with samples of their **Sentence Surgeries** can be found beginning on page 194 and continuing through page 208 in Appendix 3. These are presented in pairs, assuming two quotations per week over 15 weeks.

Always, we identify A (Action) and B (Being) verbs: Actions answer the clipped question, "Do what?" Beings are simply forms of the verb *to be*: *is, are, am, was, were, will be,* and the *beens*: *has been, have been, had been, will have been*. As I tell students, "This is enough to know for now."

A	B
Answer, "Do what?"	*is, are, am*
	was, were
	will be, shall be
	been

Signpost – Action and Being Verbs

A form to illustrate the two kinds of verbs to your class – **A = Action** and **B = Being** – is located on page 184 in Appendix 2.

We double-underline every verb and label it with a capital A for *Action* or a capital B for *Being*. Next, for each verb, we identify its subject, and single-underline it. Then we divide subject-verb combinations from others, use brackets to enclose the separate clauses, and label each one *ind* for independent or *dep* for dependent. Finally, we tally the independent and dependent clauses, studying coordinating, subordinating, and adverbial conjunctions to determine what type of sentence each is. I use these three examples of conjunctions to distinguish between the independent and dependent clauses. In fact, I tell them that training their eyes to spot the conjunctions along with verbs and subjects will give them the wherewithal to identify the grammatical type of almost any sentence they may encounter. The payoff, furthermore, is in their being able to use them in their own writing and sentence-construction to produce robust and varied types of sentences themselves.

Here's an example:

When I was a young man, they called me a liar, but now that I am older, they call me a writer.

– Isaac Bashevis Singer

Verbs:

       B   A   B   A

When I <u>was</u> a young man, they <u>called</u> me a liar, but now that I <u>am</u> older, they <u>call</u> me a writer.

Subjects:

When <u>I</u> was a young man, <u>they</u> called me a liar, but now that <u>I</u> am older, <u>they</u> call me a writer.

Clauses:

       dep   ind   dep   ind

[When I was young,] [they called me a liar,] [but [now that I am older,] they call me a writer.]

Sentence Pattern:

   [dep + ind] + [dep + ind] = cd-cx (Compound-Complex)

Of course, there are plenty of exceptions to contend with, but practicing these basic rules by applying them to a different sentence, like the motivational quotations in Appendix 3, in every class should provide students enough practice to comprehend sentence structures and help them to transfer the understanding to their own writing. To further this transfer, I also have them practice with the different conjunctions to craft their own robust sentences using independent and dependent clauses with drafts of essays.

When beginning, I like to plow ahead, assuring them that they will learn better through the hands-on practice, and probably learn more from the missed answers as they do from their initial hits. Calling on those who wish to volunteer answers as well as others who do not, I encourage their best guesses and appreciate their willingness to participate, and I attempt to ask a question to every class member at least once in each class period. I suggest that they probably will discover their success rates rising remarkably with the sentence surgeries by about the third or fourth week of practice. Furthermore, they nearly all see that by the end of the semester, not only are they able to recognize different sentence patterns, but they are also able to construct them themselves – and I make sure to call their attention to this feat around midterm and again near the end of term. It's too early to worry if they don't understand sentence structure at the outset.

Early in the term, I introduce the three, key "Not-a-Verb" signals to watch out for:

1. Negatives–such as *not, n't, never*
2. *–ing*'s occurring alone – such as *running, reaching, retching* – without B verbs like *is, are*
3. Following *to* – such as *to run, to reach, to retch*

Signpost – Not-a-Verbs

To find a form of the three types of **Not-a-Verbs** that you may photocopy or project in the classroom, turn on page 178 in Appendix 2.

Many students, although they have heard of verbals (participles, gerunds, infinitives), cannot consistently identify them or use them. Although I use the *verbals* terminology, I also continue to call them "Not-a-Verbs" for our parsing purposes, because primarily, I want them to hunt for main verbs first when practicing sentence surgery on a quotation – and so be able to differentiate between a bona fide verb and a verbal, both in our sentence surgeries on the motivational quotations as well as in their own writing and sentence construction. In addition, by beginning every class period with sentence surgery, students come to habitually weigh the relative merits of different conjunctions, verbs, and clauses while analyzing others' writings and crafting their own. They learn to consciously listen to the sounds of words and syntax as they read and write, and speak and listen.

Immediately following the clauses, I introduce the four sentence types of simple, compound, complex, and compound-complex, as well as fragments and run-ons. Usually, I identify them in the context of performing sentence surgery on a motivational quotation, as I call on individuals to ask if they happen to know what kind of sentence two independent clauses and two dependent clauses makes, as in the case of the Isaac Bashevis Singer quotation above. As often as possible, I try to teach the terminology and skills in the context of deconstructing sentences like the motivational quotations, beginning as always with (main) verbs and subjects, then clauses and conjunctions, and finally, sentence types, as follows:

> Simple (s) = ind (Independent Clause)
> Complex (cx) = ind + dep (Dependent Clause)
> Compound (cd) = ind + ind
> Compound-Complex (cd-cx) = ind + ind + dep
> Fragment (frag) = dep
> Run-on (RO) = ind + ind + ind

Afterwards, I emphasize that neither fragments nor run-ons are actually sentences, since a sentence requires at least one independent clause and is usually limited to two maximum. I note that, although the number of independent clauses in a sentence is closely governed, the numbers of dependent clauses is more flexible, so long as there's at least one in a complex or compound-complex sentence. After learning to identify different sentence types over a few weeks in parsing motivational quotations and practicing sentence combining (which I take up next), students are ready to identify them in their own writing, and they usually experience gratification at recognizing the varieties and robustness of sentences that they hadn't realized they were capable of writing. Their being able to deconstruct sentences has an added benefit of helping them recognize what causes fragments and run-ons, when they happen to write them; moreover, it gives them the terminology to identify the sentences they have written as well as to target for attention the sentence types that they may not have in a portion of their text yet.

Again, using the quotations, I vary the punctuation and the conjunctions to show them how to craft varieties of sentences. For example, by exchanging the subordinating conjunction *although* for the coordinating conjunction *but* in Singer's quotation, the sentence, which originally contained two independent clauses and two dependent clauses, now has only one independent clause with three dependent clauses, so is a complex instead of a compound-complex sentence type:

<pre>
        dep   ind   dep
[When I was a young man,] [they called me a liar,] [*but* [now that I am older,] [they
        ind
call me a writer.]
    dep + ind + dep + ind = cd-cx
        dep   ind   dep
[When I was a young man,] [they called me a liar,] [*although* [now that I am older,]
        dep
[they call me a writer.]
    dep + ind + dep + dep = cx
</pre>

Besides listening to individual clauses to judge their completeness as independent clauses worthy of standing apart as complete sentences, I like to point out how grammatically you can quickly identify an independent or dependent clause merely by recognizing the variety of conjunction that introduces it. If a clause has no conjunction or a coordinating conjunction, it is an independent clause (with the exception of quoted or reported speech, which is considered to be dependent on the reporting verb and its subject). On the other hand, if it opens with a subordinating conjunction, it is a dependent clause. An adverbial conjunction begins an independent clause, and like the coordinating conjunctions links two independent clauses. However, unlike a coordinating conjunction, which requires only a preceding comma, a loftier sounding adverbial conjunction necessitates a heftier semicolon to hold together two independent clauses, and it requires a comma afterwards, too. In fact, adverbial conjunctions always come surrounded with punctuation: a semicolon and comma when connecting independent clauses, a period in front and a comma following when functioning as a transition from one sentence to the next, or commas in front and back when functioning as a transition within a sentence.

With apologies to Isaac Bashevis Singer, here is his quotation revised to illustrate an adverbial conjunction used with a semicolon (substituted for the coordinating conjunction *but* and comma) as well as other options for use of an adverbial conjunction:

When I was a young man, they called me a liar**; however,** now that I am older, they call me a writer.
When I was a young man, they called me a liar. **However,** now that I am older, they call me a writer.
When I was a young man, they called me a liar. Now that I am older**, however,** they call me a writer.

Finally, I like to use the motivational quotations to introduce the comma-splice run-on. Again, here is the quotation from Singer used to illustrate a comma-splice, having neither a coordinating nor an adverbial conjunction between the independent clauses:

When I was a young man, they called me a liar**,** now that I am older, they call me a writer.

I also use the quotations to illustrate writing nuances, such as when the subordinating conjunction *that* is implied in a sentence. Compare the two sentences below. The first has the word *that*, but the second leaves *that* out, merely implying it. The meaning remains, as does the dependent clause.

When I was a young man, they called me a liar, but now *that* I am older, they call me a writer.

    dep + ind + dep + ind = cd-cx

When I was a young man, they called me a liar, but now I am older, they call me a writer.

    dep + ind + dep + ind = cd-cx

As much as you can exude enthusiasm over this sentence surgery, you set the tone for a positive and active class period, as well as setting an example for students' own learning through discovery and experimentation themselves. Some of your students, once acquainted with the terminology and tools to deconstruct and reconstruct these quotations – and their own constructions, too – may become captivated with this fun interplay of clauses and conjunctions.

Sentence Combining – Strong Sentences and Paragraphs Weekly

Each week, I hand out a page of sentence-combining exercises with eight clusters of 2–6 simple sentences. From each set of simple sentences, students construct a single, effective sentence by adding conjunctions and verbals, and removing any repeated words. Their goal is to form more robust sentence combinations with a variety of simple, compound, complex, and compound-complex sentence types that sound good when read aloud. In groups, they compare different arrangements with varied conjunctions, together seeking consensus on the best sounding and most meaningful sentences, ones that communicate clearly without repeating any key words or leaving out any information from the initial sentences. Usually, I begin with the first cluster as an example, often by calling on individuals to help me combine the simple sentences in one or two possible combinations. Then I suggest they decide in their groups which sounds best to them, and go on to combine the remaining clusters into sentences themselves. Normally, I project the Popular Conjunctions Mnemonics Table (page 229) for their reference before circulating among their groups to listen to their conversations, prompt possible combinations, and join in some discussions.

Signpost – Sentence-Combining Activities

Appendix 4 on pages 210–229 includes fifteen **Sentence-Combining Activities** – enough to use one each week throughout a 15-week semester – themed about the first-year college student's experience. They are arranged to practice coordinating conjunctions, subordinating conjunctions, and adverbial conjunctions in that order.

Here is an example of a cluster of simple sentences to combine:
1.   a. Richard was hired by his uncle.
     b. Richard was hired as a lawn maintenance worker.
     c. Richard was hired seasonally.
     d. His Uncle Mark owned the Green Sweep Lawn Care Company.

This is a possible combination sentence. Note that the subject *Richard* and verb *was hired* are used only once:

> Richard was hired seasonally as a lawn maintenance worker by his Uncle Mark, who owned the Green Sweep Lawn Care Company.

Once all of the simple clusters are combined into more robust sentences, I ask each group if they all have the same answers written on their worksheets, and if so, I initial and date each student's page, usually in the bottom left corner. Initialing the same corner each time allows me to quickly tally all completed worksheets and check that all have been completed satisfactorily at midterm and the end of a semester. In addition to having students combine each of the clusters into individual sentences, I often ask them to do so while including a specific number of one type of conjunction, for example, four different coordinating conjunctions. Also, I normally request that they not repeat any conjunctions on the page. I divided the fifteen Sentence-Combining Activities in Appendix 4 into a series of assignments that target coordinating conjunctions first, then subordinating, and finally adverbial conjunctions, and conclude with varied combinations using all three types of conjunctions.

Signpost – Popular Conjunctions Mnemonics Table

Table A.4.2 **Popular Conjunctions Mnemonics** includes three columns, one each for coordinating conjunctions (FANBOYS), subordinating conjunctions (Ah-Woo-Bus and Three T), and adverbial conjunctions (Major League Sports Fans), ready for you to photocopy or project in the classroom. It follows the Sentence-Combining Activities in Appendix 4 on page 229.

With different classes having varied aptitudes for sentence combining, I adapt the instructions to challenge them accordingly. For example, I may speed up the switches from coordinating to subordinating to adverbial, then spend more time on the activities that require combining all of the sentence types together. Or, I might start off with both coordinating and subordinating conjunctions, and focus on using them together to build compound-complex sentences. Let your students and groups govern your decisions as you guide them through this practice. If you realize at some point that your directions have moved ahead of a class's capabilities – and you will hear this in their conversations and see it in their completed sentence-combining worksheets – you can always scale back the expectations to keep the class members appropriately challenged within their learning zones. Of course, you may find that your teaching lags behind their abilities, too. In that case, you may have to speed up your pace or ratchet-up your instruction to work in their Zones of Proximal Development.

Signpost – Zone of Proximal Development

You may wish to review the discussion of Lev Vygotsky's **Zone of Proximal Development** on pages 122–125.

After completing their groups' sentence combinations, students copy the finished sentences as a completed paragraph into their writing notebooks. Rewriting the sentences as a paragraph not only helps them to feel ownership of the sentences themselves, it also lets them see the sentences in the context of a complete paragraph. This may aid them in listening to how the sentences they have constructed sound when combined with one another, as well as how they convey a common topic and communicate their collective meaning.

Once they have the paragraph written out, they finish by completing sentence surgeries on 3–6 of the sentences in their writing notebooks. Here's an example, using the combination from earlier:

A   ind
[Richard <u>was hired</u> seasonally as a lawn maintenance worker by his Uncle *Mark*,]
 A   dep
[who <u>owned</u> the Green Sweep Lawn Care Company.] ind + dep = cx

Performing sentence surgery on the sentence combinations grants them more practice deconstructing sentences – and this time doing so on their own sentence combinations – which may help them recheck their constructions for grammatical and syntactical correctness. Sometimes, I instruct them to select only compound sentences for sentence surgeries in their paragraphs, or I may ask for only compound sentences that use coordinating conjunctions, only compound sentences with adverbial conjunctions, or only complex sentences with subordinating conjunctions. Later, I may direct them to practice sentence surgery on all four sentence types in their paragraph: a simple sentence, a compound, a complex, and a compound-complex, and to include at least one example of all three types of conjunctions – coordinating, subordinating, and adverbial – within their chosen four sentences.

For an additional challenge, I might offer a bonus if a student or a group completes six sentence surgeries, or six surgeries that each use a separate coordinating conjunction (or subordinating or adverbial). Depending on a class's rapport, I may ask if anyone would like to guess what type of sentence or which type of conjunction they expect I will assign them that week. Also, if there is a bonus, I may ask if somebody thinks they know what the bonus activity will be. You can use this to lighten or enliven a class that could benefit from some levity or a brief break from a sentence-combining lesson.

On occasion, I may choose to type up or copy a group's sample onto the board or project it for all. Sometimes, I simply add my own surgery to a sentence, projecting it for the whole class to adopt and copy themselves, if they wish. Doing so can have an extra benefit of providing them a good sentence model to begin the lesson, or can get them thinking ahead from combining sentences towards performing surgeries on them. It could acknowledge a group's fine work merely by projecting it as exemplary, or the projected sentence may simply give the groups a sentence to help them work through the lesson.

I don't grade the lessons individually, but just as I did with the sentence-combining worksheets, I do initial and date the finished paragraphs with three to six sentence surgeries written in students' writing notebooks. In addition, I mark the number 3 or 4, 5, or 6 to indicate the number of sentence surgeries they completed in the paragraph. Simply noting and quantifying the number completed can spur some students to do more the next time. When they ask how the sentence surgeries are graded, I usually reply that three is the minimum required, and six is in the realm of a bonus-level, top grade. If letters are required, three is a C, four a B, five an A, and six is extra, normally.

As students become comfortable with the sentence-combining assignments, I give fewer and fewer directions, simply stating requirements or mentioning any optional bonus challenge. As they become more proficient at working collaboratively to combine sentences, I may delay circulating among the groups to give assistance. In fact, I might, instead of circling to assist, circle instead to search and discover groups' exemplary sentence combinations to project for the whole class. Or, I may prowl around for challenging combinations that I can project to practice performing sentence surgery. After they have begun working, I may pull up a chair and join a group to monitor its members' collaborations, check on the quality or maturity of their products, pose an appropriate question or two, or simply participate in a conversation. I usually refrain from responding to any individual questions at the outset, so students begin to work with one another using their group's resourcefulness instead of leaning on me. Since we aim to teach for independence, we must work to avoid enabling instructor dependencies. I may conclude instructions with, "Any questions?" However, if it appears that someone is asking for repetition of directions that I just gave, or a student asks for individual assistance immediately following the instructions, I generally respond by redirecting the question back to the group: For example, "Tim's group, would you explain that?" or "Kim (another member of Tim's group), could you take Tim's question?"

As much as any other activity, sentence combining accords students the benefits of addressing syntax, punctuation, transitions, and organization along with constructing, deconstructing, and reconstructing texts into sentences and paragraphs – all rather advanced writing skills. It necessitates collaboration as members discuss combinations and conjunctions to select the best sounding and most meaningful constructions. It can be readily adjusted to accommodate the learning needs of different students, groups, and classes. Their working with clusters of simple sentences to form more elaborate and diverse types of sentences, then forming sentences into paragraphs and practicing sentence surgeries on selected sentences to identify various grammatical components can help to develop knowledge and skills that build worthwhile linguistic skills which students transfer readily to their writing processes. Sentence combining offers a wide variety of writing skills to practice, yet it maintains a regular routine in weekly expectations on the part of students, both essential to sustain interest and challenge while providing comfort and the repetition required for understanding and application. Finally, when students have completed a series of sentence-combining lessons like the First-year College Student themed activities in Appendix 4, they will have accrued a collection of strong topical paragraphs with exemplary sentences in their notebooks which may produce a sense of pride in their accomplishment that leads them to treasure and revisit these course contents.

Figure 5.3. Sentence Combining Together

Trail Marker – Sentence Combining

Easy – Photocopy one of the Sentence-Combining Activities from Appendix 4 (beginning on page 214) to teach in your own class or to try yourself, preferably with a group of fellow composition instructors. Require all students in each group to discuss, agree, and write their best-sounding combinations for each of the eight clusters – either by drawing arrows to rearrange them, crossing out repeated words and unneeded capital letters and punctuation, and inserting appropriate conjunctions from the Popular Conjunctions Mnemonic Table (page 229) to combine them. Or practice carrying out these sentence combining procedures with your own cohort.

Moderate – Assign your students to combine all eight clusters into sentences (as in **Easy**, above), and copy them as a paragraph to try sentence surgery on 3–6 of their combinations, double-underlining verbs and labeling them *A* for Action or *B* for Being; single-underlining subjects; bracketing and labeling clauses as *ind* for independent or *dep* for dependent; and identifying sentences as simple, compound, complex, or compound-complex. Or practice this yourself, again preferably in a group of fellow instructors.

Difficult – Ask students to craft five compound sentences without repeating any coordinating conjunctions, or ask them to try producing all four sentence types – simple, compound, complex, and compound-complex – in their paragraphs, and then to practice sentence surgery on each. Or, try doing this yourself working alone or in a group.

Silent Socratic Dialogue (6) 5-4-3 – Paired Writing Warm-ups

Silent Socratic Dialogue is a writing prompt designed to stimulate thought through paired writings between two classmates. It is called *Silent* because students write their ideas instead of speaking them aloud to each other. It is *Socratic* since it requires purposely challenging questions that encourage deeper reflection and self-examination before responding. And it is *Dialogue*, for it necessitates written interaction through a sequence of statements and questions with another classmate. The number *6* is placed in parentheses because it represents an optional bonus point that students may choose to add by writing six sentences for their first paragraph. *5* is the number of sentences assigned for the initial writing prompt. *4* is the number of sentences written in response to the first question, and *3* is the number of sentences written to reply to the last question. Abbreviated *SSD (6) 5-4-3*, the instructions for Silent Socratic Dialogue are given in these six steps:

1. Students write 5 sentences initiated by a writing prompt provided by the instructor. A list of 15 writing prompts, one for every week of the semester, is provided in Appendix 2. (4–8 minutes)
2. They exchange with a writing partner, read the 5-sentence warm-up, skip one line, and write a one-sentence question on the same page below it to further prompt or continue the conversation. (3–4 minutes)
3. Next, they write a 4-sentence response below the partner's question. (3–7 minutes)
4. After responding, they exchange their papers with the same writing partner again, read their partner's four sentences, and write another question below. (2–3 minutes)
5. Finally, they write a 3-sentence answer to their partner's second question. (2–6 minutes)
6. Afterwards, they exchange one last time to read each other's final 3-sentence answers.

Signpost – Silent Socratic Dialogue (6) 5-4-3 Topics

A list of SSD (6) 5-4-3 writing prompts that I have used can be found on page 187 in Appendix 2.

Each writing warm-up follows the same SSD (6) 5-4-3 format: Writing 5 sentences in response to the prompt (a partner question), 4 sentences in response to the partner's question (another question from the same partner), and 3 sentences in response to the second question to finish. Usually, I adjust the times for each segment of the writing exchange to match different classes' requirements, but an SSD (6) 5-4-3 assignment typically takes 15–25 minutes to complete. When introducing an SSD (6) 5-4-3, I generally allow more time to write, but steadily contract the amounts of time for each writing and response as the semester progresses and students gain comfort and proficiency in writing their exchanges. Sometimes a more demanding prompt might require allowing additional time for students' thoughts and writing activity. I normally circulate among them to read their paragraphs and questions over their shoulders, and I often impose/set time limits during this observation. Typically, I announce, "Two-minute warning," or "Please finish your sentence before switching and asking a thoughtful Socratic question," to maintain the pace and ensure completion on schedule.

Usually, I give writing prompts that relate to essay assignments. For example, in a class in which students researched a region of the North American continent and its inhabitants as part of their research for an Ethnographic Profile paper, I asked them to write a Silent Socratic Dialogue (6) 5-4-3 in response to the question, "If you had to leave the state but remain in North America (Canada, the United States, Mexico, Central America), which city or region would you move to, why would you choose that place, and how might it change you?" I projected a map of the continent to highlight its various regions, countries, and major cities. This writing prompts many interactions about where students have traveled, what they infer different regions may be like, and some questions about what they would like to learn about people who live there. Such written interactions nudge students out of their comfort zones and often lead to shared experiences and opinions that otherwise might not surface. These writing transactions can also expand students' ideas about what to research and where to explore to learn additional information about their essay topics as well as what their reading audience would be interested in learning more about. Such a written conversation can be helpful to first-year college students who otherwise struggle to generate writing topics, or, having chosen a theme, wonder where to begin searching or researching for interesting, applicable material.

When I do grade writing notebooks, checking them usually midway through and at the end of the term, I base grades solely on the quantity of sentences written: 5 sentences for the first reply to the writing prompt + 4 sentences in reply to a partner's first Socratic question + 3 sentences to respond to the second Socratic question = 12 sentences total. Twelve sentences typically earns an A or B. To ensure an A, I suggest they write 15. For the C, they must produce at least 9 sentences. Fewer than 9 sentences is not acceptable to complete the assignment. At present, because students at all of the colleges where I currently teach classes at some time during a year must score a C to satisfactorily complete the course, be accepted in any successive English classes, or transfer credit for the course from a community college to another university or college, I design every assignment to require this minimum grade, so no one who completes the coursework can fail. If I don't have to grade an activity, I don't. Since the notebook is their collection of idea-generators and notes, motivational quotations with sentence surgeries, and collections of paragraphs composed of sentence combinations, it typically holds intrinsic value for the student-writer. Besides, the writing for SSD (6) 5-4-3 is written to communicate with their classmates, so for many, this motivates their best writing because it is for an audience of peers.

The SSD (6) 5-4-3 writing warm-up activity accentuates the dialogical process of writing to communicate and comprehend. It also allows conversational creativity while forming ties with classmates who may be very dissimilar. Their interactions often lead to further conversations and ideas for writing that otherwise may not have occurred to a student before, and it sometimes opens them to opinions and concepts that they had not encountered before writing with this partner. To take advantage of the diversity represented by students in the first-year composition classroom, have students write with as many different partners as you can. Not only does this accord them a variety of thoughts and readers, it enhances the diverse democracy within your classroom.

Figure 5.4. Silent Socratic Dialogue (6) 5-4-3

Trail Marker – Silent Socratic Dialogue (6) 5-4-3

Easy – What are three ideas for in-class writing warm-up topics that you could use with Silent Socratic Dialogue (6) 5-4-3 paired assignments?

Moderate – What are some writing prompts that you currently use in classes or are considering for future classes that you could reformat as Silent Socratic Dialogue (6) 5-4-3 writing topics? Try to list fifteen or so; in other words, aim for enough topics so that you have one for every week of a semester.

Difficult – Try to align your Silent Socratic Dialogue (6) 5-4-3 writing topics with the themes, genres, or types of essays that you plan to assign next semester, so that your students may be able to use some of the SSD (6) 5-4-3 writings towards rough drafts for assigned essays in your composition class. Try to list three different writing prompts for each of the essays that you are considering.

Figure 5.5. Exit Card

Exit Card – Ticket Out Reflective Survey

Ten or fifteen minutes before the end of the last class meeting for each week, I usually project the Exit Card, which is comprised of three statements that I ask them to respond to on only three lines in their writing notebooks:

1. Write one thing that you learned thoroughly – you understand and know how to apply it yourself – from class this week.
2. On a scale of 1–10 (1 = uncertain, 5 = developing, 10 = got it), label your understanding of one classroom concept this week.
3. Write one question about something you would like to know or learn from class, in class, or about the class.

As they finish their responses, I circle among the groups to read and initial and date their work. Typically, I note a classroom concept for question 2. For example, if students are forming compound sentences using coordinating conjunctions, I might type the phrase *coordinating conjunctions in cd sentences* beside number 2 on the Exit Card, or I may simply write it on a white board nearby. While reading their responses at the end of a class, I try to mentally tally and average their answers for number 2 to determine how confident students are about their understanding of the concept. If all or many answers fall midway or at the lower end of the spectrum, I may decide to review that concept further with an individual, a group, or a class. Also, I briefly reply verbally to every question written for number 3 on the Exit Card. Normally, I can answer quickly and move along to the next student's question. When a question requires more than a speedy reply, I ask the student if I may return after answering the others' questions, so I can provide the thorough answer that the question requires. Most students welcome this attentiveness. If not possible to return, offer to email a follow-up response. On occasion, especially if you suspect a student of dashing off a question simply to exit class without really wanting your reply, you may ask the student to send you an email with the question, so you may follow up more thoroughly. Generally, the student's response to this offer should disclose any hidden intention.

Signpost – Exit Card

The **Exit Card** form, including the three statements that I project to conclude the last class of each week, can be found on page 188 in Appendix 1. The top half has blank lines where students will write responses – if you wish to photocopy and hand out the form. The bottom half includes explanations for each of the three statements, ready to be projected in a classroom.

The Exit Card ensures that you check in with all students every week about their understandings of the course concepts, and it requires them to reflect on their own learning, too. It can be a helpful conclusion to the week's work by involving their metacognition, reviewing the week's content, and analyzing their understandings. This can be valuable to you, too, as you continually plan your teaching to align with students' learning needs. From their responses to the Exit Card, you can often gain insights into their thought processes and self-analyses. Finally, seeing what they have learned thoroughly, as well as what they ask questions about, can help you decide where and how to guide your students in future classes.

Besides the Exit Card to conclude each week, I often ask my students to complete an initial survey at the beginning of the term, asking them to complete a one-page form about their writing backgrounds and their aspirations for the first-year college composition class. Surprising to me, most respondents over the last five years – a significant plurality – chose grammar. Maybe they selected grammar because it is something they felt they didn't know as well as they should, or possibly they may have had little idea, outside of spelling, parts of speech, and punctuation, what other options there could be to a writing class. Possibly their past writing courses, or maybe the summative tests that might drive a reductionist curriculum, reduced English to the recognition of grammatical match-ups in multiple or binary choice questions, copying sentences, or filling in blanks. I wondered.

Signpost – Introductory Survey and Classwork Tally Forms

The **English Class Introductory Survey** that I photocopy and ask students to complete on the first day of class is with one of the forms in Appendix 1 on page 183. Besides an Introductory Survey form, I normally have students complete a Classwork Tally form at midterm and the end of semester to count their completed Sentence-Combining Activities and additional classwork. These (identical) forms can be found in Appendix 2 on page 189.

Yes, I do teach grammar. My students wanted it, and many claimed it was a deficit in their writing skill set, so I try to deliver. However, grammar exercises have little if any carry-over to students' own writing craft, and multiple choice, and fill-in-the-blanks exercises are inappropriate for a college writing class. So I try to teach grammar within their writing activity, or at least alongside their construction and reconstruction of sentence combinations in their weekly sentence-combining and sentence surgery activity, so students gain the additional advantage of working on grammar skills in the context of their own writing. Teaching sentence combining with sentence surgery extends students a hands-on, multi-sensory approach to grammar that is always within the context of their own writing, which is appropriate to a first-year college composition course.

Top 10 List – Sentence Surgery & Writing Warm-ups (Top 5 + 5)

Top 5 for Sentence Surgery

1. **Projecting a Quotation.** Project a motivational quotation onto an overhead screen or write a quotation on the board as students arrive to class. Sometimes students' anticipation of parsing a sentence can be as enjoyable as the actual operation. On occasion, I'll preface a quotation with a teaser, writing *cd?* (for *compound sentence?* – or *cx? cd-cx,* or *s?*) to trigger their thinking or group discussions before we begin.

Signpost – Motivational Quotations

You can find thirty **Motivational Quotations** as well as their **Sentence Surgeries**, ready to project or photocopy in class, in Appendix 3, beginning on page 190.

2. **Labeling.** Ask students to consult their groups or a partner to identify the verbs and their subjects, label clauses and conjunctions, and classify the sentence. Then call on individuals with the same questions: What is the first verb to be double-underlined? What is its subject to single-underline? What is the next verb and subject to underline? Where would you divide and bracket between these clauses? Is this first clause independent or dependent? What is the second? How many independent and dependent clauses are in this sentence, total? What type of sentence is this?

3. **Playing.** Play with the quotations and their clauses and conjunctions. I take great liberties, sometimes substituting subordinating or adverbial conjunctions where there was originally a coordinating conjunction to illustrate the different types of sentence (*s*, *cd*, *cx*, and *cd-cx*) and clauses (*ind* and *dep*).

4. **Manipulating.** Use the quotations to stitch together sentences in new ways by asking students how they might revise them from compound into complex, complex into simple, or compound-complex into complex. As they gain practice and confidence, students often enjoy revising and rearranging these example sentences. With some classes, you may want to manipulate and change conjunctions and verbals to attempt to rewrite a quotation in all four different sentence types: *s*, *cd*, *cx*, and *cd-cx*.

5. **Searching.** Invite students to search for quotations to contribute, too. Sometimes I tell students I'm on the prowl for aphorisms about homework or writing, and may even offer a bonus to anyone who furnishes a suitable one for the class.

+ Top 5 for Silent Socratic Dialogue (6) 5-4-3 Writing Warm-ups

6. **Arranging.** When seated in pairs, have students write an SSD (6) 5-4-3 with each other. The **Who Are You? Partners' Interviews and Introductions** form can be a convenient way to assign partners at the beginning of the course. When students are arranged in groups of four, you may have them write their first Silent Socratic Dialogue (6) 5-4-3 with the partner they're sitting beside, and write their second one with the groupmate they're facing. A third SSD (6) 5-4-3 may be written with the final group member whom they're sitting across from diagonally. After three paired writings, you may choose to begin over again by having students exchange with partners they're sitting beside. Otherwise, you could reassign groups or choose to wait to assign another SSD (6) 5-4-3 until you are scheduled to next rearrange classroom seating.

7. **Prompting.** Use a variety of prompts for Silent Socratic Dialogue (6) 5-4-3 paired writings, such as YouTube video clips, This I Believe essays (from the website *thisibelieve.org*), or a favorite coffee mug. Any topic that you otherwise might select for a classroom writing warm-up may make an effective SSD (6) 5-4-3

assignment. Try to align the writing prompts with your assigned essays for the course, so they can be applied logically to a rough draft, as well.

8. **Monitoring.** Continually circle, silently reading over everyone's shoulders while they write their ideas and questions. Although some instructors like to write with their students and partner with someone whenever there is an odd number in attendance, I prefer to read what they're all scribing. Besides, I can sometimes lose track of time while writing myself, and I need to be alert to their progress, as well as to the clock, to prompt the successive stops and starts for partners' questions and written responses for every one of the six steps.

9. **Rotating.** If the class does have an odd number of students, or a group contains three members, have them rotate their writing notebooks clockwise, instead of switching with a partner, so everyone responds to and writes questions for another's writing.

10. **Surveying.** Survey the students, asking them for examples of very thought-provoking, deeply Socratic questions, or for a question that steered their thinking in a new direction which they may not have been anticipating, but one that really spurred their thinking or could help them write some interesting ideas for an essay.

Lingo – Sentence Surgery on a Motivational Quotation

1. "Now that's an aphorism worth taping to your fridge!"
2. "How many verbs do you count in this sentence? Corroborate with your group before I call on somebody at random from every group."
   "Is this verb *action* or *being*? What is its *subject*?"
3. "Before we do sentence surgery, who thinks this is a *compound sentence*? What clues do you detect?"
4. "Where would you divide between these two clauses? Is this clause *independent* or *dependent*? Why? After this verb but before this next subject, where would you place a bracket to divide their separate clauses?"
5. "Two independent clauses plus two dependent clauses is what kind of sentence?" (Or writing on the board or to project: *ind + ind + dep + dep = [cd-cx (compound-complex)]*

Lingo – Silent Socratic Dialogue (6) 5-4-3 Writing Warm-ups

1. "After you've finished writing five sentences (or six for a bonus), switch your writing notebooks with your partner. Read each other's paragraph, skip one line, and write a one-sentence, Socratic-style open question, preferably beginning with the word *why* or *how*. Ask a question that cannot be answered with a single word like *yes* or *no*, or a simple phrase because it ought to generate at least a four-sentence response."
2. "After you have written your Socratic question in your partner's notebook, write your initials in front of your question, and exchange your writing notebooks back to your partner. Next, back in your own notebook, write your four-sentence answer to your partner's question."

3. "Switch notebooks with your partner again. Read each other's four-sentence paragraphs, then skip another line, and write another Socratic-style question. Keep your written conversation going."

4. "For your final exchange, write a three-sentence answer below your partner's second Socratic question."

5. "When you both have finished writing, read each other's three-sentence responses."

6. "Congratulations! You've written your first Silent Socratic Dialogue. It's *silent* because your conversation was written, not spoken; *Socratic* for our ancient Greek philosopher friend, Socrates, who taught by asking deep, demanding questions; and *dialogue* as you responded to and questioned each other to keep the written conversation flowing."

7. "Since it's difficult to grade your depth of ideas or quality of conversations, I assess instead the quantity of sentences: $5 + 4 + 3 = 12$ sentences. 12 is good. Good is B. If you keep up with the assignments, you'll earn a good, solid B."

8. "Some of you are saying, 'B? I'm not a B student. I'm average, C. Besides, I only need a C to complete this class for my program or to matriculate to Composition 2 . . . .' OK, do the math: $12 = B$, $9 = C$, so $11 = B-$ and $10 = C+$."

9. "Others are sitting here, thinking, 'Wait! I want an A.' Since $9 = C$ and $12 = B$, then $15 = A$. You completely control your grade. If you're targeting an A, add one sentence to each paragraph to make it $6 + 5 + 4$, to total 15 sentences."

10. "If necessary, return to add a sentence to your paragraphs later. If you run out of time in class, ask your partner to skip three or five lines, so you can add another sentence later when you have time to write more."

<u>Non-lingo Note</u>: Since it's *Silent* Socratic Dialogue, while I'm circulating to read over their shoulders or sitting and writing with someone myself, I have to remind myself (and here I want to remind you, too) not to speak. You may be sorely tempted (like me) – verbose folks that we are – to talk: ask, clarify, follow up, expound, wax eloquently. Don't. Keep quiet. Write. Check email. Read. Silently.

Q's – Sentence Surgery on Motivational Quotations

1. "Which groups vote that this quotation is a *compound* sentence [or *simple, complex, compound-complex*]? Why? What clues do you detect?"

2. "Who spotted the *coordinating conjunction (FANBOYS)*? What does the *comma* signify? What if I erased the *coordinating conjunction*? What is a *comma splice*?"

Q's – Silent Socratic Dialogue (6) 5-4-3 Writing Warm-up

3. "Who wrote twelve or more sentences for their first SSD (6) 5-4-3? Did anyone write fifteen or more?"

4. "Whose partner wrote an especially thought-generating question? Does anyone have a new idea that could work in your essay?"

5. "Take a few minutes to scan through your own sentences for *coordinating conjunctions* (commas with FANBOYS). Does anyone spot any *compound* or *compound-complex* sentences in your own writing?"

Chuckle – Gaming

"Yes, I used to love gaming, too, that is, until my 12-year-old son kept beating me."

Quotation with Sentence Surgery – Peter DeVries

I write when I'm inspired, and I see to it that I'm inspired at nine o'clock every morning.

–Peter DeVries

ind A   dep   B   ind   A   B   dep
[I write] [when I'm inspired,] [and I see to it] [that I'm inspired at nine o'clock every morning.]

ind + dep + ind + dep = cd-cx

Closing Conversation – Interminable Question

"Why do we have to learn this?" Irene asked, appending it with, "After all, I'm going into Radiology Tech, not English."

Why? may well be the best question we have to field, and we probably ought to be especially congenial and welcoming every time it comes, line-drive, toward us.

"Yes, that's a fine question! (Did you know that *why* is the one question never completely answered? You can always ask another *why* for follow-up.) I think the writing payoff for these activities is immense, not only for our essay assignments but also for the kinds of writings and English applications we experience in other college classes and maybe even in our careers, and the letters, applications, and interactions to gain entry to them. Can you think of a situation where you could apply this in another of your classes or on the job?"

Chapter 6. Compose – Assigning and Assessing Essays

When students were asked each year to describe their best writing experiences, two overriding characteristics emerged: (1) the opportunity to write about something that matters to the student and (2) the opportunity to engage with an instructor through written comments.
– Nancy Sommers

Figure 6.1. Tunnel Falls, Clifty Falls State Park, Indiana.
Credit: Chris Light at English Wikipedia, Creative Commons

Coffee Klatsch Collegial Conversation – Pepperoni Pinwheels

"This has to be the best set of essays I've ever received. If only I could keep this class forever!" Jorge ruffled a thumb down the length of a ream of stacked essays and reverently set them on the table. "I'd flunk them all if I could be guaranteed their reenrollment in my class next semester."

"I can't believe the schlock these students dare to turn in! Why, two of them, names I graciously withhold, had the audacity to hand in, one right after the other, their nearly identical, paragraph-to-paragraph, sentence-to-sentence, phrase-to-phrase essay about the importance of being a good student, of all things!" Patricia slapped a pile of papers down. "If they must, can't they at least plagiarize something worthwhile?"

"OK, everyone, help me think of a good way to reward their efforts," Jorge continued.

"I'd like to nail these recalcitrants, but how can I make their punishment fit the infraction?" Patricia carried on.

"What about donuts or candy? Everyone likes a treat," Blaine suggested.

"Why don't you just make them all do the essay over, from scratch?" offered Tara.

"No, I want it to fit the class, somehow to reward them with more of what they do so well. Besides, I refuse to be a contributor to the arterial-death of my prized writers," Jorge replied, tossing a derisive glance at Jimmy who was just then tossing down a leftover pepperoni pinwheels appetizer. "Where do you find that greasy squeezy stuff?"

"Nah, I can't very well punish everyone for the imbecility of a mere 75% of the class. That smacks of injustice."

"Freezer aisle …," Jimmy muttered, stopping to chew.

"Why not do a read aloud of the top excerpts from your very best essays? You could throw them some bonus points for selecting and reading a paragraph or two," Mehdi offered.

Jimmy swallowed, "… appetizers section. Want one? They're only a little stiff and cold."

"Or maybe you could require everyone below a B to rewrite from scratch, and give everybody above a B the option to revise theirs for a bonus?" Jacqui wondered.

"Cool!" Jorge exclaimed. "Sounds good."

"That's exactly what I needed!" Patricia remarked.

"Awesome, so happy to be of assistance to you two. Grease squeezin' pepperoni pinwheels for all!" Jimmy tossed one each to Jorge and Patricia.

"Ew!" Jorge and Patricia exclaimed simultaneously, dodging them.

"Jeers, you-all; here's to mud in your mug!" Jimmy raised the megamug toward Jorge and then Patricia.

"Cheers!"

Chapter Trailhead – Interactive Writing and Assessment

- Rugged Rambles – Southern Indiana's Clifty Falls State Park
- Package without Prescribing – Generating Ideas for Essays
- Step-by-Step – A Writing Process
- Troupe Trek – Peer Review
- Debriefing Essays – Labels on Typed Drafts

Rugged Rambles – Southern Indiana's Clifty Falls State Park

Just north of the Ohio River and west of the town of Madison near the southern edge of the state of Indiana, Clifty Falls State Park has four waterfalls that range from 60 to 83 feet high, along with eight difficult hiking trails. One follows a creek bed along the narrow Clifty Creek chasm, while others ramble up and along the cliffs, cross bridges and splash across creeks, climb networks of boardwalks and stairs, duck under overhangs and then switchback to ascend overhead. Try visiting in the springtime when the waterfalls and creeks are running steady, but aim for midseason because if you arrive too early, the waters may flow too strong to hike the creek bed or to scramble across, and the mud can suck the boots off your feet; too late, and the falls' water volumes may not be as appreciable, and the full foliage can block some intriguing views of precipices and vales. Regardless, expect to exit the trails with at least a few patches of rich, black mud on your shoes, and probably wet socks, too.

Like hiking trails, assigning college essays can be easy, moderate, and difficult. Course requirements may stipulate the essays you select. One course I taught necessitated my teaching a personal I-search essay (Macrorie, 1988), an expository essay, a research essay, and a persuasive essay, even dictating the numbers of pages, words, and researched sources needed for each. Sometimes, the concomitant textbook for a course will determine the essays assigned or present a menu of options from which you may choose. Some colleges require an approved textbook for the classes I am assigned to teach, so I think it important to address its contents with students since they have invested time and money to procure it, and in consideration of the departmental faculty who have devoted their energy and intellect into its acquisition – and sometimes its contents, too. I usually choose essays from a text's selections as samples, or I combine two different essay genres together into one essay assignment for students. In fairness to them, as well as to colleagues and departments, I try not to stray too far away from a department's published course guidelines.

While it's important to use a textbook to be fair to all stakeholders, as well as for any valuable content the text may contain, it's important to remember that a textbook is only one learning resource. It's there to support your instruction. Therefore, use it to select the essays that best fit your instructional methods and your students' learning needs. Use the parts that are most beneficial for your class, as well as most relevant for meeting your department's and college's requirements, and skip the rest. It is never necessary to slog through a complete text, nor is it helpful to begin at its beginning and stick with it to the very end, covering every single page. Your instruction is primary. So if your course comes with a preselected text, take from it what works for your teaching.

If you have a required textbook, I encourage you to use it, as I do mine, with reference to your own ideas about teaching and with other supplemental resources that you find useful – one of which may be this *Guide*. If your college allows adjuncts to select their own text, find one that best complements your teaching. If your college doesn't require one, opt for none. You can spare your students the expense and save yourself the additional hassles of planning by using this *Guide* instead, then supplementing it by favorite readings and sample essays.

When I am required to teach with a textbook – and I usually am assigned a text – I study the contents to see which kinds of essays it includes, and what advice it imparts about the process of writing as well as the product. While each may have its own approach to rhetoric, process, research, or content-delivery, they all have sections about writing essays to persuade, inform, profile, describe, review, and research – or something synonymous or similar. In addition, they usually have chapters or handbook-type sections on grammar, style, organization, and formatting in MLA, APA, or other formats. I find in the textbook what fits with the *Guidebook* and use it to reinforce and supplement accordingly. If the text has sample readings, I try to find an appropriate one to point out the features that I look for in the matching essays that I assign. I look for suggestions about writing as conversation or dialogue, and I seek chapters about clear, concise communication. I hunt for chapters about collaborating, interviewing, peer review, and civil and democratic discourse to support my classroom emphases. If the texts have review or handbook-type sections, I point these out to be used as guides should students want to check a sentence format, a suggestion to write with clarity, or an example of citing an electronic book in the References page for an APA-formatted essay. When a text includes a uniquely practical approach to peer review or a refreshing slant to preparing an essay, I'll probably use it. I encourage students to approach the textbook as a reference work and consult the parts that relate to those essays that they are writing.

Signpost –Democracy and Dialogism

> Look back at Chapter 3, beginning on page 75, to review the importance of conducting your class as a **pragmatic democracy** and writing as a **dialogical process**.

During the past five years, these are some of the essays I have assigned in my first-year college composition classes, in brief:

1. Self-definition (*Personal Essay*) – Identify an object, event, or experience that best represents you: a possession, a place, a life-changing occasion or insight, a job, or a hobby. Include vivid description, clear examples, and incidental narration, written in first person.

2. Portrait of Another Person (*Profile Essay*) – Write about another person, using specific and detailed observations to capture the person's character. Incorporate some dialogue and a setting or two, as well as vivid description, clear examples, and incidental narration (a brief narration about a specific incident), written in third person with some first person, as appropriate. Avoid writing about an immediate family member.

3. Restaurant Review (*Review Essay*) – Visit an eatery that you want to patronize, preferably a one-of-a-kind, local establishment that you could recommend to

fellow students. If your college has a culinary program, visit its cafeteria, bistro, or fine-dining venue, and you will have the satisfaction of supporting students' learning, too. Support your observations with vivid description, clear examples, and incidental narration, written in third person supported with plenty of first person from your own experience there.

4. Local Problem-Solution Investigation (*Proposal Essay*) – Identify a problem on campus, in your neighborhood, or within a hometown community, and then propose a solution or solutions. Investigate its background and effects by interviewing others. Broaden the scope of your investigation by researching other examples online using advanced internet searches, library databases, and electronic books as well as print resources. Thoroughly explore your topic locally and beyond through vivid description, clear examples, and incidental narration, written in third person supported with first person from your own experience and/or observations. Support your solution(s) by giving reasons backed up by the information you collected and by vivid description, examples, and narration.

5. Ethnographic Research Essay (*Ethnography Essay*) – Find an "affinity group" (Gee, 2004), preferably related to a hobby, ethnicity, religion, community, or organization that you are particularly interested in or may even be a member of yourself. Investigate its background and effects by interviewing one or more people connected with the group and observing its activities. As in the Local Problem-Solution Investigation, broaden the scope of this investigation by researching other examples online using advanced internet searches, library databases, and electronic books as well as print resources. Thoroughly explore the topic locally and beyond through vivid description, clear examples, and incidental narration, written in third person supported with first person from your own experience. Compile an Annotated Bibliography 9-6-3 of three-to-nine sources while researching your ethnography.

Signpost – Essay Assignments and Forms

Appendix 1, beginning on page 158, includes sample essay assignments and forms for peer review, turn-in, reflection, and evaluation for a **Personal Essay**, **Profile Essay**, **Review Essay**, **Proposal Essay**, and **Ethnography Essay**.

6. Downtown Tour – Select one of the topics from among the following: Architecture, Bridges, Coffee Shops, Fire and Police Stations, Museums, Outdoor Art, Places of Worship, Skyscrapers. Select representative examples for your topic that are within walking distance, then plan a circle walking tour beginning and ending on campus. Include descriptive details, historical background, recommended highlights en route, pictures with appropriate captions, and suggested times and distances.

7. Where You're From – Write about a place that is integral to who you are, maybe even defines you. Use sensory description, clear exposition, and plenty of dialogue. Try some foreshadowing, if you can, and possibly a flashback in italic text, if you wish.

8. Career Exploration – Choose an occupation to explore. Use the U.S. Bureau of Labor Statistics' Occupational Outlook Handbook website as well as a *.org*

Trail Marker – Essay Assignments

Easy – From your own or a textbook's essay assignments, list 3–5 that you have taught or would like to teach:

1. ____

2. ____

3. ____

4. ____

5. ____

Moderate – Choose 2–3 essay topics or assignments from your list above, and then write a brief set of student instructions for each. Discuss with a colleague, or respond to this question: How could these essays advance your students' writing skills, learning development, or democratic engagement?

Difficult – Discuss with another instructor or a group of cohorts which essay assignment or two do you think could best advance your students' writing, learning, and democratic engagement?

domain site to research the field. Find the university's course of study that could lead toward a related degree, and research the library's databases, subject guides, electronic, and print sources to learn what you can about the career. Interview someone working in the field or an instructor who teaches a related course on campus, if feasible. Write in third person about the field itself, and in first person about how you might prepare for a career in the field yourself, if you so choose.

9. Unsung Hero – Identify someone on campus or in the community who is an unsung hero, an altruistic, self-less, or underappreciated individual who may not get the recognition or acknowledgement deserved. Use description and exposition, then broaden your exploration to research others who may share your hero's job, situation, or background. Include your own interactions with this person and explain why the person qualifies as an Unsung Hero. Avoid immediate family members.

10. Service Learning Essay – Write a reflection about your experience volunteering at a not-for-profit organization this semester. What did you do? Whom did you serve? How did this experience benefit you? If you were to recommend it to a classmate, what would you say? Besides your own perspective, try to interview a supervisor or fellow volunteers for theirs, too. How do they compare? How could you improve the experience, or what would you do differently if you could do it over again?

Package without Prescribing – Generating Ideas for Essays

Generating ideas can be a difficult writing obstacle. Help your students surmount it with in-class assignments guiding them through conversations, lists, charts, webs, brainstorms, and sketches of their interests, experiences, places, hobbies, possible topics, and subtopics. Design related Writing Warm-ups or free-writes to assist their idea-generating. I may initiate students' idea-generation in-class with timed free-writing that I call *forced-writes*, or I might select spider-webs, mind maps, sensory maps, concept maps, bubble charts, columns-lists, ladders, Q & A, and any from the myriad of approaches to generating ideas. The trick, I suggest to my students, is to try a few new approaches and keep working with the one or two that best fit their own thinking and writing, as long as they match an assigned essay's purposes.

Signpost – Silent Socratic Dialogue (6) 5-4-3

Silent Socratic Dialogue (6) 5-4-3 is an especially effective idea-generator because it involves written reflection and engagement with another student's questions and ideas, which can anticipate an audience's interests and concerns. To find out more about this approach, turn to pages 118–119.

Resist any teacherly urge to fill lists or provide topics, yourself. Don't give answers. Instead, suggest several parameters without squelching ideas. One way that I attempt to discourage students' self-censorship while encouraging idea-generation is requiring a full column of potential topics, top-to-bottom, and sometimes as many as three or four columns of listed ideas on a page before I will initial and date the page to signal my *seal of approval* and sometimes, their *ticket out of class*. If the end of class is near, I may say that their completing a full-page list of ideas, or a full page (or two) of forced-writing about the topic with my initials is their ticket out. Some scramble to finish, borrowing ideas from group members, and gathering suggestions from the textbook's samples, just to shave 2–5 minutes off the remaining class time. Everyone is dismissed by the end of the period, but if some want to stay and finish their work before leaving, they're welcome to remain as long as I am able to and as long as no other class or instructor is scheduled in that room. When time runs out, I normally offer to initial their finished work at the beginning of our next class meeting.

Step-by-Step – A Writing Process

In a way, no writing should ever really be completely finished. Every essay (not to mention chapter or book) can be continually revised, improved, updated. Ultimately, there is no such thing, then, as a final copy or a last draft. Always, it could be returned to for additional revisions. Even the best writing theoretically could see some improvement. How do we effectively communicate this to our students? One way is to require separate turn-ins of several drafts for each essay. Usually, I ask to see students' rough drafts, revised drafts, edited and formatted copies before grading an essay. After reading the rough draft, revised drafts, and edited copy, I initial and date it in class, then ask them to produce the earlier copies before I'll read and assess an essay. For each step in this writing process, I ask the class to focus on a separate skill. First, we work on the theme or focus of the essay, and then I ask them to divide it into individual topics and subtopics within that theme. This is done at the idea-generation stage. For a rough draft, they write about the topics of their theme, using strategies of description, explanation, examples, exploration, and maybe also making some Notes to Self for later research or possible topics. The revision (i.e., a revised draft) adds changes, such as additional topics with examples, maybe illustrations, rearrangements, clearer explanations, more descriptive details. Often, I suggest that students write an additional two pages or so between the rough draft and revised draft. For this revision draft, I have them target writing style, syntactic structures, paragraph organization, introduction, conclusion, and format. For editing and formatting, I suggest they use their word processing program to spell-check and grammar-check, and submit their essay for a plagiarism scan using the school's online plagiarism-detection program, as well.

Requiring separate drafts can target students' writing toward the different requirements of producing a worthwhile essay. First, selecting a theme that has personal relevance helps to generate ideas and sustain a writer's interest through the writing process and also helps to generate and sustain a reader's interest and ideas. Second, developing writing at a collegiate level and meeting the demands for content, style, and organization that will communicate both creatively and clearly requires substantial revision. Third, making a specific last stage for editing and formatting keeps these activities from sabotaging the writing process by jumping ahead of content and organizational concerns, thereby sidetracking the deep topical reflection and revision that should occur before attention is focused on surface-level concerns. One effective way to keep the sequence may be to require an additional page length with each successive draft/version: assigning another three pages after the rough draft necessitates more detail, additional paragraphs, and probably some rearrangement and revision that will affect the length, too. Another technique is asking students to list 3–5 *Notes-to-Self* following a peer review session, with ideas to add or change, then asking them when checking the next draft which of these notes they followed in their revision. One more option is to ask students to review a draft with a tutor or consultant in a writing center or other campus academic support center, possibly requiring documentation such as a report or reflection.

I allow the class size to govern how much of every draft I read. Nearly always, I read their drafts in class while students peer review one another's work. When a class is small, I often have the leisure to thoroughly read their drafts and offer comments, recognize achievements, and suggest a few revisions. When a class is packed, I may read only an introductory paragraph, some topic sentences, a thesis statement, a passage of dialogue, 2–3 sentences that the students themselves select, or another portion of the assignment. If this is the case, I usually announce beforehand what I intend to review, or I ask students to suggest what would be most helpful to them. In some classes, I may have a student tutor or consultant assigned. In that situation, I ask the tutor to read the drafts of half the class, and I review the other half.

On the due date for an assignment, I plan a ritual routine for students' turn-in of their essays. On occasion, I have them attach my initialed and dated copies of the essay's rough draft, revised draft, and edited/formatted final copy, too. When I do so, I normally supply a pile of large, colorful paper clips for them to select one to conjoin their drafts. The color adds a celebratory touch to the often large stack of drafts students can accumulate – and often appreciate at turn-in. Sometimes, I simply ask to see these drafts before accepting the essay for grading. Sometimes, I ask them to fill in a Essay Reflection Form, too, to add to their stack of drafts. The reflection is a half-page of questions that encourages them to self-reflect on their own writing process while it is still immediate.

Signpost – Essay Reflection Form and Essay Review Form

A copy of the half-page, **Essay Reflection Form**, to be completed and turned in with an essay, can be found on the top half of page 177. A copy of the **Essay Review Form**, completed by the student after an essay is returned with the instructor's mark-up, is on the bottom half of page 177.

Always, I aim to return their essays as they arrive at the next class meeting. With every returned paper, I typically hand students another half-page sheet, this one called the Essay Review Form. The Essay Review Form guides their thorough reading of my suggestions as they review their essay while reading my written feedback on it. To encourage additional revision, I typically offer them up to 10% bonus for rewriting it again, that is, going through a second revision, and submitting it by the next class meeting. Usually, I will give up to a 5% bonus for sentence-level and stylistic improvements, and another up to 5% for organizational, paragraph-level changes. This promotes deep revision more than simply surface or superficial editing of mechanics. Even when their changes may weaken an essay, I add points for the attempts, because all revision can be beneficial experimentation, and therefore good learning – even when students have learned when it's better not to arrange a sentence in a particular way again.

Normally, as few as three and as many as eight students choose to revise their essays a second time to turn in by the next class meeting. Although not everyone takes advantage of this opportunity to improve both a grade and their writing, all appreciate the offer and welcome my generosity as well as the follow-through on my assertion that the more we practice writing, the better writers we become. Typically, I don't grant the offer to revise an essay to a student who didn't turn in an essay when it is due, so it can prod those who turned in a late essay to submit the next one on time to receive an opportunity for revising that next essay for a subsequent improvement. On the other side, it does, for a few, undermine their quality, leading them to believe, mistakenly, that they will be able to make up any slovenliness after-the-fact, so slopping together a mish-mash essay to turn in first. Rarely have I experienced this, however. I don't require nearly as much time for second readings of essays, instead aligning them side-by-side with my already-marked copy, and making ink-dots beneath the changes, offering only one or two additional suggestions for revision.

Troupe Trek – Peer Review

Besides the student's own drafts of each essay, I collect a Peer Review page. For every essay, I assign an hour or so of one class period to read and assess a few aspects of one draft. For example, in the Personal Essay, usually the first I assign, I have students staple a blank page onto the back and exchange their rough drafts with a partner. Usually, I encourage them to switch with someone who has written a similar amount as they have. Then, I project a list of items for them to uncover in their partner's paper and answer five or so questions, such as:

1. What metaphor – an item, event, or place – has the writer chosen to represent her/himself? What examples of it does the author include?
2. What personal anecdote, a vivid yet brief narrative, best expresses the writer's character?
3. What detailed description gives you the most vivid picture of the writer?
4. Which paragraphs are about the past, the present, the future? Does the writer begin the introduction in the past or the present? Does the author end the conclusion in the present or the future?
5. What would you like to learn more about? What seems incomplete? What might better express the writer's personality?

They write their names on the Peer Review page attached to the back of the drafts, numbered 1–4, and write a brief response including an example for each. After twenty minutes, they return the drafts to their authors, or maybe I have them take another turn at peer review, exchanging essays with another classmate, usually a fellow group member, and write their answers for the same questions below the first reviewer's. Finally, they return the drafts to their authors and discuss them to clarify any comments or ask any further questions. After they've completed the reviews, under the heading "Notes to Self," all write 3–5 ideas or suggestions to improve their next draft of the essay.

Signpost – Peer Review Activity Forms

Appendix 1 includes a form for five **Peer Review** activities to align with each of five essays: **Personal Essay – Rough Draft**, page 161; **Profile Essay – Rough Draft + Revised Draft**, page 164; **Review Essay – Revised Draft**, page 167; **Proposal Essay – Revised Draft**, page 171; and **Ethnography Essay – Revised Draft**, page 174. I usually project these forms on the days when students review one another's essays in class.

Peer Review, besides providing writers multiple perspectives and suggestions about their drafts, offers the reviewers models of different ideas, organizational structures, and language that they may want to attempt or emulate in their own writing. To encourage this, I sometimes suggest they include an item in their Notes to Self that they learned from another student's essay. In addition, Peer Review helps guide students' critique of others' idea-generating, drafting, revising, and editing, reinforcing and informing their own understanding and implementation of writing processes. Finally, it shows them that there is always more than one good way to craft and revise an essay through multiple drafts. For some students, reading one another's writing can be a stronger learning experience than hearing instructions from an instructor or reading exemplary essays in a textbook.

Debriefing Essays – Labels on Typed Drafts

Self-assessment is helpful for students to internalize their learning. When they submit their essays, I have them mark up their final drafts to reflect about and review assigned content – or to *debrief* while their writing of the essay is still fresh in their minds – on the day that they turn them in for evaluation. First, I ask them to label four items on their finished copies using a carat for each, pointing up, down, left, and right: <, ^, >, and ∨. For example, in the Personal Essay, I ask them to write a carat pointing left (<) in the left margin before a representative thing, event, or place that they include as a topic. If they include more than one, they're invited to mark more than one <. They then put a carat pointing up (^) beside a brief narrative, story, or anecdote used as illustration. Although the Personal Essay is not a narrative or story itself, it uses a succession of brief stories to further its purpose, so I ask them to label these brief stories with an upward pointing carat in their Personal Essay. Next, they are to place a right-pointing carat (>) beside especially clear and succinct explanations or expositions. Finally, I ask them to mark downward pointing carats (∨) before their most vivid, sensory descriptions.

In addition to placing carats to identify topics, narrative, exposition, and description, they apply sentence surgery to 3–6 sentences, by double-underlining its verbs, single-underlining their subjects, bracketing and labeling the clauses as *independent* or *dependent*, and identifying the sentences as *simple, compound, complex*, or *compound-complex*, so they gain facility in recognizing the different sentence types, and will include them in their own writing. Finally, they are to identify and circle their 3–6 best college-level, $10 words. To preempt anyone's displeasure about marking on their final drafts, I add, "As perfect and pristine as your typed essay appears, once I get my pen on it, I'll have it all marked and inked up right away. Besides, this is your opportunity to show me you can apply what we have been learning together, as well as a chance to check and correct anything that may need fixing before submitting the essay for the grade. Anything you catch counts before I check it, even if it's penned in above the typed text." Rarely do I write lengthy comments. The single word *yes* is probably my most noted comment. Sometimes, I don't write any closing remarks; however, I make always a suggestion or two, usually posed as a question, such as "Could you make this sentence your introductory hook, instead?"

Often, I use a scoring rubric using ten criteria that are adapted to each essay's genre and requirements. Generally, nine of the criteria remain the same – or very similar – for every essay, but one evaluates the features of its specific genre. For example, the Personal Essay Evaluation Form includes a "Features of the Genre" row to include these items: explanation, examples, description, and dialogue. Dividing each of the ten components into four descriptors of excellent, good, satisfactory, and poor writing, aligns readily with A, B, C, and D-E grades, so students can understand the values placed on each assessed feature. As an example, an excellent "Theme," the first criterion of the Review Essay, is described this way, "My thesis sentence is robust, included in the introduction, and contains three or more detailed topics." While admittedly prescriptive and, therefore, a bit limiting, the rubrics allow me to circle, tally, and score an essay rapidly, allowing me to devote time toward assessing multiple copies of essays with students and reviewing them more frequently.

Signpost – Labeling Final Drafts for Turn-in

Appendix 1 also includes forms with instructions for students to label each of the five different essays: **Personal Essay Turn-in Labels**, page 162; **Profile Essay Turn-in Labels**, page 165; **Review Essay Turn-in Labels**, page 168; **Proposal Essay Turn-in Labels**, page 172; and **Ethnography Essay Turn-in Labels**, page 175.

For those semesters when I happen to have some extra assessment time, I may select 3–5 exemplary introductory paragraphs, vivid descriptions, character-revealing dialogue, thesis sentences, or another topic from among the students' turned in essays to highlight in the class by reading it aloud, asking the student-author to read it aloud, or projecting it for the class. After these readings, I praise the essay's laudable traits. Sometimes, I ask authors of the exemplary work to stand and remain standing while each reads or has read her/his excerpts, and after all have finished, we applaud them all together as they sit. When I scout out these exceptional samples in students' essays, I seek a diversity among both writers and writing styles to be able to accentuate the variety to the other students. I want to clearly communicate that all succeed through effort, experimentation, and exploration, and I hope to demonstrate the value of such diversity in a democratic classroom.

Finally, just a note about fielding the perpetual question, "How many pages do you want?" On the one hand, I understand any umbrage at the question. Why can't students just let the assignment's topic carry them through a thorough treatment? On the other hand, if they were trained to write on a treadmill of five-paragraph essays or three-page formulaic assignments, how could they be expected to realize the rigors of writing a college-level composition? Besides, when have we teacher-writers ever written an essay ourselves that didn't require an assigned number of words as well as an imposed deadline in our own writing? Why not simply respond, "four pages," or "fourteen pages," and just get on with the process? Instead of insisting on word counts or page productions, you can always hedge with the exclamation, "Since your essay is so well written, I can always make an exemplary exception – your quality far exceeds the quantity!"

Sometimes, this is how I reply, "Did you write any five-paragraph formula essays in your high school? Introduction, three body paragraphs, conclusion? Since this is college, give me at least six strong paragraphs for a first draft, OK? If you're planning to write your book, let me tell you that after eight pages (or four – or whatever – if a class is overbooked with students that term), I skip to the conclusion and mark what I've read, fair enough?" I like to add for a bit of levity, "By the way, if you do happen to write your book and it does get published, be sure to remember your good old English professor when the royalties start pouring in, eh?"

Top 10 List – Student Essay Revisions

1. **Assigning Essays.** Students benefit from more assigned essays of varied genre than fewer, longer ones because they practice applying different approaches, and the range helps keep them interested and engaged. If time constraints restrict the number of essays you assign, try combining a couple of genres together, such as adding some personal narrative to introduce and conclude every expository and review essay. It probably will make them much more interesting, and it grants you some insight about your student-authors, too.

2. **Selecting Themes.** Within specified parameters, students should select their own themes. Choosing topics helps them practice generating ideas, a critical first step in the writing process. It increases motivation to write, which can engage both student-writers and their peer- and instructor-readers. In addition, the option of using first-person voice in personal narrative helps student writers select individually meaningful topics and write about them in a way that avoids the risk of plagiarism.

3. **Dividing Tasks.** Dividing a daunting college composing task into a step-by-step procedure is useful, and four or five steps seem plenty to accentuate students' writing as a process.

4. **Generating Ideas.** Try a new idea-generator with every essay: a list, a cluster, a forced-write, free-write, mind-map, brainstorm, and others. Encourage students to select one or two of these ways of generating ideas that matches best with their own writing process and with the strictures of different writing assignments.

5. **Drafting.** For the Rough Draft, suggest that writers note their own experiences, ideas, interests, and knowledge about a topic, then add some Notes-to-Self listing what they need to find out and where they plan to discover it. A list of Notes-to-Self can be beneficial when concluding Peer Review activities, too.

6. **Revising.** For a Revised Draft, encourage experimentation and exploration with the formation and arrangements of paragraphs. I typically suggest students wait until this draft (after a Rough Draft) to write an introduction and conclusion for an essay, both because they can be more difficult to write, and often an essay's body content, once developed at the rough draft stage may suggest an appropriate

opening and closing. Mention, too, that conjunctions – like those on the Popular Conjunctions Mnemonics list on page 229 – make effective transitions to link paragraphs as well as supplying necessary connectors between clauses and helping to vary sentence style.

7. **Peer Reviewing.** Assign Peer Review for every essay, so students learn to offer constructive criticism to their peers, to glean good ideas and techniques from classmates, and to accept critique about improving their compositions.

8. **Editing.** Require a spell-check, grammar-check, and plagiarism-check wherever possible. Encourage visits to writing and other assistance centers, tutorial sessions, and libraries whenever expedient: local, free, and beneficial.

9. **Checking.** Check every draft of every essay, from the preliminary sketch or idea-generator to the latest, typed copy, as well as the Peer Review and Essay Reflection forms. Even if you don't read every portion of every draft, find something to review in every one. Checking them accentuates the importance of every step in the writing process.

10. **Assessing.** Allow students opportunities to revise their essays after you have returned them with mark-ups and grades. For some, a chance to improve the grade may be the single greatest motivator to rewrite an essay, and any additional revision is good practice. Besides, especially when your students aren't familiar with your comments and assessments, granting them the opportunity to earn a better grade through revision is integral to fair play in guiding students' writing.

Lingo – Great Arrangements

1. "When you're ready to turn in the drafts of your completed essay, staple each draft individually – List of Ideas, Rough Draft, Revised Draft, Peer Review, and Edited/Formatted Copy – but use a paper clip to attach them all together: Last Draft on top, down to the first Idea-Generator on the bottom. Remember, the last shall be first."

2. "Welcome to writing! I'm returning the essays you turned in last class. Remember, I warned you that I'd mark all over them. My goal of course is to provide you far too much feedback to correct all in one try. You may want to revise it again and resubmit it by our next class meeting for some more input as well as an improved score if you like."

3. "You know my philosophy: the more writing you practice and the more additional revisions you do, the more experimenting you try, the greater your reward in learning and writing – and also in grading. Fair is fair."

4. "Whether or not you decide to revise your graded essay another time, please fill out the half-page Essay Review Form, so I can see what you attempted and what you plan to target in your next essay writing."

5. "Today, I have chosen three superb selections of introductory paragraphs with first-person narrative openings that immediately hook the reader [or another writing topic you want to accentuate from their writing]. Listen and follow along on the projector screen while I read them aloud. Would the student-authors please stand up, so we can acknowledge you with our applause after I've finished reading all three?"

Q's – Poignant Anecdote?

1. "Why do you think it is essential for students to select a theme that interests you, the writer? What might happen if the writer becomes uninterested in a topic?"
2. "Which is more important, an introduction that hooks the readers and pulls them into the essay or a conclusion that summarizes clearly yet thoroughly? Why?"
3. "Would you rather read a poignant anecdote that includes a brief personal story to open an essay, or a factual explanation with an abundance of statistics? Why?"
4. "What is the purpose of writing a Personal Essay [or Profile, Review, Proposal, Ethnography]? What do you want your readers to think or do? How could you make this as effective and purposeful for your readers as possible?"
5. "Do you plan to rewrite this Personal Essay [or Profile, Review, Proposal, Ethnography] after you have read my suggestions? You are going to try rewriting at least one section of your essay for our next class, right?"

Chuckle – Skip the Flick

"No, I doubt that I'll go see that movie; instead, I think I'll just wait for the book to come out."

Sentence Surgery on a Motivational Quotation

Writing is an exploration, so you start from nothing and learn as you go.

– E. L. Doctorow

      B   ind   A   ind   A   dep A
[<u>Writing</u> <u>is</u> an exploration,] [so you <u>start</u> from nothing and <u>learn</u>] [as you <u>go</u>.]
ind + ind + dep = cd-cx

Closing Conversation – A Healthy Dose

"Can't you let us write personal narratives all the time?" Andrew pleaded.

"Wouldn't that be nice? Actually, I'm aiming to give you all a healthy dose of every possible essay you may encounter in your college career here. When you graduate, you'll have to be sure to let me know how I did, OK? In the meantime, please do slip in some first-person narrative to open and close every essay that you can in our class."

Figure 6.2. *I think it's a compound-complex sentence.*

Chapter 7. Confab – Being Collegial

As I look back on what I have written, I can see that the very persons who have taken away my time are those who have given me something to say.
– Katherine Paterson

Figure 7.1. Big Sable Point Lighthouse, Ludington State Park, Michigan.
Credit: Rachel Kramer at Flickr Creative Commons

Coffee Klatsch Collegial Conversation – Scraped PBJ

"Whew, so we managed to make it through another one!" Nina exulted.

"You and me, two," Roberto pulled up a stool.

"Me, too, too!" Mehdi called out. "What are we signing up for?"

"End of semester clean-out-the office KP?" Jimmy volunteered.

"Not for me! Did you see that PBJ still stuck beneath the corner workstation in the common office?" Jacqui asked.

"Why didn't you clean it up?" accused Kim.

"Why didn't you?" Roberto replied. "You sat there every Tuesday after all."

"Ah, it appears my nefarious little experiment is working!" Jimmy crouched, sinisterly waving his hands over the steam rising from his beverage.

"It was you! You …!" Kim declared.

"Not to worry, I scraped it off and ate it before walking over here this afternoon – still good."

"Ew, you!" Jacqui pushed away a carrot bran muffin. "That annihilated my appetite."

"So, has anyone heard when we find out what we're assigned to teach next semester?" Patricia asked.

"Here's to mud in your mug." Jimmy raised the megamug, "Jeers, you-all!"

"Cheers!"

Chapter Trailhead – Gather for Blather

- The Extra Mile – Western Michigan's Ludington State Park
- Pick Pleasures – Avoid Poisons
- Catch a Cup of Coffee – Small-Talk to Shop-Talk
- Congregate and Confabulate – And Celebrate!

The Extra Mile – Western Michigan's Ludington State Park

If you like to hike around circumferences of sand dune blow-outs, the great bowls of sand blasted into the white-sand dunes of Michigan's west coast by wind and weather, visit P. J. Hoffmaster (Michigan) State Park, south of Muskegon, or North Ottawa (County) Dunes Park, next door. Hoffmaster Park's Gillette Nature Center offers a fine explanation of dune ecology and the unique circumstances that happen to cause a dune blow-out. But if you continue north of Muskegon on US-31 to Ludington, then follow signs to Ludington State Park, north of the city of Ludington, between Lake Michigan and inland Hamlin Lake, there, you can experience three exceptional hiking trails, either individually, or all together if you have the whole day.

When I visited one chilly day in early spring, the campgrounds nearly empty, and the beach houses and concessions all closed for the season, only a handful of hardy canoers and kayakers all bundled in winter water gear were launching their crafts into the canoe trail canals that wind along Hamlin Lake. I set off alongside the Hamlin Lake launch site, taking the Island Trail's boardwalk between Lost Lake to the left, and Hamlin Lake on my right. Skirting little Lost Lake's shoreline, I watched a couple of mute swans and their brood of cygnets dipping for breakfast, seeming unmindful of my passing. Once past Lost Lake, I turned up the Ridge Trail to climb the forested tertiary dune to take the trail along its crest back to the trailhead. When it intersected with the Lighthouse Trail, I turned onto that path and set off towards the black-and-white banded Big Sable (pronounced Sah'-bul) Point Lighthouse on the Lake Michigan shore. I'm glad I did, since this trail accorded me an inimitable pleasure of descending to a lighthouse from a ridgeline high above, after periodically sighting it off in the distance, then ever nearer, down along the coastline's edge. Then hiking down to the shore, I was lucky enough to discover the lighthouse open, so I circled the stairwell up to its summit and out on its platform. Even though I had been looking down at it from a ridgeline, I admit a touch of vertigo out on that narrow metal ledge 112 feet above the beach up in the winds and hearing the waves below. After circling the top, I circled the stairs back down, I opted to walk the Lake Michigan shoreline for the couple of miles back south to the state park. From Island Trail to Ridge Trail and Lighthouse Trail (and lighthouse climb), I prized Ludington State Park's varieties of landforms and sceneries, happy to have added the extra few miles to its lighthouse.

Like finding and climbing a lighthouse, expect the serendipitous in your job as a writing teacher. You may feel rewarded and refreshed after you've taken a break and started a conversation. Try to think of it as a success when you made a moment lighthearted enough to laugh out loud. Although a number of years ago now, I vividly and fondly recollect the shared desks and spaces in the basement of the dated English Department hall that served as my graduate school's TA (Teaching Associates) office. Suspended from the drop-ceiling was an ancient, lidless beer stein dangling from a string, and filled with pennies. At particularly unproductive moments or times of high anxiety, someone climbed onto a central desk to tip the cup, empty all the pennies and toss them among whoever was occupying the office. All work stopped. Then the TA twisted the string to spin the stein as all attempted to toss pennies into its spinning mouth. "Losers" at times were tabbed to buy a round for everyone uptown after the last afternoon class. Rarely was there any "winner." Simply hitting the cup, anywhere, elicited fist-thrusts with cheers of victory. Spinning stein or not, nearly always there was a hum of activity and a shared conviviality in that cramped, basement, shared space. Maybe I'm simply attempting to recapture those younger days.

Adjunct instructors at the various colleges where I now work share a couple of offices with a half dozen desks, several PCs, conference tables, file cabinets, and phones scattered against the walls – in many respects, they look just like the TA office back in my grad school days. All they need is a broken beer stein filled with pennies dangling from the ceiling. That, and somebody brave enough to climb atop a desk to set it spinning. Although adjuncts come and go, checking emails, marking essays, preparing lessons and Power Point slides, many enter and exit stealthily with nary a word spoken or cordial greeting exchanged. Sure, they may value a silent spot to study, plan, mark, or write. However, teaching already can be a solitary task, with so many going it doggedly alone, desperately driving to and from campuses, planning and assessing lessons and essays, closing the classroom doors, opening them only to depart when done. Adjuncts need to create opportunities to gather together with peers to commiserate, celebrate, and collaborate in the company of part-time colleagues. In other words, adjuncts could benefit from a little more *adjunction*.

Signpost – Adjunction

For some more about *adjunction*, turn back to the Introduction to find **Adjunction – Teaching Composition on the Run**, beginning on page 3.

Why not create an office of conversation, collaboration, and now-and-then some little hijinks? This is a whole lot more welcoming than stepping into a silent sepulcher of blue faces illumined at antiquated terminals. There is too much collective wisdom available for adjuncts to silently, stoically go it alone. Greet your colleagues, be collegial, and pop a few questions whenever you enter your shared offices. Instead of whispering around, skulking in silence, introduce and then reintroduce yourself as many times as necessary. Ask others their names, what they teach, which texts they use, what essays they assign. You may gain some new ideas, some good friends. Many of my best practices are begged, borrowed, and adapted from friends and associates. Initiate a conversation. Start some small-talk, and then move along to shop-talk. In my experiences, most instructors don't just offer unsolicited their best ideas, for that could come across as forward, cocky even, among us humbletons. Still, most relish an opportunity to talk about what they're doing, and they may appreciate your initiating their opportunity. Although counterintuitive, asking for others' ideas, advice, and accomplishments may make you more respected than giving your own.

Usually familiar with neglect, disregard, and discount, adjunct instructors should regard and acknowledge one another. Although it may seem paradoxical, give the recognition that you would like to receive. You can be the one who cranes your neck to spot and greet your colleagues when they enter the shared office. That newby slinking over to the corner checking her phone? She may be wondering how to grab the reins of classroom management in her late afternoon class, but she is hesitant to ask anyone for fear that she appears incompetent in her first assignment. The Haight-Ashbury looking dude slouched over the PC? He's worried he may never get the gist of the college's new online program. Step over and introduce yourself, and acknowledge your peers when you step into your shared adjunct spaces. Yes, you can get stepped on sometimes, but risking a little collegial democracy may help to break down a few despotic, departmental fiefdoms. Try to clear open some pathways by becoming a clearinghouse to your department's resources, both human and non. Live the congenial collaboration you seek to inspire in your students and classrooms. And why not have some fun and stir up a little adjunction-collusion among your part-time colleagues in the meantime, too? Short of spinning beer steins from a ceiling, maybe you'll find yourself able to relive some of your own TA glory days back when.

Pick Pleasures – Avoid Poisons

One of the shining beauties of adjunction-instruction is you get to choose to participate in those extracurricular activities you want, and equally glorious, you get to skip what you don't. You might be invited to join a faculty reading group, to serve on the assessment norming committee, or to attend a departmental party. And as inclinations, time, and coffers allow, you may welcome any or all of these opportunities. If angling for a full-time position, you may want to wrangle invitations to participate in as many departmental or college gatherings as you can. Some institutions may expect or solicit participation on the part of adjunct instructors that aren't contractual obligations, and then your choosing whether to attend may get dicey. Still, it's yours to decide: you get to pick.

What's more, whatever you choose to invest yourself in should be appreciated by administrators and full-time colleagues who may feel pressure to pick up ever more tasks if budgets constrain, personnel and benefits whittle back, or revenues shrink with enrollments. Let's face it, some institutions seem bent on reducing higher education to an economic commodity instead of what might better be considered an acculturating loss leader, one that humanizes and democratizes successive generations. In a sense, adjuncts do contribute to this reductionist commodification of higher education; after all, we are hired at a discount for an institution to bank benefits and save salaries. Of course, adjuncts contribute valuable talents, distinctive abilities, and inimitable experiences to students' learning and colleges' offerings. Adjuncts are the subcontracted specialists without whom colleges couldn't compete, and certainly wouldn't contribute all their coursework and classes to constituencies and communities. Besides, adjuncts can be freed up from extra institutional obligations and so focus on teaching and students.

Of course, I've heard of some schools and administrators that use stipends, food, and threats to coax and coerce adjuncts into participating in meetings, training sessions, or departmental or college events. One college dangled this carrot: adjuncts who attend professional development offerings get bumped up the pecking order for class assignments in the next semester's class-assignments dole. Another promised a feed furnished by the culinary program. Occasionally, a collegial friend may invite some cohorts to go to an orientation or professional development session together – that is likely worth attending. The good news is that adjuncts usually aren't required to attend – except sometimes they are. When told you have to be there, it may pay to see how seriously it's stipulated: if you don't go, then what? Ask how many grade-norming meetings are required of adjuncts when the expectation isn't specified. It's OK to beg off an event because another institution presents an obligation. Administrators may understand. After all, some of them have swum in adjunct pools, too.

Trail Marker – Pick Your Poisons

Easy – Choose one of your department's or college's social gatherings to participate in. Invite one or two adjunct colleagues to go along with you.

Moderate – Up the ante: invite a half-dozen colleagues to an on-campus cafeteria, food court, or coffee shop at a time when you can all gather together – just to socialize. Don't only focus on peers just like you. Try to target some diversity among your colleagues.

Difficult – Post a sign in your adjunct office and send an email invitation to all your fellow adjuncts in the department to a luncheon, coffee break, or happy hour – to celebrate payday, midterm, or finals. Ask them to RSVP with you beforehand, so you can make a reservation at a nearby restaurant, coffee shop, or brew pub.

As you demonstrate your versatility – and if an adjunct, you certainly are agile – administrators and colleagues should recognize and respect it – and you. When they don't, do what you must, but choose what is just. Besides infrequent hobnobs with colleagues in nearby coffee shops, I enjoy the chances I get to mentor new adjunct instructors and being mentored whenever I pick up a new class or break into a new department. I like to plan and lead professional development trainings, participate in curriculum reviews as well as horizontal and vertical alignments of courses, and I take pleasure in putting into practice new theories, designing new themes, units, and lessons for composition courses. Fortunately, I am blessed with supervisors who often encourage my different endeavors and full-time colleagues who welcome my working alongside them – as well as a plethora of fascinating and fun fellow adjuncts.

Catch a Cup of Coffee – Small-Talk to Shop-Talk

Maybe more than anything else, the gratification of genuine conversation with a like-minded colleague or flourishing student over a cup of java invigorates me. Do nurture your coffee (or tea) habit. Or foster one. One year I set the goal to complete a Mug Club punch card entitling me to one free cup of coffee having purchased a previous seven. It may be because I resolved to invite a colleague every week to "catch a cup of coffee." Or it may be because one of my favorite coffee shops closed, and the other two had been discovered by so many others that the seats were always packed when I tried to snag one. Whichever, I sent emails, caught colleagues, and sometimes shanghaied compadres into conversing at the campus coffee shop.

I'm still surprised by the enthusiasm that many express at getting a simple, one-line email or spoken invitation to break for coffee. Once a week for one semester, when the majority of my courses met on the main campus, I made an effort to invite someone every week for a coffee break to catch up. From former students to a former mentor, a dean and a department chair, full-time faculty and adjunct instructors, support staff and office employees, and even a book publisher's rep, the only ones who wouldn't meet me couldn't because of persistent schedule conflicts – at least that was the claim they made.

Of course, it is good for me, too. Besides the coffee's warmth and caffeine boost, getting out of the classroom and the office, and sometimes off campus, is a rejuvenating change of venue. Conversations with many different individuals permit me participation in widely divergent and fascinating subjects, as well as insightful shop-talk about assignments and approaches instructors take to planning and practice. In addition, I often find out news that otherwise I wouldn't know, such as the new edition of a composition textbook being adopted next semester, announced in the departmental meeting I happened to miss the previous month due to a scheduling conflict.

Part-time colleagues don't often collect for coffee breaks anymore. Maybe it's due to the staggering schedules they keep, or possibly it's caused by the staggered schedules of classes that they're assigned. Three-hour classes, two-hour, one-, one-and-a-half, multiple campuses and online courses – all can result in a dizzying number of arrivals and departures, sometimes without encountering counterparts met at a last orientation or seen every week throughout a preceding term. It doesn't always work out, or work out well, but you may be gratified at their gratitude for your initiative or invitation, or at least at your generosity if you offer to spring for their cup of coffee. By the way, I usually do offer to pay for a cup for former students, whom I tell that they may reciprocate after they graduate if their salary starts to climb. If nothing else, you may gain the satisfaction of accumulating enough stamps on your punch card to earn a free, steaming cup of joe, eh?

Congregate and Confabulate – And Celebrate!

Sometimes adjuncts have to schedule their own socials. Several, long-term adjunct instructors that I know gather for a celebratory luncheon to conclude each semester. They had been arranging this for years when I happened upon them one day, planning in a corner of our train depot shaped adjunct office. "Is anyone invited," I called over, grinning, "or is this an exclusive club?" What could they say? "Of course, you're welcome to join us!" The next semester, we invited everyone through departmental email, and we posted a sign-up sheet on an office door. It drew a small crowd, a baker's dozen, occurring on an afternoon at a local, newly opened restaurant during the last week of the semester, and everyone – at least all who talked with me – appreciated the invitation.

Celebrate and share your successes. Celebrations used to be woven into the fabric of school life, but many part-timers missed out. They may not have been invited. Or, with all their scrambling to cobble together a career, they may not have been able to fit it into their schedules. Nevertheless, resolve to gather a few colleagues into a vanguard and arrange a celebratory get-together once a term if nothing is already going on. And open it up to all your fellows, so your colleagues don't consign themselves into little, exclusive clubs. They will appreciate it, and appreciate you for it. You probably will, too.

Top 10 List – Confabulate

1. **Augmenting Collaboration.** The traditional conclaves of academia may leave out adjuncts, so take advantage of the ones that work to your benefit and create others to augment collegial collaboration.
2. **Introducing Yourself.** Go an extra mile and get to know your colleagues. Start by introducing yourself to those you haven't met.
3. **Sharing Place for Conversations.** If your school has one, make the shared adjunct office a place to initiate and instigate collegial conversations.
4. **Participating to Interact.** Participate in departmental meetings and orientations that allow you to interact with peers when time, transportation, and treasury allow.
5. **Skipping Meetings.** Skip any meetings or training sessions that devolve into hoop-jumping or mouse-mazes that benefit you or colleagues little or none.
6. **Inviting Collegiality.** Invite a colleague or two for a cup of coffee and use the opportunity for small-talk and shop-talk. Set a calendar goal for regular coffee klatches.
7. **Celebrating Milestones.** Celebrate the successful completion of every semester with a cohort of colleagues – and invite all the adjuncts in the department, preferably personally.

8. **Expanding Participation.** Attempt to expand your cohort of participants by widening the team of inviters.
9. **Accentuating Enjoyment.** Remain flexible, accentuate the events you enjoy, and invite someone or two along to a worthwhile professional development module.
10. **Confabulating to Celebrate.** Regularly congregate to confabulate and celebrate one another's accomplishments and ideas.

Lingo – Sail with Strengths, Shore up Weaknesses

1. "I'm devoted to professional development, so I read widely in the field. Have you read [recommended book], yet?"
2. "I'm committed to collegial collaboration: I love mentoring, observing classes, and talking shop over a strong beverage. Have you been to [name of coffee shop or brew pub], yet?"
3. "We sail with our strengths, and shore-up the weaknesses."
4. "Let's take a pass on that meeting, so we can divert ourselves over to the new watering hole instead."
5. "Let's start a coffee club! Who else could use a regular break?"

Q's – Coffee Klatsch

1. "Care to catch a cup of coffee?"
2. "Sorry, but I am teaching during the required professional development day. When might it be rescheduled?"
3. "May I visit your class? I'd love to see how you discuss service learning. Do you teach on Wednesday mornings?"
4. "What are you teaching this semester? What is your schedule?"
5. "Can you join us for lunch to help celebrate the end of the term?"

Chuckle – It's All an Act

"Why do we tell actors to *break a leg*? Because every play has a *cast*."

"And did you hear about the actor who fell through the floorboards? He was just going through a stage."
— Brandon Specktor (10 short jokes anyone can remember, Readersdigest.com)

Sentence Surgery on a Motivational Quotation – Katherine Paterson

As I look back on what I have written, I can see that the very persons who have taken away my time are those who have given me something to say.
— Katherine Paterson

```
      A dep          dep    A          ind  A        dep                      A
[As I look back on [what I have written,]] [I can see [that the very persons [who have
      dep        B              A     dep
taken away my time] are those] [who have given me something to say.]
5 dep's + ind = cx
```

Closing Conversation – Calendar Concierge

"You know, Jimmy, you're becoming my social calendar concierge!" Kim chuckled.
  "You-all know me: happy to help out, every way I can!" Jimmy replied.
  "So, which coffee shop are we going to patronize next semester?" Jacqui asked.

Figure 7.2. Revising the Essay

OVERVIEW

Appendix 1. Essay Assignments and Review, Turn-in, and Evaluation Forms

It is less important what we make of student writing than that we make something, something principled, of it. The writing teacher must believe that student texts are intrinsically worthy of being valued.
– James Thomas Zebroski

Figure A.1. Lake Champlain Villages Ramble, Vermont.
Credit: Cathy Mulder

Appendix Trailhead – Student Essays

- Sample Essay Assignments
- Personal Essay Sample Forms
  - Peer Review
  - Turn-in Labels
  - Evaluation
- Profile Essay Sample Forms
  - Peer Review
  - Turn-in Labels
  - Evaluation
- Review Essay Sample Forms
  - Peer Review
  - Turn-in Labels
  - Evaluation
- Proposal Essay Sample Forms
  - Peer Review
  - Turn-in Labels
  - Evaluation
- Ethnography Essay Sample Forms
  - Peer Review
  - Turn-in Labels
  - Evaluation
- Essay Reflection Form
- Essay Review Form

Sample Essay Assignments

Self-definition (*Personal Essay*) – Identify an object, event, or experience that best represents you: a possession, a place, a life-changing occasion or insight, a job, or a hobby. Include vivid description, clear examples, and incidental narration, written in first person.

Signpost – Essays

A list and brief descriptions of 10 different essays from different genres that includes these five can be found on pages 132–133 in Chapter 6.

Portrait of Another Person (*Profile Essay*) – Write about another person, using specific and detailed observations to capture that person's character. Incorporate some dialogue and a setting or two, as well as vivid description, clear examples, and incidental narration (a brief narration about a specific incident), written in third person with some first person, as appropriate. Avoid writing about an immediate family member.

Restaurant Review (*Review Essay*) – Visit an eatery that you want to patronize, preferably a one-of-a-kind, local establishment that you could recommend to fellow students. If your college has a culinary program, visit its cafeteria, bistro, or fine-dining venue, and you will have the satisfaction of supporting students' learning, too. Support your observations with vivid description, clear examples, and incidental narration, written in third person supported with plenty of first person from your own experience there.

Local Problem-Solution Investigation (*Proposal Essay*) – Identify a problem on campus, in your neighborhood, or within a hometown community, and then propose a solution or solutions. Investigate its background and effects by interviewing others. Broaden the scope of your investigation by researching other examples online using advanced internet searches, library databases, and electronic books as well as print resources. Thoroughly explore your topic locally and beyond through vivid description, clear examples, and incidental narration, written in third person supported with first person from your own experience and/or observations. Support your solution(s) by giving reasons backed up by the information you collected and by vivid description, examples, and narration.

Ethnographic Research Essay (*Ethnography Essay*) – Find an "affinity group" (Gee, 2004), preferably related to a hobby, ethnicity, religion, community, or organization that you are particularly interested in or may even be a member of yourself. Investigate its background and effects by interviewing one or more people connected with the group and observing its activities. As in the Local Problem-Solution Investigation, broaden the scope of this investigation by researching other examples online using advanced internet searches, library databases, and electronic books as well as print resources. Thoroughly explore the topic locally and beyond through vivid description, clear examples, and incidental narration, written in third person supported with first person from your own experience. Compile an Annotated Bibliography 9-6-3 of three-to-nine sources while researching your ethnography.

Personal Essay Peer Review
On the Clock - Rough Draft

Writer
1.   Staple a blank sheet of paper to the back of your rough draft.
2.   Write your name and the working title of your Personal Essay on top.
3.   Pass your essay to the group member to your left (clockwise).

Readers
Look for, number, and write down these five items (one or two lines for each) as you read <u>two</u> Personal Essays:

1.   First, write your name, and today's date.

2.   Find the most poignant <u>vignette</u> (one-or-two paragraph anecdote). Write its first sentence and paragraph number.

3.   Locate the most vivid <u>description</u>, and write down its first sentence and paragraph number.

4.   Write down the first sentence and paragraph number of the most detailed <u>explanation</u>.

5.   Identify writing that is <u>too obvious</u> to write because everyone knows this already, unrelated to the person who wrote the essay, lacking specifics and details, or repeating something that was already said. Write down its first sentence and the paragraph number.

Personal Essay Turn-in Labels

Please label these items in the formatted draft of your essay:

∧   Introductory Hook

>   Best Vivid Description

∨   Poignant Vignette

<   Most Detailed Explanation

Do sentence surgery on one <u>compound (cd)</u> or <u>compound-complex (cd-cx)</u> sentence that uses a coordinating conjunction.

Circle 3–5 <u>$10 words</u> (5-4-3) selected from your S-A-G-E-S Vocabulary cards.

Turn-in Order: (Attached with a <u>paper clip</u>)

- (Optional) Writing Center tutorial report or reflection form
- MLA-formatted, edited, typed copy on <u>top</u>
- Revised and organized copy <u>second</u>
- Rough draft <u>third</u>
- Prewriting <u>fourth</u>
- Personal Essay Evaluation Form – with your name, title, and date – <u>fifth</u>
- Essay Reflection Form – completed – on <u>bottom</u>

Personal Essay Evaluation Form

Name ____ Date __________

	Excellent 9–10 A	Good 8–9 B	Satisfactory 7–8 C	Poor 1–6 D/E
Process	5+ drafts of my essay demonstrate substantial changes at every level.	4 drafts of my essay show good changes at every step from idea-generating.	3 drafts of my essay show ideas, rough draft, revised draft, editing with MLA format.	Fewer than 3 drafts, or demonstrate little change or limited process.
Theme	My theme is robust and personal, and it has 5+ descriptive and detailed topics that develop it.	My essay's theme is worthwhile with 4 detailed topics that develop it.	My theme is clear and includes 3 well-explained topics to illustrate it.	My theme is impersonal, unclear, uninteresting, too dramatic, or only tells a story instead.
Support	Every ¶ has specific, creative, and personal examples in support. 7+¶s	Each ¶ includes a "visual" example and vivid details to support its topic. 6+ ¶s	Paragraphs include good examples or clear explanations. 5 ¶s	My ¶'s aren't supported with a relevant, clear example or explanation. <5 ¶s
Coherence (Paragraphs)	My writing has an inviting opening, an intriguing middle, and a satisfying conclusion, all united by one image. 5 sentences in each ¶	It has a good beginning, middle, and end, with appropriate transitions between 4+ ¶s, all focused on the theme. 4 sentences/¶	My writing is printed in paragraphs, mostly focused on the theme, and using limited transitions to begin ¶s. 3 sentences/¶	My writing isn't printed in paragraphs, is unfocused or disorganized.
Sentence Skills	All my sentences are clear, complete, and of varying lengths and types in each ¶. 4 sentence types/ ¶	I have well-constructed and varied sentences with fewer than 3 run-ons or fragments. 3 sentence types/¶	4–6 of my sentences are awkward, or contain run-ons or fragments, making my style clumsy. 2 sentence types/¶	More than 6 run-ons, fragments, or awkard sentences make my style hard to read. 1 sentence type/¶
Word Choice	My words are college-level: striking but natural, varied and vivid, including 5+ $10 Words.	I make good, varied word choices with 4+ $10 Words, and fewer than 3 key words repeated.	3+ $10 Words, 3–6 of my key word choices are repeated, or I choose uninspired or slang words.	I repeat the same words over and over, or my words are confusing, dull, or inappropriate.
Voice and Tone	My passion for the theme and topics shows, and I also creatively apply how each has shaped me.	It sounds like I care about my theme, and I use < 3 clichés, casual or awkward phrases.	My tone is clear, and my voice sounds real, but I have 3–6 clichés, casual or awkward phrases.	I have > 6 clichés, casual or awkward phrases, or my writing sounds fake – too casual or formal.
Features of the Genre	My writing is a dialogical process that creatively uses personal memories, experiences, and thoughts.	My writing shifts logically and smoothly from descriptive and detailed past events to current ideas.	My writing is personal, and uses effective examples and interesting explanations.	My writing doesn't explain well, give personal examples, or apply any insights.
Conventions	I use 1st person and have < 3 grammar, spelling, or punctuation errors.	I write in 1st person and use correct conventions with < 6 errors.	I have < 9 errors in my essay, enough to distract a reader, or switch persons.	Many errors (> 9) make my paper hard to read, or I don't use 1st person.
Title and Labels	My title is creative, and I type in MLA format with correct Works Cited page.	Good title and Works Cited, every page has a running head with my last name and p#.	My title and Works Cited are satisfactory but with some errors, or every page is not labeled correctly.	My title or Works Cited is missing, pages are unlabeled, and/or paper is unformatted.

☐ **Academic Service Learning**   ☐ **30-Minute Tutorial**

Total

Grade

Profile Essay Peer Review
Beside-and-Across – Rough Draft + Revised Draft

Writer

1. Staple a blank sheet of paper to the back of your rough and revised drafts.
2. Write your name and the working title of your Profile Essay on top.
3. Exchange essays with the person on your left.
4. Afterwards, switch with the person sitting across from you.

Reader

Look for, number, and write down these six items (one or two lines for each) as you read two Profile Essays:

1. First, write your name and today's date.

2. Find a <u>poignant anecdote</u> relating to the profile's theme (a short story, observation, example, or snapshot) in every paragraph. Write its first sentence and paragraph number in a list.

3. Locate a vivid description of <u>the person's setting</u>, and write down its first sentence and paragraph number.

4. Write down the first sentence and paragraph number of the most <u>descriptive and expressive passage</u>.

5. Note the beginning of the best <u>dialogue</u>, or conversation. (Yes or No – Is it punctuated appropriately with quotation marks and commas?)

6. Identify any writing that is <u>too obvious</u> to write because everyone knows this already, <u>unrelated</u> to the person who wrote the essay, <u>lacking specifics and details</u>, or <u>repeating</u> something that was already said. Write down its first sentence and the paragraph number.

Profile Essay Turn-in Labels

Please label these items in the formatted draft of your essay:

∧   Introductory <u>Hook</u>

\>   Best Vivid <u>Description</u>

∨   Poignant <u>Anecdote</u>

\<   Expressive <u>Dialogue</u>

Do sentence surgery on 3–5 (OK, 6 if you insist!) <u>compound-complex (cd-cx)</u> sentences that use different coordinating and subordinating conjunctions.

Circle 3–5 <u>$10 words</u> (5-4-3) selected from your S-A-G-E-S Vocabulary cards.

Turn-in Order (Attached with a <u>paper clip</u>)

- (Optional) Writing Center tutorial report or reflection form
- MLA-formatted, edited, typed copy on <u>top</u>
- Any revised and organized copy <u>second</u>
- Rough draft, <u>third</u>
- Two Beside-and-Across Peer Reviews with 3–5 (OK, 6 if you wish!) Notes-to-Self List, <u>fourth</u>
- Profile Essay Evaluation Form – with your name, title, and date – <u>fifth</u>
- ½ sheet Essay Reflection Form – completed – on bottom

Profile Essay Evaluation Form

Name ____   Date __________

	Excellent 9–10 A	Good 8–9 B	Satisfactory 7–8 C	Poor 1–6 D/E
Process	5+ drafts of my essay demonstrate substantial changes at every level.	4 drafts of my essay show good changes at every step from idea-generating.	3 drafts of my essay show ideas, rough draft, revision, editing with MLA format.	Fewer than 3 drafts, or demonstrate little change or limited process.
Theme	My theme is robust and personal, and it has 5+ descriptive and detailed topics that develop it.	My essay's theme is worthwhile with 4 detailed topics to develop it.	My theme is clear and includes 3 well-explained topics to illustrate it.	My theme is impersonal, unclear, uninteresting, too dramatic, or only tells a story instead.
Support	Every ¶ has specific, creative, and personal examples in support. 7+¶s	Each ¶ includes a "visual" example and vivid details to support its topic. 6+ ¶s	Paragraphs include good examples or clear explanations. 5 ¶s	My ¶'s aren't supported with a relevant, clear example or explanation. <5 ¶s
Coherence (Paragraphs)	My writing has an inviting opening, an intriguing middle, and a satisfying conclusion, all united by one image. 5 sentences in each ¶	It has a good beginning, middle, and end, with appropriate transitions between 4+ ¶s, all focused on the theme. 4 sentences/¶	My writing is printed in paragraphs, mostly focused on the theme, and using limited transitions to begin ¶s. 3 sentences/¶	My writing isn't printed in paragraphs, is unfocused or disorganized.
Sentence Skills	All my sentences are clear, complete, and of varying lengths and types in each ¶. 4 sentence types/ ¶	I have well-constructed and varied sentence lengths and types with fewer than 3 run-ons or fragments. 3 sentence types/¶	4–6 of my sentences are awkward, or contain run-ons or fragments, making my style clumsy. 2 sentence types/¶	More than 6 run-ons, fragments, or awkward sentences make my style hard to read. 1 sentence type/¶
Word Choice	My words are college-level: striking but natural, varied and vivid, including 5+ $10 Words.	I make good, varied word choices with 4+ $10 Words, and fewer than 3 key words repeated.	3+ $10 Words, 3–6 of my key word choices are repeated, or I choose uninspired or slang words.	I repeat the same words over and over, or my words are confusing, dull, or inappropriate.
Voice and Tone	My passion for the theme and topics shows, and I also creatively apply how each has shaped me.	It sounds like I care about my theme, and I use < 3 clichés, casual or awkward phrases.	My tone is clear, and my voice sounds real, but I have 3–6 clichés, casual or awkward phrases.	I have > 6 clichés, casual or awkward phrases, or my writing sounds fake – too casual or formal.
Features of the Genre	My writing is a dialogical process that creatively captures my subject's character.	My writing logically and smoothly includes details to describe my subject's deeper character.	My writing is purposeful with effective examples, detailed descriptions, and interesting explanations.	My writing doesn't give varied examples or balanced assessments, or apply any insights.
Conventions	I use 1st and 3rd persons, with < 3 grammar, spelling, or punctuation errors.	I write in 1st and 3rd person and use correct conventions with < 6 errors.	I have < 9 errors in my essay, enough to distract a reader, or use 2nd person.	Many errors (> 9) make my paper hard to read, or I don't use 1st person.
Title and Labels	My title is creative, and I type in MLA format with correct Works Cited page.	Good title and Works Cited, every page has a running head with my last name and p#.	My title and Works Cited are satisfactory (with some errors), or every page is not labeled correctly.	My title or Works Cited is missing, pages are unlabeled, and/or paper is unformatted.

☐ **Academic Service Learning**   ☐ **30-Minute Tutorial** | **Total** | **Grade**

Review Essay Peer Review
Read-Aloud Quads – Revised Draft

Everyone will need 2 sheets of paper besides the Review Essay: one full page and two half-pages. Your roles – Writer, Reader, Questioner, and Listener – rotate around the group with every essay, so everyone practices each role once.

Writer

1. Take out a full sheet of paper.
2. Write down the date and the names and roles of the other members of your group.
3. Pass your essay to the person beside you – the <u>Reader</u>.
4. While listening to the Reader read your essay, write at least <u>3–5+ Notes-to-Self</u>, such as things you might have missed while writing or things you want to add or change after hearing it read aloud.
5. After the Reader has finished reading, collect the Questioner and Listener's ½-sheets to attach onto the <u>back</u> of your Notes-to-Self.

Reader

At a moderate pace, in careful, crisp, clear intonation, and briefly pausing between paragraphs, read the Writer's essay aloud to the rest of your group. Start with the title, and end with the References.

Questioner

On a ½-sheet of paper, while listening to the Reader read the essay, write down <u>3–5 details that you wonder about</u>, such as prices, hours, directions, entrees, features, apps, year of release, etc. When the essay is finished being read, give the ½-sheet with your details to the essay's Writer.

Listener

On a ½-sheet of paper, while listening to the Reader read the essay, <u>list these 3 things</u>:
*   To whom does the writer <u>recommend</u> the movie, restaurant, phone, car…? Why?
*   What <u>five topics</u> does the writer discuss?
*   Does the writer include <u>both positive and negative</u> examples?

When the essay is finished being read, give the ½-sheet with your details to the essay's Writer.

Learning is the lifelong expression of our wonder and worth. –Roland Barth

Review Essay Turn-in Labels

Please label these items in the formatted draft of your essay:

∧   Introductory <u>Hook</u>

>   Thesis Sentence in Introduction (cd-cx)

∨   Thesis Sentence Restated

<   Memorable Statement

Do sentence surgery on 3–5 sentences, including the <u>compound-complex (cd-cx)</u> thesis sentence, a compound (cd) sentence that uses a different coordinating conjunction (FANBOYS), and a complex (cx) sentence using a different subordinating conjunction.

Circle 3–5 <u>$10 words</u> (5-4-3) selected from your S-A-G-E-S Vocabulary cards.

Turn-in Order (Attached with a <u>paper clip</u>)

- (Optional) Writing Center tutorial report or reflection form
- APA-formatted, edited, typed copy with 3 APA-cited References on <u>top</u>
- Revised and organized copy <u>second</u> with Quads peer reviews and notes-to-self
- Rough draft <u>third</u>
- 5 Ladders Chart (next page) prewriting <u>fourth</u>
- Review Essay Evaluation Form – with your name, title, and date – <u>fifth</u>
- Essay Reflection Form – completed – on <u>bottom</u>

Five Ladders Chart

Note five <u>topics</u> about your theme at the top of each "ladder," and list five or six <u>examples</u> for each topic, then write your <u>thesis sentence</u> in the box below:

☐ Topic	☐ Topic	☐ Topic	☐ Topic	☐ Topic
Example 1	Example 1	Example 1	Example 1	Example 1
2	2	2	2	2
3	3	3	3	3
4	4	4	4	4
5	5	5	5	5

Sources:

Working Thesis:

Review Essay Evaluation Form

Name ____   Date __________

	Excellent 9–10 A	Good 8–9 B	Satisfactory 7–8 C	Poor 1–6 D/E
Process – Drafts	In-depth 5 Ladders Chart Draft with peer reviews Revised ¶s, sentences 2+ cc. with ample changes APA-formatted copy	Thorough 5 Ladders Chart Draft with peer reviews Revised ¶s and sentences APA-formatted copy	5 Ladders Chart complete Draft with peer reviews APA-formatted copy	5 Ladders Chart incomplete Fewer than 3 drafts Few changes or attempts
Theme – Thesis Sentence	Creative thesis: cd-cx Thesis ends introductory ¶ At least 4 creative topics Rewritten to begin last ¶	Robust thesis: cd-cx Thesis ends introductory ¶ At least 3 good topics Rewritten in concluding ¶	Clear thesis: cd or cx Thesis in introductory ¶ At least 2 satisfactory topics	Simple, incomplete, unclear, misplaced, or missing thesis sentence
Support – Examples	Specific, thorough details Creative comparisons Vivid, visual examples 8+ Paragraphs	Good, personal examples Supporting, related details 7+ ¶s	Sufficient examples Clear explanations 6+ ¶s	Insufficient support Irrelevant examples, Unclear explanations ≤ 6 ¶s
Organizational Coherence – Paragraphs	Opening hook and thesis Introductory vignette Creative order to body ¶s Thesis restated in conclusion Memorable final point All paragraphs fully developed with strong transitions	Good introduction, body, and conclusion Logical order to body ¶s Good, varied transitions in ¶s Well-developed paragraphs	Satisfactory overall structure and coherence Sufficient transitions between ¶s ¶ topics focus on theme Some paragraphs not well developed	Weak introduction and/or conclusion Incomplete paragraphs Purposeless theme Disorganized topics Unfocused organization
Sentence Skills	Creative sentence types Several types in each ¶ No run-ons or fragments 5+ sentence surgeries 4 sentence types/ ¶	Well-constructed sentences Varied sentence types ≤ 3 run-ons or fragments 4+ sentence surgeries 3 sentence types/¶	Satisfactory sentences ≤ 6 awkward sentences ≤ 6 run-ons or fragments 3+ sentence surgeries 2+ sentence types/¶	Unclear sentences ≥ 6 awkward sentences ≥ 6 run-ons or fragments ≤ 3 sentence surgeries 1+ sentence type/¶
Word Choice – $10 Words	Varied, vivid vocabulary Striking yet natural terms 5+ $10 Words	Good variety of words ≤ 3 words repeated ≤ 3 clichés, awkward terms 4+ $10 Words	Satisfactory use of vocabulary ≤ 6 words repeated ≤ 6 clichés, awkward terms 3+ $10 Words	Dull, unclear, inapt words ≥ 6 words repeated ≥ 6 clichés, awkward terms ≤ 3 $10 Words
Voice and Tone	Unique, specific audience Creative, intriguing tone 1st person intro, conclusion 3rd person body	Clear, relevant audience Good voice and tone 1st and 3rd person pronouns	Appropriate audience Satisfactory voice and tone 1st and 3rd person pronouns ≤ 3 2nd person pronouns	Inappropriate audience Too casual or formal tone Inconsistent voice ≥ 3 2nd person pronouns
Features of the Genre	Balanced assessment Interesting comparisons Exceptional details 3+ Sources	Good comparisons Specific examples Good supporting details 2+ Sources	Purposeful writing Effective examples Satisfactory descriptions, explanations 1+ Source	Little purpose, direction Few examples, details Little assessment, insight 0 Sources
Conventions – Mechanics	Exact challenging spellings Varied punctuation Excellent mechanics	Good spelling, grammar, punctuation, capitalization ≤ 3 conventions errors	Satisfactory conventions Few misplaced modifiers ≤ 6 conventions errors	Errors hinder understanding ≥ 6 errors
Title and Labels – APA Format	Creative two-part title Correct APA format Excellent References page	Good two-part title Complete running header Good References page	Satisfactory two-part title Correct running header Appropriate references	Incomplete title Unfinished running header Missing references
☐ **Academic Service Learning** ☐ **30-Minute Tutorial**			**Total**	**Grade**

Proposal Essay Peer Review
Revision Circle – Revised Draft

<u>Writer</u>

1. Staple a blank sheet of paper to the back of your revised draft.
2. Write your name and the two-part working title of your Proposal Essay on top.
3. Number every paragraph, including your introduction and conclusion.
4. Pass your essay around your group's circle.

<u>Readers</u>

Look for, number, and write down these eight items (one or two lines for each) as you read your group members' essays:

1. Write your name and today's date at the top.

2. a. What is the problem being explored?
   b. Whom does it affect? How?
   c. Is it a local to our campus, a neighborhood, the city, or another town?

3. a. What would happen if nothing is done?
   b. Why is it happening?

4. What <u>3–5 perspectives</u> does the writer explore about the problem? List them.

5. a. How many sources are interviewed?
   b. How many of them are quoted?
   c. Who is the most rational source? Why?

6. Which paragraph has the best <u>anecdote</u> or <u>vignette</u>? How does it start?

7. Does the <u>hook</u> catch your attention?

8. Does the <u>thesis sentence</u> give a "roadmap" of the essay? Does it include 3 topics? Is it a compound-complex sentence? Is it at the end of the 1st or 2nd paragraph?

9. Is/Are the proposed solution(s) well-supported?

Learning is the lifelong expression of our wonder and worth. –Roland Barth

Proposal Essay Turn-in Labels

Please label these items in the formatted draft of your essay:

∧   Introductory <u>Hook</u>

>   Thesis Sentence in Introduction (cd-cx)

∨   Thesis Sentence Restated

<   Memorable Statement

Do sentence surgery on 3–5 sentences, including <u>all four sentence patterns</u> within one paragraph (¶): a compound-complex (cd-cx), compound (cd), complex (cx), and simple (s) sentence.

In addition, complete the sentence surgery on the <u>thesis sentence</u> in your introduction that uses a different coordinating conjunction or adverbial conjunction from the other cd-cx sentence you chose for surgery.

Circle 3–5 <u>$10 words</u> (5-4-3) selected from your S-A-G-E-S Vocabulary cards.

Turn-in Order (Attached with a <u>paper clip</u>)

- (Optional) Writing Center tutorial report or reflection form
- APA-formatted, edited, typed copy on <u>top</u>
- Revised and organized copy <u>second</u> with peer reviews
- Rough draft <u>third</u>
- Any prewriting (list, bubble chart, outline, or 5 Ladders Chart) <u>fourth</u>
- Proposal Essay Evaluation Form – with your name, title, and date – <u>fifth</u>
- Essay Reflection Form – completed – on <u>bottom</u>

Proposal Essay Evaluation Form

Name ____ Date __________

	Excellent 9–10 A	Good 8–9 B	Satisfactory 7–8 C	Poor 1–6 D/E
Process – Drafts	Qs, notes of 5+ interviews Draft with peer reviews Revised ¶s, sentences 2+ cc. with ample changes APA-formatted copy	Qs, notes for 4+ interviews Draft with peer reviews Revised ¶s and sentences APA-formatted copy	Qs, notes of 3+ interviews Draft with peer reviews APA-formatted copy	Incomplete interviews Fewer than 3 drafts Few changes or attempts
Theme – Thesis Sentence	Creative thesis: cd-cx Thesis ends introductory ¶ At least 4 creative topics Rewritten to begin last ¶	Robust thesis: cd-cx Thesis ends introductory ¶ At least 3 good topics Rewritten in concluding ¶	Clear thesis: cd or cx Thesis in introductory ¶ At least 2 satisfactory topics	Simple, incomplete, unclear, misplaced, or missing thesis sentence
Support – Examples	Specific, thorough details Creative comparisons Vivid, visual examples 8+ Paragraphs	Good, personal examples Supporting, related details 7+ ¶s	Sufficient examples Clear explanations 6+ ¶s	Insufficient support Irrelevant examples, Unclear explanations ≤ 6 ¶s
Organizational Coherence – Paragraphs	Opening hook and thesis Introductory vignette Creative order to body ¶s Thesis restated in conclusion Memorable final point All paragraphs fully developed with strong transitions	Good introduction, body, and conclusion Logical order to body ¶s Good, varied transitions in ¶s Well-developed paragraphs	Satisfactory overall structure and coherence Sufficient transitions between ¶s ¶ topics focus on theme Some paragraphs not well-developed	Weak introduction and/or conclusion Incomplete paragraphs Purposeless theme Disorganized topics Unfocused organization
Sentence Skills	Creative sentence types Several types in each ¶ No run-ons or fragments 5+ sentence surgeries 4 sentence types/ ¶	Well-constructed sentences Varied sentence types ≤ 3 run-ons or fragments 4+ sentence surgeries 3 sentence types/¶	Satisfactory sentences ≤ 6 awkward sentences ≤ 6 run-ons or fragments 3+ sentence surgeries 2+ sentence types/¶	Unclear sentences ≥ 6 awkward sentences ≥ 6 run-ons or fragments ≤ 3 sentence surgeries 1+ sentence type/¶
Word Choice – $10 Words	Varied, vivid vocabulary Striking yet natural terms 5+ $10 Words	Good variety of words ≤ 3 words repeated ≤ 3 clichés, awkward terms 4+ $10 Words	Satisfactory use of vocabulary ≤ 6 words repeated ≤ 6 clichés, awkward terms 3+ $10 Words	Dull, unclear, inapt words ≥ 6 words repeated ≥ 6 clichés, awkward terms ≤ 3 $10 Words
Voice and Tone	Unique, specific audience Creative, intriguing tone 1st person intro, conclusion 3rd person body	Clear, relevant audience Good voice and tone 1st and 3rd person pronouns	Appropriate audience Satisfactory voice and tone 1st and 3rd person pronouns ≤ 3 2nd person pronouns	Inappropriate audience Too casual or formal tone Inconsistent voice ≥ 3 2nd person pronouns
Features of the Genre	Balanced assessment of problem Striking examples Exceptional quotations Strongly supported solution(s) 5+ Sources	Good supporting details Memorable examples Numerous quotations Well-reasoned solution(s) 4+ Sources	Purposeful details Effective examples Satisfactory quotations Sensible solution(s) 3+ Sources	Little purpose, direction Few examples, details Limited quotations Weakly argued solution(s) ≤ 3 Sources
Conventions – Mechanics	Exact challenging spellings Varied punctuation Excellent mechanics	Good spelling, grammar, punctuation, capitalization ≤ 3 conventions errors	Satisfactory conventions Few misplaced modifiers ≤ 6 conventions errors	Errors hinder understanding ≥ 6 errors
Title and Labels – APA Format	Creative two-part title Correct APA format Excellent References page	Good two-part title Complete running header Good References page	Satisfactory two-part title Correct running header Appropriate references	Incomplete title Unfinished running header Missing references

☐ **Academic Service Learning**   ☐ **30-Minute Tutorial**

Total	**Grade**

Peer Review Ethnography Essay
Partner Switch – Revised Draft

Writer

1. <u>Wait</u> to staple the blank sheet of paper onto your revised copy.
2. Write your name and the two-part working title on top.
3. Number every paragraph including your introduction and conclusion.
4. Switch your essay with your partner.

Reader & Writer

Read each other's Ethnography Essays:

1. <u>Writer</u>, write down your "Notes to Self" as you discuss one essay together.

2. Which affinity group does the essay discuss? Where are they?

3. How are your paragraphs arranged? What is your organization?

4. What hook did you use?

5. Does the <u>thesis sentence</u> give a "roadmap" of the essay? Does it include 3 topics? Is it a compound-complex sentence? Is it at the end of the 1st or 2nd paragraph?

6. Does every page have an adverbial conjunction? $10 word? Quotation?

7. Does the conclusion restate the thesis sentence? Have a good memorable statement?

8. Together discuss the same questions for the second essay while the other writer writes "Notes to Self" in one ¶ 5-4-3.

Ethnography Essay Turn-in Labels

Please label these items in the final draft of your essay:

∧   Introductory Hook

>   Thesis Sentence in Introduction (cd-cx)

∨   Thesis Sentence Restated

<   Memorable Statement

Do sentence surgery on 3–5 sentences, including <u>all four sentences patterns</u> within one paragraph (¶): a compound-complex (cd-cx), compound (cd), complex (cx), and simple (s) sentence.

In addition, complete the sentence surgery on the <u>thesis sentence</u> in your introduction that uses a different coordinating conjunction or adverbial conjunction from the other cd-cx sentence you chose for surgery.

Circle 5–7 <u>$10 words</u> (5-4-3) selected from your S-A-G-E-S Vocabulary cards.

Turn-in Order (Attached with a <u>paper clip</u>)

- APA-formatted, edited, typed copy on <u>top</u> – with References at the end
- Any revised and organized copy <u>second</u> with peer review
- <u>Do not</u> turn in the Annotated Bibliography or rough draft
- <u>Do not</u> turn in any prewriting (list, bubble chart, outline, 5 Ladders Chart)
- Ethnography Essay Evaluation Form – <u>third</u>
- Essay Reflection Form – completed – on <u>bottom</u>

Learning is the lifelong expression of our wonder and worth. –Roland Barth

Ethnography Essay Evaluation Form

Name ____ Date __________

	Excellent 9–10 A	Good 8–9 B	Average 7–8 C	Poor 1–6 D/E
Process – Drafts	In-depth 5 Ladders Chart Draft with peer reviews Revised ¶s, sentences 2+ cc. with ample changes APA-formatted copy	Thorough 5 Ladders Chart Draft with peer reviews Revised ¶s and sentences APA-formatted copy	5 Ladders Chart complete Draft with peer reviews APA-formatted copy	5 Ladders Chart incomplete Fewer than 3 drafts Few changes or attempts
Theme – Thesis Sentence	Creative thesis: cd-cx Thesis ends introductory ¶ At least 4 creative topics Rewritten to begin last ¶	Robust thesis: cd-cx Thesis ends introductory ¶ At least 3 good topics Rewritten in concluding ¶	Clear thesis: cd or cx Thesis in introductory ¶ At least 2 OK topics	Simple, incomplete, unclear, misplaced, or missing thesis sentence
Support – Examples	Specific, thorough details Creative comparisons Vivid, visual examples 8+ Paragraphs	Good, personal examples Supporting, related details 7+ ¶s	Sufficient examples Clear explanations 6+ ¶s	Insufficient support Irrelevant examples, Unclear explanations ≤ 6 ¶s
Organizational Coherence – Paragraphs	Opening hook and thesis Introductory vignette Creative order to body ¶s Thesis restated in conclusion Memorable final point All paragraphs fully developed with strong transitions	Good introduction, body, and conclusion Logical order to body ¶s Good, varied transitions in ¶s Well-developed paragraphs	Satisfactory overall structure and coherence Sufficient transitions between ¶s ¶ topics focus on theme Some paragraphs not well developed	Weak introduction and/or conclusion Incomplete paragraphs Purposeless theme Disorganized topics Unfocused organization
Sentence Skills	Creative sentence types Several types in each ¶ No run-ons or fragments 5+ sentence surgeries 4 sentence types/¶	Well-constructed sentences Varied sentence types ≤ 3 run-ons or fragments 4+ sentence surgeries 3 sentence types/¶	Satisfactory sentences ≤ 6 awkward sentences ≤ 6 run-ons or fragments 3+ sentence surgeries 2+ sentence types/¶	Unclear sentences ≥ 6 awkward sentences ≥ 6 run-ons or fragments ≤ 3 sentence surgeries 1+ sentence type/¶
Word Choice – $10 Words	Varied, vivid vocabulary Striking yet natural terms 5+ $10 Words	Good variety of words ≤ 3 words repeated ≤ 3 clichés, awkward terms 4+ $10 Words	Satisfactory use of vocabulary ≤ 6 words repeated ≤ 6 clichés, awkward terms 3+ $10 Words	Dull, unclear, inapt words ≥ 6 words repeated ≥ 6 clichés, awkward terms ≤ 3 $10 Words
Voice and Tone	Unique, specific audience Creative, intriguing tone 1st person intro, conclusion 3rd person body	Clear, relevant audience Good voice and tone 1st and 3rd person pronouns	Appropriate audience Satisfactory voice and tone 1st and 3rd person pronouns ≤ 3 2nd person pronouns	Inappropriate audience Too casual or formal tone Inconsistent voice ≥ 3 2nd person pronouns
Features of the Genre	I include 6+ in-text citations and 9+ research sources in a balanced, dialogical writing style.	I include 3+ in-text citations and 6+ research sources on my References page in a clear style.	I include 2–3 in-text citations and 3+ research sources on my References page in a satisfactory style.	I include <2 in-text citations, <3 research sources, or it's unclear, unrelated, uninteresting.
Conventions – Mechanics	Exact challenging spellings Varied punctuation Excellent mechanics	Good spelling, grammar, punctuation, capitalization ≤ 3 conventions errors	Satisfactory conventions Few misplaced modifiers ≤ 6 conventions errors	Errors hinder understanding ≥ 6 errors
Title and Labels – APA Format	Creative two-part title Correct APA format Excellent References page	Good two-part title Complete running header Good References page	Satisfactory two-part title Correct running header Appropriate references	Incomplete title Unfinished running header Missing references
☐ Academic Service Learning ☐ 30-Minute Tutorial			Total	Grade

Writer ____ Date ____/____/____

Essay Reflection Form

Honestly **evaluate** your own preparation and practice writing this essay; turn in this form with all copies of your essay.

1. Which draft of your essay was most challenging? Why?
    Prewriting   Rough Draft   Revised Draft   Editing   Final Copy

2. Which draft of your essay was most enjoyable? Why?
    Prewriting   Rough Draft   Revised Draft   Editing   Final Copy

3. For which draft of your essay did you make most changes?
    Prewriting   Rough Draft   Revised Draft   Editing   Final Copy

4. What part of your paper are you most confident about?
    Sentences   Paragraphs   Introduction   Conclusion   Editing

5. On a scale of 1 (poor) – 10 (excellent), how is your essay overall? ______
    What would you do differently?

____
Learning is the lifelong expression of our wonder and worth. –Roland Barth

Writer ____ Date ____/____/____

Essay Review Form

Analyze your returned essay by completing this form; review this form with your instructor and have the instructor initial it here: _________

1. Which type of sentence did you write most?
    Simple   Complex   Compound   Compound-Complex

2. Which type of sentence will you try to add to your next essay?
    Simple   Complex   Compound   Compound-Complex

3. Which mistake, comment, or problem occurred most often on your evaluation?
    ____

4. If you decided to add, rearrange, or delete any paragraphs, what would you change? Why?

5. If you rewrote this essay for next week, what grade could you earn? ________
    Do you want to rewrite it? Yes No

____
Learning is the lifelong expression of our wonder and worth. –Roland Barth

Figure A.2. Reviewing the Essay

Appendix 2. Classroom and Assignment Protocols

Appendix Trailhead – Sacred Class Time

- Tom's Promise

- Tom's Top 10 Writing Tips

- Who Are You? Partners' Interviews and Introductions

- English Class Introductory Survey

- Not-a-Verbs and A and B Verbs

- S-A-G-E-S Vocabulary Cards 5-4-3

- Silent Socratic Dialogue (6) 5-4-3 Prompts

- Exit Card

- Classwork Tally Forms

Tom's Promise

1. **You will succeed in this class.**
   I promise to help you achieve your writing goals and the grade you seek. Success is 90% attitude and 10% aptitude. Believe in yourself – I do! Never quit on yourself – I won't! Attend and *attend*.

2. **You will get your money's worth from this course.**
   I promise to challenge you to do your best by selecting the most worthwhile, purposeful, and targeted assignments that focus your learning on what most benefits your writing development. I promise to plan courses thoroughly and teach them the best I can. I promise to teach every class period – the whole period – as well as I can. I promise to grade and return papers and post them to you online before the next class period.

3. **You will meet the course objectives.**
   I promise that we will meet all course objectives and cover all class content. Because no one can eat a pizza in one bite, I promise to divide all writing assignments into bite-sized pieces to chew one bite at a time. I promise to conduct this class primarily as a workshop, so you will learn through practice and application of skills.

4. **You will improve your writing abilities.**
   I promise to assign writing activities and assignments that help you strengthen your composing skills and target any weaknesses.

5. **You will strengthen grammar skills.**
   I promise to teach grammar and language skills to help you craft stronger sentences and better essays.

6. **You will advance other English talents, too.**
   I promise to integrate reading, speaking, listening, thinking skills, conversation, and technology with writing to apply and advance every area of your language arts usage.

7. **You will use the textbook.**
   With the high price of college textbooks, I promise that we will use the course's text. However, I promise, too, to give you some tips to keep it pristine if you wish to resell it after class.

8. **You will receive any extra help you seek.**
   I promise to arrive at class at least fifteen minutes beforehand and stay afterwards to be available for any questions you have. In addition, I promise to respond to your email within twenty-four hours. Finally, I promise to help you get any additional help you want through college resources if you ask my assistance.

9. **You will have fun.**
   I promise to do my very best to make writing – which is hard work – as enjoyable and relevant as I can. Depending on your interests (and the course's assignments), I promise to let you choose your own writing topics and explorations. I promise to be positive and encouraging.

10. **You may ask for help with other English applications, too.**
    I promise to help with any English questions (such as other course's essays, job resumes or applications and letters) during and after this class is finished because I always enjoy hearing from students – you're my success, and I take pride in you!

I promise, **Tom**

Tom's Top 10 Writing Tips

1. Write a variety of sentences, balancing simple, compound, complex, and compound-complex types, so your writing doesn't sound repetitive, simplistic, or sing-songy. If you can, aim to include all four sentence types in every paragraph of an essay.

2. Hook your reader with a specific, personal, vivid observation or example, if possible: "Yesterday, checking email, I bumped my mug, cascading coffee all over my keyboard." Or ask an intriguing question like, "What happens when you dump coffee on a keyboard?" before jumping into your essay about the trials of coffee dependency. Avoid broad generalities, especially in an introduction: "Liquids can harm computers." Ho-hum.

3. Incorporate your own experiences as examples. Yes, it's good to use first person – *I, me, my* – to support all the third person perspective, explanation, proposal, and description.

4. Try not to use second person, *you*, very much. Definitely avoid any unspecified you, like "*You* know that wars help the economy," or "When *you* get married, *you* become a different person." *Who, me?* Stay away from understood *you*, too: "Think about it."

5. Don't write what is obvious. "In today's world" doesn't mean anything because nobody really knows any other worlds. "In my opinion," too, is irrelevant since it's your essay. Who else's opinion would you be writing?

6. Write about your theme, not about your essay or writing itself. "The topic of my essay is . . ." is writing about the essay, not the topic. "In conclusion …" is stating something that should be obvious to a college reader and amounts to words wasted.

7. Stay away from the word *there*. "There are …" and "There is…" usually begin dull, boring, nebulous, unsubstantiated statements, like "There are a lot of expensive college textbooks." Don't we all know it?

8. Avoid unspecific words like *thing* and *something*. "One bad thing about skipping class is all the work a student has to catch up" can be more clearly said, "Skipping class has the detrimental effect of requiring a student to catch up all the missed work."

9. Replace contractions with each word written out and choose standard English over slang in formal essays. "I will not!" sounds clearer and more authoritative than "I won't!" And "is not" is better than "ain't."

10. Match up your subjects with verbs, and do not repeat key words if you can help it within a paragraph or on a page. Instead of "He don't," write "He does not."

Email Address ____

Who Are You? Partners' Interviews and Introductions

Interview your partner, write her/his responses, and prepare an oral introduction.

1. First-and-Last **Name** (and any Nickname!) ________________________

2. Up to 3 Top **Jobs** You've Worked:
    (Examples: Clerk, piano teacher, paper route, computer programmer, baby sitter, wait staff, reception) ____
    ____
    ____

3. Up to 3 **Hobbies**:
    (Examples: Hiking, visiting coffee shops, driving, B & W movies, gardening, watching Cubs games) ____
    ____
    ____

4. **Job, Degree**, and **College Program** You're Seeking:
    (Examples: English, art, history, nurse, teacher, engineer, business, science, criminal justice, culinary) ____
    ____
    ____

5. Up to 3 **Writing Skills** That You Most Want to Learn in This Class:
    (Examples: Hooking readers, stylizing sentences, organizing paragraphs, getting ideas, grammar, typing) ____
    ____
    ____

6. **Favorite Thing about School** or Learning: ________________________
    (Examples: Studying, note-taking, discussing, reading, projects, planning, tests, researching, typing)

7. **Least-Favorite Thing about School** or Learning: ________________________
    (Examples: Studying, note-taking, discussing, reading, projects, planning, tests, researching, typing)

8. **Favorite Pizza**:
    (Examples: Chicago-style, pepperoni, olives, meat-lovers, vegetarian, delivery watching Cubs on TV) ____

9. **One Unique Characteristic** or experience that distinguishes you from everyone else in class. ____

When you're both finished, decide who goes first, and practice what you're going to say.

Student ____ Date ____/____/____

English Class Introductory Survey

Please complete this form honestly.

1. Do you have access to a computer or a printer to type essays at home? ☐ Computer ☐ Printer ☐ None

2. What college-level English classes have you taken? ☐ None ☐ Comp ☐ ESL ☐ Other ________________

3. How long ago did you take your last English class? ☐ 0–1 Year ☐ 2–3 Years ☐ 4–6 Years ☐ 7+ Years

4. How much time do you spend reading for pleasure in an average week? ☐ 0–1 Hour ☐ 2–4 Hours ☐ 5–8 Hours ☐ 9–14 Hours ☐ 15+ Hours

5. What genre do you read most? ☐ Novels ☐ Short Stories ☐ Poetry ☐ Articles – Fiction ☐ Articles – Non-fiction ☐ Correspondence ☐ News ☐ Other ___________________________________

6. What format do you read most? ☐ Print Book ☐ Electronic Book ☐ Magazine or Journal ☐ Newspaper ☐ Social Media ☐ Email ☐ Listserv ☐ Website ☐ Other ___________________________

7. How would you rate each of the following:

	Poor		Fair		Satisfactory		Good		Excellent	
a. Your <u>enjoyment</u> of writing classes	1	2	3	4	5	6	7	8	9	10
b. Your <u>success</u> in writing classes	1	2	3	4	5	6	7	8	9	10
c. Your <u>confidence</u> in your writing ability	1	2	3	4	5	6	7	8	9	10
d. Your <u>motivation</u> to succeed in class	1	2	3	4	5	6	7	8	9	10
e. Your <u>commitment</u> to attend classes	1	2	3	4	5	6	7	8	9	10

8. Check the <u>two</u> that you find most <u>difficult</u> about writing essays: ☐ Getting ideas ☐ Organizing ☐ Researching ☐ Forming paragraphs ☐ Forming sentences ☐ Punctuating ☐ Spelling ☐ Writing in a flowing style ☐ Crafting a thesis sentence ☐ Using college-level vocabulary ☐ Other ___________________________

9. Check the <u>two</u> that would most <u>benefit</u> your writing: ☐ Strategies for getting ideas ☐ Techniques for researching ☐ A teacher whose style matches my learning ☐ Arrangements for organizing essays ☐ Crafting sentences ☐ Ideas for forming paragraphs ☐ Punctuation exercises ☐ Spelling exercises ☐ Learning writing styles ☐ Crafting thesis sentences ☐ Vocabulary ☐ Other ___________________________

10. In which year of college are you? ☐ 1st ☐ 2nd ☐ 3rd ☐ 4th How many years do you plan to go? ☐ 1–2 ☐ 3–4+

Three Not-a-Verbs

Infinitives

1.   to _______

Any word immediately following the word *to* is an infinitive-verbal; in other words, it's <u>not a verb!</u>

Participles

2.   -ing (alone)

Any word that ends in *-ing* but doesn't have a helping verb *is*, *are*, *am…* in front, is <u>not a verb!</u>

Negatives

3.   no, not, never…

Verbs are always positive, so any negative word like these is <u>not a verb!</u>

Two Verbs

1. *A* = Action

Action verbs answer…

"Do what?"
"Does what?"
"Did what?" or
"Will do what?"

2. *B* = Being

Being verbs:

Is
Are
Am
Were
Will be
Has been
Have been
Had been
Will have been…

Figure A.3. Essay Labeling for Turn-in

S-A-G-E-S Vocabulary Cards 5-4-3

Synonym   **A**ntonym

| **Vocabulary Word** |

General Context
• Definition
• Source Sentence
• Part of Speech

Example

Sketch
(on back)

Each week, seek 3–5 $10, college-level words worth adding to your vocabulary, and complete an index card to enhance your memory of each.

5 = Excellent; 4 = Good; 3 = Average

Try including them in your essay writing, as opportunities arise.

15 Silent Socratic Dialogue (6) 5-4-3 Prompts

1. *Great Generations*. News anchor and author Tom Brokaw called those who lived during the Great Depression and World War II the *Greatest Generation*. How is your generation great, too? Begin with those things that you yourself are good at. Then write another 1–3 things that the people your age are generally good at. What is a positive name that you could use for your generation?

2. *GOAT TV/Film* (*Greatest of All Time*). What is the greatest (or your personal favorite) TV show or film? Make the case for: theme, acting, production, soundtrack, special effects, or other aspect.

3. *GOAT Book*. What is the greatest (or your personal favorite) book? Make the case for: genre, plot, characters, theme, creativity, author, or other aspect.

4. *GOAT Person*. Who is the greatest (or your personal favorite) person (e.g., historical figure, artist, athlete, etc.)? Choose one individual, and make the case with plenty of examples to support your choice.

5. *GOAT Place*. Which is the greatest (or your personal favorite) place? Choose an international locale or a national, state, or local site to make the case, using ample details and description.

6. *Appreciation 1*. Listen to Sarah Adams' "Be Cool to the Pizza Dude" on NPR's *This I Believe* <https://www.npr.org/2005/05/16/4651531/be-cool-to-the-pizza-dude>. Besides the Pizza Dude, whom else should people be cool to? Who often goes unappreciated in your city or on your campus? How should people show their appreciation?

7. *Appreciation 2*. Listen to Eve Burch's "The Art of Being a Neighbor" on NPR's *This I Believe* <https://www.npr.org/templates/story/story.php?storyId=102961694>. Whom do you know who demonstrates this art of neighborliness? How do they show it? How would you define "The Art of Being a Neighbor'? What examples would you give?

8. *Effects of Technology 1*. Consider: Is technology making us smarter or stupider? Explore both sides with some examples, then state your opinion.

9. *Effects of Technology 2*. Consider: Does the internet make us safer or put us more at risk? Explore both sides with some examples, and then state your opinion.

10. *Pay It Forward*. What is one small thing you could do to brighten someone›s day today? What is something you could say to encourage a classmate? Can you think of enough things to do and say for an entire week?

11. *Positivity*. What is a hobby or sport that has the potential to offset the isolation, selfishness, depression, and narcissism that many suffer? How might this succeed?

12. *Foodies*. If you were to prepare a special meal, what would it include? Describe its preparation, ingredients, presentation, and maybe the occasion and guests for serving it.

13. *Foodies 2*. What would make the ultimate tailgate or picnic menu? Where would you enjoy it if you could?

14. *Foodies 3*. What local restaurant could you recommend? Where is it? How would you describe its menu, prices, service, atmosphere, patrons, and any other characteristics?

15. *Emigrate*. If you could move out of this state or country, where would you go? Why?

---

learning is the lifelong expression of our wonder and worth. –Roland Barth

Exit Card

Name ____ Date __________

1. ! ____

2. *x*/10 ____

3. ? ____

Get **Exit Card** initialed by your instructor at the end of class.

____

Learning is the lifelong expression of our wonder and worth. –Roland Barth

Exit Card

Name ____ Date __________

1. **!** On one line, write one thing that you learned thoroughly – you understand and know how to apply it yourself – from class this week.

2. ***x*/10** On a scale of 1–10 (1 = uncertain, 5 = developing, 10 = got it), label your understanding of a classroom concept your instructor mentions.

3. **?** Write one question about something you would like to know or learn from class, in class, or about the class.

Get **Exit Card** initialed by your instructor at the end of class today.

____

Learning is the lifelong expression of our wonder and worth. –Roland Barth

Writer ____ Date ____/____/____

Midterm Classwork Tally

Complete this form and then staple it after the last written page of your written reflection. Thank-you!
1. a. Number of SSD 5-4-3 Writing Warm-ups <u>completed</u>: _____/_____
    b. Number of <u>different</u> Writing Partners: _____/_____
    c. Average Number of Sentences that you wrote for each one: _____
    d. Initials of the Writing Partner who wrote the most thought-provoking, <u>Socratic-thinking</u> style of questions: _____
2. a. Number of Quotations completed: _____/_____
    b. Number of completed Sentence Surgeries on Quotations: _____/_____
    c. Favorite Quotation and Author: Date ____/____/____
    d. Favorite Sentence Surgery on a Quotation: Date ____/____/____
3. a. Number of Sentence-Combining Activities completed: _____/_____
    b. Avg. Number of Sentence Surgeries on each: _____/5-4-3
4. Number of completed S-A-G-E-S Vocabulary Cards: _____/_____

Learning is the lifelong expression of our wonder and worth. –Roland Barth

Writer ____ Date ____/____/____

End-of-Term Classwork Tally

Complete this form and then staple it after the last written page of your written reflection. Thank-you!
1. a. Number of SSD 5-4-3 Writing Warm-ups <u>completed</u>: _____/_____
    b. Number of <u>different</u> Writing Partners: _____/_____
    c. Average Number of Sentences that you wrote in each one: _____
    d. Initials of the Writing Partner who wrote the most thought-provoking, <u>Socratic-thinking</u> style of questions: _____
2. a. Number of Quotations completed: _____/_____
    b. Number of completed Sentence Surgeries on Quotations: _____/_____
    c. Favorite Quotation and Author: Date ____/____/____
    d. Favorite Sentence Surgery on a Quotation: Date ____/____/____
3. a. Number of Sentence-Combining Activities completed: _____/_____
    b. Avg. Number of Sentence Surgeries on each: _____/5-4-3
4. Number of completed S-A-G-E-S Vocabulary Cards: _____/_____

Learning is the lifelong expression of our wonder and worth. –Roland Barth

Appendix 3. Motivational Quotations and Sentence Surgeries

I write when I'm inspired, and I see to it that I'm inspired at 9:00 every morning.
– Peter DeVries

Appendix Trailhead – Refrigerator-Worthy Quotations

- 30 Motivational Quotations
  - Compound (cd) Sentences
  - Complex (cx) Sentences
  - Compound-Complex (cd-cx) Sentences

Appendix 3 is a compilation of thirty of the quotations that I use to introduce most class meetings. At the beginning of the semester, I ask students to be on the lookout for inspiring quotations, quotations about college learning or English or writing, and quotations that are robust and chock full of fun conjunctions for us to play with together. I ask them to add each one to a collection in their writing notebooks, so we can practice sentence surgeries and revisions to begin our classes with some playtime. In addition, I suggest that they keep track of their favorites because they may encounter a couple that are so motivational that they may want to tape them on their dashboard or computer monitor, or possibly attach them with a magnet to the fridge. They are drawn from my collection, gathered by myself and students from many and sundry sources, and as such, I've discovered that they occasionally take different forms from those quoted elsewhere. Nevertheless, these are the forms I use in class, and even when they may not be completely accurate, I've tried to credit their sources and keep them true. Wherever they may differ from those originals, please accept my humble apologies.

Typically, I project the day's quotation before students arrive to class, so they can copy and begin discussing it beforehand. Many attempt their own surgeries, discussing them with classmates as they arrive, often anticipating my sequences of questions. At the beginning of the semester, I start by asking individuals to identify the verbs, in order, classify each one as an *action* or *being* verb, and then state its subject. Everyone is required to double-underline and label as A (*action*) or B (*being*) the verbs, then single-underline their subjects. Often I instruct them to discuss the verbs and how many there are with groupmates before calling on one member of each group to share the group's responses. As we continue along in the semester, I ask them, too, to make predictions about how many and what kinds of clauses the quotation contains, and what grammatical type of sentence they predict this one is. Generally sticking with patterns, I help them pick up on sentence types, so they may identify them rapidly while searching for key markers like coordinating and subordinating conjunctions. In addition, I like to rearrange clauses, switch conjunctions, insert not-a-verbs, and pose questions about how such adjustments affect sentence style and the meanings of the quotations. I like to conclude with declarations like, "Wow, that was fun!" "Life just doesn't get any better than that!" and "It's always good to begin with some playtime before we get down to work!"

Midway through the semester, I collect the writing notebooks to tally their writings, including the quotations and sentence surgeries we practice together. I always like to ask them to write down which quotation was their favorite – and which surgery was their favorite, too.

Table A.3. Motivational Quotations for Sentence Surgery

Motivational Quotations for Sentence Surgery Author, Theme, Page, Sentence Type			
Frank Herbert	Experience Life	194	cd
James R. Sherman	Brand New Ending	194	
Andy Rooney	Working Hard	195	
Eleanor Roosevelt	Curiosity	195	
John Dewey	Democracy	196	
Ann Voskamp	Practice	196	
Daniel Burnham	Plans	197	
Alfred, Lord Tennyson	Wisdom	197	
Wolfgang Goethe	Encouragement	198	
Marva Collins	Success	198	
Marva Collins	Expectations	199	cx
Charles Beard	Stars	199	
J. K. Rowling	Grow	200	
J. R. R. Tolkien	Wander	200	
Robert Orben	Education	201	
Abraham Lincoln	Resolution	201	
Desmond Tutu	Injustice	202	
Freeman Dyson	Diversity	202	
Booker T. Washington	Help	203	
Barack Obama	Change	203	
Helen Keller	Happiness	204	cd-cx
Oprah Winfrey	Opportunity	204	
Oprah Winfrey	Possibility	205	
Walt Disney	Encouragement	205	
Walt Disney	Creativity	206	
Samuel Goldwyn	Applause	206	
Jintao Hu	Diversity	207	
E. L. Doctorow	Exploration	207	
Charles Dickens	Procrastination	208	
Batman (C. Bale)	Definition	208	

Figure A.4. Another Mode of Dialogism

The mystery of life isn't a problem to solve, but it is a reality to experience.

– Frank Herbert

You can't go back and make a new start, but you can start right now
and make a brand new ending.

– James R. Sherman

                       B   ind   B   ind
[The mystery of life isn't a problem to solve,] [but it is a reality to experience.]

– Frank Herbert

             A   ind   A   A
[You can't go back and make a new start,] [but you can start right now

       A   ind
and make a brand new ending.]

– James R. Sherman

Hoping and praying are easier, but they do not produce as good results as hard work.

– Andy Rooney

Life was meant to be lived, and curiosity must be kept alive.

– Eleanor Roosevelt

<pre>
          ind   B   ind   A
[Hoping and praying are easier,] [but they do not produce as good
results as hard work.]
</pre>

– Andy Rooney

<pre>
        A   ind   ind   A
[Life was meant to be lived,] [and curiosity must be kept alive.]
</pre>

– Eleanor Roosevelt

A democracy is more than a form of government, for it is primarily a
mode of associated living, of conjoint communicated experience.

– John Dewey

Practice is the hardest part of learning, and training is the essence
of transformation.

– Ann Voskamp

           B   ind   B   ind
[A democracy is more than a form of government,] [for it is primarily a
mode of associated living, of conjoint communicated experience.]

– John Dewey

         B   ind   B   ind
[Practice is the hardest part of learning,] [and training is the essence
of transformation.]

– Ann Voskamp

Make big plans, and aim high in hope and work.

– Daniel Burnham

Knowledge comes, but wisdom lingers.

– Alfred, Lord Tennyson

<u>(You)</u> A   ind   <u>(you)</u> A   ind
[^ <u>Make</u> big plans,] [and ^ <u>aim</u> high in hope and work.]

– Daniel Burnham

      ind   A   ind   A
[<u>Knowledge</u> <u>comes</u>,] [but <u>wisdom</u> <u>lingers</u>.]

– Alfred, Lord Tennyson

Instruction does much, but encouragement does everything.

– Wolfgang Goethe

Success is not coming to you, so you must go to it.

– Marva Collins

          A   ind   A   ind
[Instruction <u>does</u> much,] [but encouragement <u>does</u> everything.]

– Wolfgang Goethe

    ind   A   ind   A
[<u>Success</u> <u>is</u> not <u>coming</u> to you,] [so <u>you</u> <u>must go</u> to it.]

– Marva Collins

If you don't give anything, don't expect anything.

– Marva Collins

When it is dark enough, you can see the stars.

– Charles A. Beard

```
    dep      A           (you)     A     ind
[If you don't give anything,] [ ^ don't expect anything.]
```

– Marva Collins

```
        B      dep             A     ind
[When it is dark enough,] [you can see the stars.]
```

– Charles A. Beard

It matters not what someone is born but what they grow to be.

– J. K. Rowling

Not all those who wander are lost.

– J. R. R. Tolkien

<pre>
        A   ind   dep   A   dep   A
[It matters not] [what someone is born] [but what they grow to be.]
</pre>

– J. K. Rowling

<pre>
          dep   A   B   ind
[Not all those [who wander] are lost.]
</pre>

– J. R. R. Tolkien

If you think education is expensive, try ignorance.

– Robert Orben

Always bear in mind that your own resolution to succeed is more important than any one thing.

– Abraham Lincoln

   dep A   (that)   B   dep   (you) A ind
[If you think] [^ education is expensive,] [^ try ignorance.]

– Robert Orben

(you)   A   ind   dep   B
[Always ^ bear in mind] [that your own resolution to succeed is more important than any one thing.]

– Abraham Lincoln

If you are neutral in situations of injustice,
you have chosen the side of the oppressor.

                        – Desmond Tutu

When we look at the glory of stars and galaxies in the sky and the glory
of forests and flowers in the living world around us, it is evident
that God loves diversity.

                        – Freeman Dyson

        B   dep   A
[If you are neutral in situations of injustice,] [you have chosen

     ind
the side of the oppressor.]

                        – Desmond Tutu

      A   dep
[When we look at the glory of stars and galaxies in the sky and the glory

                               B   ind
of forests and flowers in the living world around us,] [it is evident]

  dep   A
[that God loves diversity.]

                        – Freeman Dyson

I think I have learned that the best way to lift one's self up is to help someone else.

– Booker T. Washington

Change will not come if we wait for some other person or if we wait for some other time.

– Barack Obama

ind A   (that)   A dep   dep   B
[I think] [^ I have learned] [that the best way to lift one's self up is to help someone else.]

– Booker T. Washington

       ind   A   A   dep
[Change will not come] [if we wait for some other person] [or if we

 A   dep
wait for some other time.]

– Barack Obama

When one door of happiness closes, another opens, but often we look so long at
the closed door that we do not see the one which has been opened for us.

– Helen Keller

If you look at what you have in life, you'll always have more, but if you
look at what you don't have in life, you'll never have enough.

– Oprah Winfrey

               dep   A   ind   A   ind   A
[When one door of happiness closes,][another opens,][but often we look so long

              dep   A   dep   A
at the closed door] [that we do not see the one] [which has been opened for us.]

– Helen Keller

   dep A   dep   A   ind   A
[If you look at] [what you have in life,] [you'll always have more,] [but

   dep A   dep   A   ind   A
if you look at] [what you don't have in life,] [you'll never have enough.]

– Oprah Winfrey

You are your possibilities, so if you know that, you can do anything.

– Oprah Winfrey

We need to be life-enhancers, people who reach out to enrich the lives
of others, to lift them up and inspire them, and we need to surround ourselves
with life-enhancers.

– Walt Disney

      B   ind   dep   A   ind   A
[You are your possibilities,] [so if you know that,] [you can do anything.]

– Oprah Winfrey

   ind A   A   dep
[We need to be life-enhancers,] [people who reach out to enrich the lives

                                      ind   A
of others, to lift them up and inspire them,] [and we need to surround
ourselves with life-enhancers.]

– Walt Disney

We keep moving forward, opening up new doors and doing new things,
because we're curious, and curiosity keeps leading us down new paths.

> – Walt Disney

When someone does something good, applaud, and you will make
two people happy.

> – Samuel Goldwyn

```
        A                    ind
[We keep moving forward, opening up new doors and doing new things,]

  dep       B                    A              ind
[because we're curious,] [and curiosity keeps leading us down new paths.]
```

> – Walt Disney

```
  dep            A                   (you) A ind        ind    A
[When someone does something good,] [ ^ applaud,] [and you will make
two people happy.]
```

> – Samuel Goldwyn

Diversity is a basic characteristic of human society; moreover, it is the key condition for a lively and dynamic world as we see today.

– Jintao Hu

Writing is an exploration; therefore, you start from nothing and learn as you go.

– E. L. Doctorow

     ind   B   ind   B
[Diversity is a basic characteristic of human society;] [moreover, it is the

                                     dep   A
key condition for a lively and dynamic world] [as we see today.]

– Jintao Hu

 ind   B   ind   A   A
[Writing is an exploration;] [therefore, you start from nothing and learn]

 dep   A
[as you go.]

– E. L. Doctorow

Never do tomorrow what you can do today, for procrastination is the thief of time.

– Charles Dickens

It's not who I am underneath, but it's what I do that defines me.

– Batman (C. Bale)

    (you) A   ind   dep   A   ind   B
[Never ^ do tomorrow] [what you can do today,] [for procrastination is the thief of time.]

– Charles Dickens

   B ind dep   B   ind B dep   A dep   A
[It's not] [who I am underneath,] [but it's] [what I do] [that defines me.]

– Batman (C. Bale)

Figure A.5. Sentence Surgery

Appendix 4. Sentence-Combining Activities

Sentence combining gives students the flexibility of options, revision fluency, and confidence.
– Jeff Anderson and Deborah Dean

Appendix Trailhead – 15 Sentence-Combining Activities

- Arranged by Conjunctions and Sentence Types

  ◦ Coordinating Conjunctions (FANBOYS) – Compound (cd) Sentences

  ◦ Subordinating Conjunctions (AAAWWWWUBIS) – Complex (cx) Sentences

  ◦ <u>Note:</u> AAAWWWWUBIS is derived from Jeff Anderson's "AAAWWUBBIS – The Subordinating Conjunction" (Anderson, 2005: 91–92).

  ◦ Adverbial Conjunctions (MLB…) – Compound-Complex (cd-cx) Sentences

- Popular Conjunctions Mnemonics Table

Table A.4.1. Sentence-Combining Activities

First-Year College Student Learning Skills Theme		
Title	**Topic**	**Conjunctions**
1. First Year – First Day	Classroom and Book	Free Choice
2. College Value	Costs and Earnings	Free Choice
3. College Schedules	Schedule, Syllabus, Studies	Coordinating: FANBOYS
4. College Balance	Nontraditional, Men, Women, and Minority Students	Coordinating: FANBOYS
5. College Costs	Tuition, Loans, Budgets	Coordinating: FANBOYS
6. Divergent Directions	Attendance, Lectures, Homework Preparation	Subordinating: AAAWWWWUBIS
7. Notes	Classroom Notes	Subordinating: AAAWWWWUBIS
8. Prep Resolutions	Diet and Exercise	Subordinating: AAAWWWWUBIS
9. Composing Calisthenics	Writing Process	Subordinating: AAAWWWWUBIS
10. Alone Together	Student Study Group	Subordinating: AAAWWWWUBIS
11. Alcohol Stats	Use and Effects	Adverbial: MLBNFLFIFA…
12. Smoking Stats	Use and Effects	Adverbial: MLBNFLFIFA…
13. Student Stress and Sleep Stats	Numbers and Effects	Adverbial: MLBNFLFIFA…
14. Online Learning	Numbers and Effects	Adverbial: MLBNFLFIFA…
15. Essential College Skills	Thinking, Communicating, Ethics	Adverbial: MLBNFLFIFA…

Note: See Popular Conjunctions Mnemonics Table at the end of the Appendix to see what the abbreviations stand for.

Appendix 4 includes the fifteen Sentence-Combining Activities and Popular Conjunctions Mnemonics Table that I use one-a-week in English 100 classes with first-year students. Each has eight simpler sentences to combine into more robust compound, complex, or compound-complex sentence-combinations. All together, they may be used to form a complete, college-level paragraph of nicely transitioned sentences. Or they may simply be constructed into series of compound, complex, and compound-complex sentences– as you see fit for your classes or groups of students. Normally, I begin by asking students to work together to form sequences of compound sentences using coordinating conjunctions and commas in the first lessons. Next, I switch them to a series of complex sentences with subordinating conjunctions. Then, I have them use both coordinating and subordinating conjunctions to form compound-complex sentences. The exercises are designed to incrementally reinforce sentence styles and paragraph organization as students interact with classmates in small groups, together discussing and analyzing the relative merits of different combinations. Through their spoken interplay, they are planning and reflecting, thinking and revising their syntax, while synthesizing individual sentences into a coherent and cohesive paragraph.

As students develop and demonstrate their mastery of the several conjunctions and sentence types, I change the instructions to target their learning needs. Sometimes, I skip whole lessons, but usually, I add combinations by asking them to construct an equal number of compound and complex sentences using a variety of coordinating and subordinating conjunctions. Or I ask them to try to package a balanced ratio of all four sentence types. As they progress, I introduce semicolons and comma patterns, to illustrate the varieties of sentence types and how they influence writers' tone and balance as they plan communications with their audiences. For example, I like to accentuate compound sentences by encouraging students' use of coordinating conjunctions to emphasize a healthy balance when they are introducing themselves in a personal essay. When they wish to show depth, I ask them to try demonstrating it with compound-complex or complex sentences with multiple clauses. Staccatoed simple sentences can be used to target attention or point out simplicity, straightforwardness, even immaturity, as they will. In addition, I ask students to form simple sentences by using Not-a-Verbs to reduce the clauses of the sentence combinations into phrases, so they form single, independent clauses of each. Finally, I have them consider individual clusters of sentences within a sentence-combining exercise and attempt to form them into all four sentence varieties: simple, compound, complex, and compound-complex. On occasion, depending on the groups, I may have them form fragments and run-ons, to learn from their nonexamples.

I've found that sentence-combining practice when it is taught as a grouped, dialogical interaction and then applied to students' own writing assignments and essays, is especially effective in their learning the whole package together: syntax, topic organization, grammar, and punctuation. For many of my students, these are the most challenging aspects of writing. In addition, students who have taken developmental writing classes at one of the colleges where I teach receive a sentence-combining unit in which they're given the rudimentaries of forming completed, longer sentences. This background assures their initial successes in my first-year college class since they often discover themselves to be ahead of their peers and sometimes able to lead their groups' discussions, which can bolster their confidence and boost their willingness to continue contributing to groupwork and classwork.

Usually, I seek to stir up some fun by announcing extra credit opportunities, such as any group that is able to use all seven FANBOYS earns three bonus points. Or, the teams who can find a way to construct five compound-complex sentences without repeating any conjunctions whatsoever can gain three points. Or, any group that forms an equal number of all four sentence types gets bonus points that day. You get the idea.

Normally, I do nothing with the sentence content, leaving them to speak for themselves. Often, though, my students react to them. I frequently hear their exclamations: "Ooooh, Tina's so not together!" regarding Lesson 6, or "So that's what that is: I always wondered what a *hookah* was!" in response to Lesson 12. Where used, sources for all facts or statistics communicated in the sentence-combining forms are noted at the bottom of the page.

Sentence-combining lessons of course are mere resources whose value is appropriated only when they're adapted to the learning and writing needs of individual classes, groups, and students by a discerning instructor – you!

Figure A.6. Sentence Combining in Writing Notebook

Sentence Combining

1.   First Year – First Day

Working with your group members, combine each of these clusters into one, well-written sentence, by including every item without repeating any key words. Change punctuation and capitalization, draw arrows to move text, and cross out words to craft your best combination; or if you prefer, rewrite your constructions in the space on the page. Read your answers aloud to hear how your sentences sound.

1.1 Students arrive at Main Hall.
1.2 Students study signs posted in the building.

2.1 Suzette stops in the entryway.
2.2 Suzette stops between the stairs and elevators.
2.3 Suzette checks her course schedule.

3.1 She pauses at the crest of the stairs.
3.2 She wonders if she should turn left.
3.3 She wonders if she should turn right.
3.4 She joins the surge of students down a hallway.

4.1 She arrives outside the classroom.
4.2 She confirms her schedule.
4.3 Suzette steps inside the classroom.
4.4 A dozen other students are quietly sitting at desks.

5.1 Suzette chooses a desk across the room.
5.2 She chooses a desk beside a window.
5.3 She takes out her notebook.
5.4 She takes her notebook out of her backpack.

6.1 She opens her textbook.
6.2 She scans the Table of Contents.
6.3 The Table of Contents lists fifteen chapters.

7.1 Among the book's fifteen chapters are explanations about how to write five essays.
7.2 Included, too, are sample essays for each of the five.

8.1 In the back of the book, Suzette discovered something.
8.2 She discovered an appendix with a review of grammar.
8.3 She discovered an appendix with suggestions for effective sentences.
8.4 And she discovered an appendix with suggestions for a clear writing style.

Copy your sentence combinations into a writing notebook. Try sentence surgery on them: double-underline all <u>verbs</u>, single-underline their <u>subjects</u>, bracket and label [clauses] independent (*ind*) or dependent (*dep*), and label each sentence simple (*s*), complex (*cx*), compound (*cd*), or compound-complex (*cd-cx*).

Note: In speech, we combine ideas automatically. In writing, however, we study and try connecting words in various arrangements, so we can arrange and rearrange them in a multitude of forms, and continually revise them until we discover a combination that sounds best.

Learning is the lifelong expression of our wonder and worth. –Roland Barth

Sentence Combining

2.   College Value

Working with your group members, combine each of these clusters into one, well-written sentence, by including every item without repeating any key words. Change punctuation and capitalization, draw arrows to move text, and cross out words to craft your best combination; or if you prefer, rewrite your constructions in the space on the page. Read your answers aloud to hear how your sentences sound.

1.1 Four-year college graduates averaged nearly $50,000 per year.
1.2 Two-year college associate degree graduates averaged $38,000.
1.3 This was in 2016.
1.4 This was according to the National Center for Educational Statistics.

2.1 High school graduates averaged $31,800.
2.2 High school dropouts averaged $22,200.

3.1 79% of college graduates worked full time jobs.
3.2 69% of high school graduates worked full time jobs.
3.3 The graduates were young adults.

4.1 One of the fastest growing occupations is a *Windtech*.
4.2 *Windtech* is short for Wind Turbine Technologist.
4.3 The number of *Windtechs* needed is expected to double.
4.4 *Windtechs* are expected to double in the next ten years.
4.5 This is according to the U.S. Bureau of Labor Statistics.

5.1 *Windtechs* earn more than $53,000 per year.
5.2 *Windtechs* may graduate with a two-year college associates degree.

6.1 Some of the fastest growing occupations are in the health field.
6.2 They include Physical Therapists, Physical Therapist Assistants, and Physical Therapist Aides.
6.3 They include Occupational Therapists, Occupational Therapist Assistants and Aides.

7.1 Top paying jobs include anesthesiologists, psychiatrists, and judges.
7.2 Top paying jobs earn over $130,000 per year.
7.3 Lowest paying jobs are hairdressers, preschool teachers, and nursing aides.
7.4 Lowest paying jobs earn below $35,000.

8.1 Of course, income is only one benefit of a college education.
8.2 College gains knowledge and wisdom.
8.3 College gains perspective and insight.

Sources

Wind Turbine Technicians: Occupational Outlook Handbook. U.S. Bureau of Labor Statistics. (2018, April 13). Retrieved from https://www.bls.gov/ooh/installation-maintenance-and-repair/wind-turbine-technicians.htm

National Center for Education Statistics. (2018). Annual earnings of young adults – Indicator April 2018. The Condition of Education - Population Characteristics and Economic Outcomes – Economic Outcomes. Retrieved from https://nces.ed.gov/programs/coe/indicator_cba.asp

Copy your sentence combinations into a writing notebook. Try sentence surgery on them: double-underline all <u>verbs</u>, single-underline their <u>subjects</u>, bracket and label [clauses] independent (*ind*) or dependent (*dep*), and label each sentence simple (*s*), complex (*cx*), compound (*cd*), or compound-complex (*cd-cx*).

Note: Say your sentences to yourself, talk them over with classmates, and select those that sound best. Listen for the smooth resonances of some sentences and the rhythmic reverberations of others.

Learning is the lifelong expression of our wonder and worth. –Roland Barth

Sentence Combining

3.   College Schedules

Combine each of these clusters into one, well-written sentence, by including every item without repeating any key words. Use coordinating conjunctions, *for*, *and*, *nor*, *but*, *or*, *yet*, and *so* (FANBOYS) with commas to connect independent clauses.

1.1 In college, students select their courses.
1.2 Students have to take required classes.

2.1 College students enjoy many freedoms.
2.2 Students choose morning classes.
2.3 Students select afternoon and evening classes.
2.4 Students pick evening or weekend classes.

3.1 In high school, the schedule normally began at the same time.
3.2 In high school, the schedule usually ended at the same time.
3.3 Class changes were announced with bells.
3.4 In college, class schedules often vary from day to day.

4.1 In high school, many students were dependent on adults.
4.2 Students waited for teachers to tell them assignments.
4.3 Students waited for teachers to tell them due dates.

5.1 In college, students must consult a syllabus.
5.2 In college, students must plan ahead.

6.1 College students are treated as adults.
6.2 College students are responsible for assignments.
6.3 Many college students use a calendar to record due dates.
6.4 Many college students use a planner to note homework.

7.1 College students averaged 15–17 hours studying every week.
7.2 Students review class notes.
7.3 Students complete homework.
7.4 Students work on assignments.
7.5 This was according to the American Association of Colleges and Universities.

8.1 Most students study one hour a week for every hour spent in class.
8.2 About 10% study two hours or more for every hour spent in class.

Source

McCormick, A. C. (2017, March 10) It's about time: What to make of reported declines in how much college students study. Retrieved from https://www.aacu.org/publications-research/periodicals/its-about-time-what-make-reported-declines-how-much-college.

Copy your sentence combinations into a writing notebook. Try sentence surgery on them: identify and double-underline all <u>verbs</u>, single-underline their <u>subjects</u>, bracket and label [clauses] as independent (*ind*) or dependent (*dep*), and label each sentence as simple (*s*), complex (*cx*), compound (*cd*), or compound-complex (*cd-cx*).

Note: In speech, we combine ideas automatically. In writing, however, we study and try connecting words in various arrangements, so we can arrange and rearrange them in a multitude of forms, and continually revise them until we discover a combination that sounds best.

Sentence Combining

4.   College Balance

Combine each of these clusters into one, well-written sentence, using coordinating conjunctions, *for*, *and*, *nor*, *but*, *or*, *yet*, and *so* (FANBOYS).

1.1 Marc returned to college to get a degree.
1.2 Marc worked in the construction industry.
1.3 Marc wanted to have more control over his career.

2.1 Marc worked for his dad.
2.2 His dad was foreman of a construction company.
2.3 His dad's construction crew built new houses.
2.4 Sometimes, his dad's crew had to remodel rooms.

3.1 Usually, Marc kept busy.
3.2 Marc nailed framing and siding.
3.3 Marc prepared and cleaned work sites.

4.1 Marc wanted something more.
4.2 Marc wanted to run his own business someday.
4.3 The business could be construction.
4.4 Marc wanted to earn a degree.

5.1 Marc enrolled in a construction management program.
5.2 The program is at his local college.
5.3 He has been out of high school seven years.
5.4 He wonders if he will feel out of place.

6.1 Marc is one of nearly 8 million students returning to college.
6.2 These students are age 25 and older.
6.3 This number is projected to grow by 20% in the next decade.
6.4 This is according to the National Center for Educational Statistics.

7.1 Marc is one of almost 9 million men enrolled in college.
7.2 Nearly 12 million women are enrolled in college.

8.1 Marc is one of about 3 million Hispanic students enrolled in college.
8.3 This is about 14% of all college students.
8.4 Another 14% is African Americans.
8.5 Nearly 57% is whites.
8.6 Almost 6% is Asian Americans.

Source

National Center for Educational Statistics (2016, October) Total fall enrollment in degree-granting postsecondary institutions, by level of enrollment, sex, attendance status, and race/ethnicity of student: Selected years, 1976 through 2015. Table 306.10. Institute of Education Sciences. U.S. Department of Education. Retrieved from https://nces.ed.gov/programs/digest/d16/tables/dt16_306.10.asp?current=yes.

Try sentence surgery on 3–5 combinations in your writing notebook: double-underline verbs, single-underline subjects, bracket and label [clauses] as *ind* or dependent *dep*, and identify each sentence as *s*, *cx*, *cd*, or *cd-cx*.

Learning is the lifelong expression of our wonder and worth. –Roland Barth

Sentence Combining

5.   College Costs

Combine each of these clusters into one, well-written sentence, using coordinating conjunctions, *for*, *and*, *nor*, *but*, *or*, *yet*, and *so* (FANBOYS). Try using all seven.

1.1 The National Center for Education Statistics (NCES) reported something.
1.2 The average two-year college cost over $9,500 in 2012–13.
1.3 The average four-year college cost over $23,800 in 2012–13.

2.1 College is expensive.
2.2 College provides learning opportunities.
2.3 College provides career opportunities.
2.4 The opportunities are valuable.

3.1 In 2013, *US News* reported something.
3.2 Four-year college graduates averaged almost $30,000 in debt.
3.3 Some averaged as little as $2,700.
3.4 Others averaged as much as $71,000.

4.1 Students in the five states averaged the highest college-debt.
4.2 The college-debt was over $30,000.
4.3 The five states were Delaware, Minnesota, New Hampshire, Pennsylvania, and Rhode Island.
4.4 Students in only one state averaged below $20,000.
4.5 That state was New Mexico.

5.1 The *Atlantic Monthly* reported something.
5.2 Investment in a college education is the best deal.
5.3 It pays nearly 10–20% in financial returns.
5.4 It is better than stocks, bonds, gold, and housing.

6.1 College students must learn to budget money.
6.2 They complete FAFSA forms for financial aid.
6.3 They apply for scholarships and loans.
6.4 This is to invest in their futures.

7.1 Many college students borrow money.
7.2 They borrow money from the government and other lenders.
7.2 Most advisers suggest borrowing no more than one year's wages.
7.4 The year's wages equals the annual salary for their job after graduation.

8.1 College students have confidence.
8.2 Their confidence is in the labor market.
8.3 Their confidence is in their own commitment to learn.

Sources

Bidwell, A. (2014, November 13) Average student loan debt approaches $30,000. Retrieved from https://www.usnews.com/news/articles/2014/11/13/average-student-loan-debt-hits-30-000.

National Center for Educational Statistics (2015) Tuition costs of colleges and universities. Fast Facts. U.S. Department of Education. Retrieved from https://nces.ed.gov/fastfacts/display.asp?id=76.

Weissmann, J. (2013, June 11). Is going to college still worth it if you drop out? Retrieved from https://www.theatlantic.com/business/archive/2013/06/is-going-to-college-still-worth-it-if-you-drop-out/276757/.

Try sentence surgery on 3-5 combinations in your writing notebook: double-underline <u>verbs</u>, single-underline <u>subjects</u>, bracket and label [clauses] as *ind* or dependent *dep*, and identify each sentence as *s*, *cx*, *cd*, or *cd-cx*.

Sentence Combining

6.   Divergent Directions

Combine each of these clusters into one, well-written sentence, using subordinating conjunctions, such as *after, although, as, when, while, which, who, unless, until, because, before, if, since, that, then, though* (AAAWWWUBBIS).

1.1 Tina raced around the vast parking lot.
1.2 She searched for an available parking space.
1.3 She had overslept.

2.1 Anthony sat at a desk.
2.2 The desk was near a window.
2.3 He talked to James about a ballgame.
2.4 He waited for class to begin.

3.1 Tina slunk into the classroom.
3.4 The door slammed behind her.
3.5 The door interrupted the professor's lecture.
3.6 Tina slouched into a front seat.

4.1 Anthony usually arrived at class ten minutes early.
4.2 He liked to have a little extra time.
4.3 He liked to converse with his classmates.
4.4 Sometimes he liked to ask a question about an assignment.

5.1 In her hurry, Tina had forgotten her assignment.
5.2 She worried that the professor might call on her.
5.3 She worried that he might be annoyed by her tardiness.
5.4 She wondered what the other students thought about her.

6.1 Sometimes Anthony struggled with homework.
6.2 He wrote notes to remember the readings.
6.3 He reread passages that were difficult.
6.4 He wrote questions to ask the professor.

7.1 Tina didn't dare to look around.
7.2 She couldn't concentrate on the lecture.
7.3 She thought the lecture was boring.

8.1 Anthony was grateful for college's opportunities.
8.2 He listened for information to write.

Try sentence surgery on 3–5 combinations in your writing notebook.

Learning is the lifelong expression of our wonder and worth. –Roland Barth

Sentence Combining

7.   Notes

Combine each of these clusters into one, well-written sentence, using subordinating conjunctions, such as *after*, *although*, *as*, *when*, *while*, *which*, *who*, *unless*, *until*, *because*, *before*, *if*, *since*, *that*, *then*, *though* (AAAWWWUBBIS).

1.1 William wondered what to write.
1.2 All the other students were noting down words in notebooks.

2.1 William's professor was talking about paragraphs and sentences.
2.2 She was marking a sample on the whiteboard.
2.3 She was marking with different colored dry erase markers.
2.4 She was calling on individuals to supply answers.

3.1 Professor O'Neill noticed William.
3.2 She saw he was examining the whiteboard.
3.3 She asked him a question.

4.1 Professor O'Neill could see William was listening.
4.2 William knew the answer.
4.3 He appreciated her questioning him.
4.4 He worried that he wouldn't remember.
4.5 He wouldn't remember how to do the problem on his own tomorrow.

5.1 He remembered the professor in his college studies class.
5.2 The professor said that they're notes if they're written on the board.
5.3 They're notes if repeated in a professor's lecture.
5.4 Notes should be reviewed 10–20 minutes.
5.5 Notes should be reviewed immediately following every class session.

6.1 William opened his spiral-bound notebook.
6.2 He wrote down the date in the upper right corner.
6.3 He began jotting the sample sentences from the board.
6.4 William smiled at his memory.

7.1 His professor saw William's smile.
7.2 She noticed he had begun writing notes.
7.3 She smiled, too.

8.1 She watched until William paused in his writing.
8.2 She called upon him with a second question.
8.3 She knew he would respond correctly.

   Try sentence surgery on 3–5 combinations in your writing notebook.

Sentence Combining

8.   Prep Resolutions

Combine each of these clusters into one, well-written sentence, using subordinating conjunctions, such as *after, although, as, when, while, which, who, unless until, because, before, if, since, that, then, though* (AAAWWWUBBIS).

1.1 Wendy made a New Year's resolution.
1.2 She made a resolution for the new school year.
1.3 She resolved to take good care of herself.
1.4 She resolved this to do her best in college.

2.1 Wendy stopped at the vending machines before classes last semester.
2.2 She usually bought chips and a soda pop.
2.3 Sometimes she drove through a fast food restaurant.
2.4 She usually ate hamburgers and fries for lunch.

3.1 Wendy decided to replace French fries with fresh fruit and vegetables.
3.2 She decided to join the 89% of college students.
3.3 These students eat at least one or two servings of fruit and vegetables every day.
3.4 This is according to the American College Health Association.
3.5 This was in 2015 (American College Health).

4.1 She would make a menu and shopping list every weekend.
4.2 She would buy all her food at the grocery store and farmers market.
4.3 She would prepare nutritious dinners for the whole week on Sundays.
4.4 She would prepare healthful lunches for the whole week on Sundays.

5.1 Wendy wanted no longer to belong to the 43%.
5.2 43% of college students did not exercise.

6.1 Wendy resolved to exercise 5 days a week, too.
6.2 She resolved to join the 46% of college students.
6.3 These students met the exercise recommendations for healthy adults.

7.1 A healthy exercise regimen for college students is 30 minutes of moderately intense exercise.
7.2 The exercise is cardio or aerobic.
7.3 The exercise is 5 days per week.
7.4 A healthy exercise regimen can be 20 minutes of vigorously intense exercise.

8.1 Wendy set a calendar on her kitchen counter.
8.2 She blocked 30 minutes for exercise.
8.3 The exercise was Monday through Friday at 7:30 until 8:00 am.

Sources

American College Health Association (2015, Fall) National College Health Assessment
    II: Reference Group Undergraduates Report. Retrieved from
    https://www.acha.org/documents/ncha/NCHA-II_FALL_2015_REFERENCE_
    GROUP_DATA_REPORT_UNDERGRADS_ONLY.pdf.
Try sentence surgery on 3–5 combinations in your writing notebook.

Sentence Combining

9.   Composing Calisthenics

Combine each of these clusters into one, well-written sentence, using subordinating conjunctions, such as *after, although, as, when, while, which, who, unless, until, because, before, if, since, that, then, though* (AAAWWWUBBIS).

1.1 Philip thought writing was difficult.
1.2 It looked easy.
2.1 It looked like lining up words on paper.

2.2 The words made sentences.
2.3 The sentences made paragraphs.
2.4 The paragraphs made essays.

3.1 Writing essays for class, he realized something.
3.2 The class was English composition.
3.3 Things are usually more complex than simple.

4.1 Birds can fly in straight lines toward their destinations.
4.2 Cars generally have to follow roads.
4.3 The roads sometimes curve around hills.
4.4 The routes sometimes require turns.

5.1 Writing rarely occurs in straight lines.
5.2 It, too, often takes turns.
5.3 Often, it requires going over a route more than one time.

6.1 Philip thought writing was like calisthenics.
6.2 It improved the more he practiced.
6.3 He liked to try different words and combinations.
6.4 He liked to try arranging and rearranging them.

7.1 Philip used writing to express his thoughts.
7.2 He used writing to explore new ideas.
7.3 The ideas usually started out undeveloped.
7.4 The ideas frequently gained form.
7.5 Their form was gained through revisions.

8.1 Philip discovered something.
8.2 Writing is a process.
8.3 The process is multi-step.
8.4 The process allows composers to think deeply.
8.5 The process allows composers to explore thoroughly.

Try sentence surgery on 3–5 combinations in your writing notebook.

Sentence Combining

10. Alone Together

Combine each of these clusters into one, well-written sentence, using subordinating conjunctions, such as *after, although, as, when, while, which, who, unless, until, because, before, if, since, that, then, though* (AAAWWWUBBIS).

1.1 Annie looked up from her homework.
1.2 The homework was English.
1.3 She had dozed in the library.
1.4 She had dozed after class.

2.1 Every class she sat in the same seat.
2.2 She sat by the same students.
2.3 She didn't speak to anyone.

3.1 Today, she was struck by something.
3.2 A thought had struck like a missile.

4.1 Annie looked around the library.
4.2 Everyone sat at tables.
4.3 Everyone sat at carrels.
4.4 Everyone sat at chairs.
4.5 Everyone sat separately.

5.1 One student was typing at his keyboard.
5.2 Another had headphones attached to an electronic device.
5.3 A third was holding her head.
5.4 She studied a thick textbook.
5.5 The textbook was English composition.

6.1 Annie recognized the students.
6.2 They had all walked from the same class.
6.3 They had walked to the library.

7.1 They were working on the same assignment.
7.2 She didn't know any of their names.

8.1 She decided to ask the students something.
8.2 Would they like to form a study group?
8.3 Would they like to study together after class?
8.4 Annie stood.
8.5 They all looked up to her.

Try sentence surgery on 3–5 combinations in your writing notebook.

Sentence Combining

11. Alcohol Stats

Combine each of these clusters into one, well-written sentence, using a semicolon with an adverbial conjunction like *moreover, however, nevertheless, therefore, furthermore* (See *Popular Conjunctions Mnemonics*).

1.1 Moderate alcohol consumption may have beneficial consequences.
1.2 Moderate alcohol consumption is defined as 1 drink for women and 1–2 drinks for men.
1.3 Beneficial consequences may be for coronary heart disease and ischemic stroke.
1.4 Beneficial consequences are for middle aged and older men and women.
1.5 This is according to the National Institute of Health.

2.1 Alcohol abuse is the primary cause of premature mortality and injury.
2.2 It is the primary cause of mortality and injury to people 15-49 years old.
2.3 It is the cause of about 25% of the deaths among 20–39 year olds.

3.1 23% of people in the U.S. reported drinking some alcohol in the past month.
3.2 These people were ages 12–20.
3.2 Underage drinking can interfere with normal brain development.
3.3 Underage drinking increases the risk of developing Alcohol Use Disorder.
3.4 Underage drinking contributes to acute injuries, sexual assaults, and premature deaths.

4.1 About 60% of college students drank alcohol in the past month.
4.2 These students were ages 18–22.
4.3 This was in 2014.

5.1 About 38% of college students participated in binge drinking within the past month.
5.2 Binge drinking is defined as drinking 4–5 or more drinks.
5.3 Binge drinking is defined as drinking them within about 2 hours.
5.4 This pattern of drinking brings the blood alcohol content to 0.08 g/dL.

6.1 Over 12% of college students were heavy drinkers.
6.2 Heavy drinkers is defined as drinking 4–5 or more drinks.
6.3 Heavy drinkers is defined as drinking them on at least 5 occasions per month.

7.1 Researchers have identified several consequences of college students' alcohol consumption.
7.2 Every year, 1,825 die from alcohol-related injuries, including car crashes.
7.3 Every year, 696,000 students are assaulted by others.
7.4 Every year, 97,000 report sexual assault and date rape.

8.1 Around 25% of college students suffer academic consequences for drinking.
8.2 Academic consequences include poor grades, low scores on tests and essays, missed classes, and falling behind.
8.3 About 20% of college students actually qualify as having an Acute Use Disorder.

Source

National Institute on Alcohol Abuse and Alcoholism (2018, August) Alcohol facts and statistics. Retrieved from https://www.niaaa.nih.gov/alcohol-health/overview-alcohol-consumption/alcohol-facts-and-statistics.

Try sentence surgery on 3–5 combinations in your writing notebook.

Sentence Combining

12. Smoking Stats

Combine each of these clusters into one, well-written sentence, using a semicolon with an adverbial conjunction like *moreover*, *however*, *nevertheless*, *therefore*, *furthermore* (See *Popular Conjunctions Mnemonics*).

1.1 78% of college students have never smoked tobacco.
1.2 82% of college women have never smoked tobacco.
1.3 73% of college men have never smoked tobacco.
1.4 This is according to the American College Health Association.
1.5 This was in 2015.

2.1 83% of college students have never smoked an e-cigarette.
2.2 78% of college students have never smoked a water pipe.
2.3 A water pipe is also called a hookah.

3.1 20% of all deaths in the U.S. are caused by tobacco consumption.
3.2 Cigarette smoking is the number 1 cause of preventable deaths.
3.2 Cigarette smoking is the number 1 cause of preventable diseases.
3.3 Cigarette smoking is the number 1 cause of preventable disabilities.

4.1 Smoking results in severely poor health for 16 million people in the U.S.
4.2 30 people are harmed by tobacco for every one person who dies.

5.1 Smoking can affect nonsmokers, too.
5.2 88 million Americans are exposed to secondhand smoke.
5.3 41 thousand people are killed by illnesses caused by secondhand smoke.

6.1 Tobacco contains nicotine.
6.2 Nicotine is addictive.
6.3 Nicotine causes the adrenal glands to release the hormone epinephrine.
6.4 Epinephrine affects the central nervous and the cardiopulmonary systems.
6.5 Nicotine raises the level of dopamine.
6.6 Dopamine influences the brain's networks of gratification.

7.1 Nonsmokers live 10 years longer than smokers, on average.
7.2 Cigarette smokers contract 33% of all cancer diagnoses.
7.3 Cigarette smokers contract 90% of all lung cancer diagnoses.
7.4 Cigarette smokers also can contract heart and vascular diseases and emphysema.

8.1 Women cigarette smokers who are pregnant run several risks for their infants.
8.2 Probabilities of miscarriage, premature births, and low birth weights increase.
8.3 Possible increases in children's learning and behavioral problems have been detected.

Source

National Institute on Drug Abuse (2018, June) Cigarettes and other tobacco products. Retrieved from
https://www.drugabuse.gov/publications/drugfacts/cigarettes-other-tobacco-products.

Try sentence surgery on 3–5 combinations in your writing notebook.

Sentence Combining

13. Student Stress and Sleep Stats

Combine each of these clusters into one, well-written sentence, using a semicolon with an adverbial conjunction like *moreover*, *however*, *nevertheless*, *therefore*, *furthermore* (See *Popular Conjunctions Mnemonics*).

1.1 Almost 86% of college students reported feeling overwhelmed by all they had to do.
1.2 This was during the past 12 months.
1.3 More than 11% experienced tremendous stress.
1.4 This is according to the American College Health Association.
1.5 This was in 2015.

2.1 About 18% sought treatment for anxiety.
2.2 Nearly 15% were diagnosed with depression.

3.1 Almost 60% felt very anxious within the past year.
3.2 Almost 60% felt very lonely within the past year.
3.3 About 65% were mentally exhausted in the last 12 months.

4.1 Within the last year, college students found three things especially challenging.
4.2 45% of students were stressed by college academics.
4.3 Almost 37% were stressed by finances.
4.4 Nearly 30% were stressed by sleep difficulties.

5.1 Nearly 8% of college students report insomnia or a sleep disorder.
5.2 About 7% of college men experience insomnia or sleep disorder.
5.2 About 8% of college women experience insomnia or sleep disorder.

6.1 9% of women get enough rest to feel refreshed at least 6 nights per week.
6.2 12% of men get enough rest to feel refreshed at least 6 nights per week.
6.3 10% of all college students are getting enough sleep to feel rested 6 or more nights each week.

7.1 Almost two-thirds of college students feel "tired, dragged out, or sleepy."
7.2 This is 3 or more days of the week.
7.2 More than two-thirds of college women feel weary at least half of the week.
7.3 More than half of college men feel weary at least half of the week.

8.1 Less than 10% of college students consider themselves to have no problems with sleep.
8.2 13% think that sleep causes a big problem for their daytime activity.
8.3 About 6% think that sleep causes a very big problem for their daytime activity.

Source

American College Health Association (2015, Fall) American College Health Association-National College Health Assessment II: Reference Group Undergraduates Report. Retrieved on from https://www.acha.org/documents/ncha/NCHA-II_FALL_2015_REFERENCE_GROUP_DATA_REPORT_UNDERGRADS_ONLY.pdf.

Try sentence surgery on 3–5 combinations in your writing notebook.

Sentence Combining

14. Online Learning

Combine each of these clusters into one, well-written sentence, using a semicolon with an adverbial conjunction like *moreover, however, nevertheless, therefore, furthermore* (See *Popular Conjunctions Mnemonics*).

1.1 Many colleges nationwide are experiencing annual reductions in student enrollments.
1.2 Many colleges are experiencing reductions in annual budgets.
1.3 Online college classes have grown 21% since 2002.
1.4 Online college classes continue to increase about 5% every year.

2.1 More than 5.5 million students took online classes in 2013.
2.2 Almost 15 million college students didn't take any online classes.
2.3 This is according to the National Center for Education Statistics.

3.1 13% take all their classes online.
3.2 14% take at least one of their courses online.

4.1 Online students take 6.5% of their classes at a college in their state.
4.2 Nearly 6% take their classes out-of-state.
4.3 Less than 1/2% enroll distance learning courses outside of the U.S. or at an unknown location.

5.1 Students appreciate the convenience of taking distance learning classes.
5.2 Distance learning classes can reduce the amount of time students require to complete a degree.
5.2 Distance learning classes can increase the number and availability of courses.

6.1 Some students may do better in online classes.
6.2 Students take an online orientation class.
6.3 Students are motivated to persist in learning how to learn in each class.
6.4 Students with good time management skills do better.

7.1 Between 10–20% more web-based learning college students drop out.
7.2 This is compared to traditional face-to-face, on-site college classes.
7.2 Some web-based classes have reported attrition as high as 80%.

8.1 Students report significant differences between distance and in-class learning.
8.2 Interactions among classmates and with professors is one variable.
8.3 Deep and critical thinking and improving writing skills are others.

Sources

Institute of Education Sciences. (2014, December) Distance learning: Digest of educational statistics table 311.15. U.S. Department of Education. Retrieved from https://nces.ed.gov/fastfacts/display.asp?id=80.

Neumann, Y., and Neumann, E. (2016, 3 May) Lessons of online learning: What we've learned after several decades of online learning (essay). *Inside Higher Ed*. Retrieved from https://www.insidehighered.com/views/2016/05/03/what-weve-learned-after-several-decades-online-learning-essay.

Smith, A. A. (2016, April 21) The increasingly digital community college: Survey shows participation in online courses growing. *Inside Higher Ed*. Retrieved from https://www.insidehighered.com/news/2015/04/21/survey-shows-participation-online-courses-growing.

Ya Ni, A. (2013, Spring) Comparing the effectiveness of classroom and online learning: Teaching research methods. *Journal of Public Affairs Education* 19(2): 199–215.

Try sentence surgery on 3–5 combinations in your writing notebook.

Learning is the lifelong expression of our wonder and worth. –Roland Barth

Sentence Combining

15. Essential College Skills

Combine each of these clusters into one, well-written sentence, using a semicolon with an adverbial conjunction like *moreover, however, nevertheless, therefore, furthermore* (See *Popular Conjunctions Mnemonics*).

1.1 Nearly 75% of business and non-profit leaders thought the liberal arts was most important.
1.2 Liberal arts abilities are more important than any college major.
1.3 Over 100 college presidents and 150 business and non-profit leaders made a pledge.
1.4 The pledge was to ensure that college students get a good liberal-arts education.
1.5 The education prepares students for working, living, and participating as citizens.

2.1 Nationwide, employers want something.
2.2 They want quality learning to be a national priority in colleges.
2.3 They want college graduates to have wider skills and knowledge.
2.4 They want this so that they are flexible and creative in our innovative information culture.

3.1 93% of business leaders claim three things are most important in college.
3.2 They claim students should learn to think deeply.
3.3 They claim students should learn to communicate clearly.
3.4 They claim students should learn to solve problems that are complex.

4.1 95% say they prefer to hire college graduates who can do two things.
4.2 They prefer college graduates who think creatively and imaginatively.
4.3 They prefer college graduates who can assist with workplace innovation.

5.1 Of all who were surveyed, 95% said something.
5.2 They employ college graduates who make moral and principled decisions.
5.2 They employ college graduates who are comfortable with different cultures.
5.3 They employ college graduates who keep learning new things.

6.1 Over 75% want colleges to do more teaching of five key areas.
6.2 Key areas are critical thinking and challenging problem-solving.
6.3 Additional key areas include written and oral communications.
6.4 Another key area is using learning in actual applications.

7.1 The hundreds of leaders surveyed were from many different employment sectors.
7.2 They represented business, engineering, healthcare, finance, media, marketing, and energy.
7.2 They included leaders of two-year, four-year, private, and public colleges and universities.

8.1 Mildred Garcia is the president of California State University in Fullerton.
8.2 Mildred Garcia is the president of the board of directors of the AACU.
8.3 She said, "Business leaders who hire graduates are urging us to prioritize the cross-cutting capacities a college education should develop in every student."

Source

Association of American Colleges and Universities (2014, May) Employers more interested in critical thinking and problem solving than college major. Retrieved from https://www.aacu.org/press/press-releases/employers-more-interested-critical-thinking-and-problem-solving-college-major.

Try sentence surgery on 3–5 combinations in your writing notebook.

Table A.4.2. Popular Conjunctions Mnemonics

Coordinating Conjunctions	**Subordinating Conjunctions**	**Adverbial Conjunctions**
For	**After**	**Moreover**
And	**Although**	**Likewise**
Nor	**As**	**Besides**
But	**When**	**Nevertheless**
Or	**Where**	**Furthermore**
Yet	**While**	**Last**
So	**Which**	**First**
	Who	**Instead**
	Unless	**Finally**
	Until	**Afterward**
	Because	**In fact**
	Before	**Therefore**
	If	**For instance**
	Since	**In other words**
	That	**However**
	Then	**Lately**
	Though	**In addition**
		Before
		Also

*Use a comma (,) + a FANBOYS to join two independent (ind) clauses in a compound (cd) or compound-complex (cd-cx) sentence.

*Use an *Ah-Woo-Bus* or *Three-T* to introduce a dependent (dep) clause in a complex (cx) or compound-complex (cd-cx) sentence.

**Ah-Woo-Bus* comes from Anderson, Jeff. *Mechanically Inclined.* Portland, ME: Stenhouse, 2005.

*Use a semicolon (;) + an adverbial conjunction (Sports Fans—Major League Baseball, National Football League, Fédération Internationale de Football Association, International Tennis Federation, National Hockey League, National Basketball Association) + a comma (,) to join two independent (ind) clauses in a compound (cd) or compound-complex (cd-cx) sentence.

References – Epigraph Quotations for Chapters and Appendices

Anderson, J., & Dean, D. (2014). *Revision decisions: Talking through sentences and beyond*. Portland: Stenhouse, p. 5.

Barth, R. S. (1990). *Improving schools from within: Teachers, parents, and principals can make a difference*. San Francisco: Jossey-Bass, p. 18.

Burton, P., & Pennington, M. C. (2011). Tools of the trade: The college writing teacher in a new age. In M. C. Pennington & P. Burton (eds.), *The college writing toolkit: Tried and tested ideas for teaching college writing* (pp. 1–18). Sheffield, UK and Oakville, CT: Equinox, p. 3.

DeVries, P. (1980, September 28). Sayings of the week. *The London Observer*, p. L3.

Elbow, P. (1986). *Embracing contraries: Explorations in learning and teaching*. New York: Oxford University Press, p. x.

Gere, A. R. (1987). *Writing groups: History, theory, and implications*. Carbondale: Southern Illinois University Press, p. 73.

Harbour, C. P., & Ebie, G. (2011). Deweyan democratic learning communities and student marginalization. In E. M. Cox & J. S. Watson (eds.), *Marginalized students: New directions for community colleges*. San Francisco: Jossey-Bass, p. 12.

Orben, R. (1974, July 28). *The Gallup Independent*, Family Weekly Section: Quips & Quotes. Gallup, New Mexico, p. 15, column 2.

Paterson, K. (1981). *Gates of excellence: On reading and writing books for children*. New York: Dutton Books for Young Readers, p. 84.

Power, B. (2016, October 22). Talking is not teaching, *The Big Fresh Newsletter*. Choice Literacy. Retrieved from https://choiceliteracy.com/article/the-big-fresh-october-22-2016talking-is-not-teaching/

Sommers, N. (2013). *Responding to student writers*. Boston: Bedford/St. Martin's, p. xiii.

Zebroski, J. T. (1989). A hero in the classroom. *Encountering student texts: Interpretive issues inreading student writing*. Urbana: National Council of Teachers of English, p. 46.

References – Motivational Quotations for Sentence Surgeries

Batman (Played by C. Bale). (2005). In Nolan, C. (Director). *Batman begins*. USA: Warner Bros.

Beard, C. A. (1941, February). Quoted in Secord, A. H. Condensed history lesson. *Readers' digest, 38*(226), p. 20.

Burnham, D. (1907). Quoted in Moore, C. (1921). *Daniel H. Burnham: Architect, planner of cities*. Vol. 2, p. 147.

Collins, M. (1990). *Marva Collins' way*. New York: Tarcher/Putnam, p. 22.

Dewey, J. (1916). *Democracy and education: An introduction to the philosophy of education*. New York Macmillan. Quoted from Scottsville, CA: CreateSpace Independent Publishing reprint (2018), p. 54.

Dickens, C. (1849). *David Copperfield*. Quoted from Penguin Classics Paperback edition (2004). New York: Penguin, p. 185.

Disney, W. (no date). Quoted in Anderson, S. J. (Director). (2007). End credits, *Meet the Robinsons*. Burbank, CA: Walt Disney Pictures.

Disney, W. (no date). Quoted in Maxwell, J. C. (2008). *Encouragement changes everything*. Nashville: Thomas Nelson, p. 19.

Doctorow, E. L. (1985, October 20). Quoted in Weber, B. The myth maker. *The New York Times Magazine*. Retrieved from
https://www.nytimes.com/1985/10/20/magazine/the-myth-maker.html

Dyson, F. (2000, May 16). *Progress in religion: A talk by Freeman Dyson*. Acceptance speech for the Templeton Prize, Washington National Cathedral. Retrieved from
https://www.edge.org/conversation/freeman_dyson-progress-in-religion

Goethe, J. W. (1768, November 9). Letter to A. F. Oeser. In E. Bell (ed.) (2012). *Early and miscellaneous letters of J. W. Goethe, including letters to his mother. With notes and a short biography. Classical Reprint*. London: Forgotten Books.

Goldwyn, S. (no date). Quoted in Maxwell, J. C. (2008). *Encouragement changes everything*. Nashville: Thomas Nelson, p. 20.

Herbert, F. (1990). *Dune*. New York: Berkley, p. 508.

Hu, J. (2003, October 24). Speech given to Australian Parliament. *The Sydney Morning Herald*. Retrieved from
https://www.smh.com.au/national/full-text-hus-speech-20031024-gdhnfs.html

Keller, H. (1929). *We bereaved*. New York: Leslie Fulenwider, Inc. Quoted from Internet Archive digitized version (2014), p. 23.
https://archive.org/stream/webereaved00hele/webereaved00hele_djvu.txt

Lincoln, A. (1855, November 5). Letter to I. Reavis. In D. E. Fehrenbacher (ed.) (1989). *Lincoln: Speeches and writings, 1832–1858*. New York: Library of America, p. 364.

Obama, B. (2008, February 5). Super Tuesday speech, Chicago, IL. Retrieved from
http://obamaspeeches.com/E02-Barack-Obama-Super-Tuesday-Chicago-IL-February-5-2008.htm

Rooney, A. (2010). *60 Years of wit and wisdom*. New York: Public Affairs, p. 372.

Roosevelt, E. (1961). *The autobiography of Eleanor Roosevelt*. New York: Harper & Brothers. Quoted from Harper Perennial edition (2014), p. xv.

Rowling, J. K. (2000). *Harry Potter and the goblet of fire*. New York: Scholastic, p. 708.

Sherman, J. R. (1982). *Rejection*. La Grange, IN: Pathway Books, p. 45.

Tennyson, A. (1842). *Locksley Hall*. Boston: W. D. Ticknor, Stanza 141.

Tolkien, J. R. R. (2005). *Lord of the rings: 50th anniversary edition*. New York: Mariner, p. 170.

Tutu, D. (1984). Quoted in Brown, R. A. *Unexpected news: Reading the Bible with third world eyes*. Philadelphia, PA: Westminster Press, p. 19.

Voskamp, A. (2011). *One thousand gifts: A dare to live fully right where you are*. Grand Rapids: Zondervan, p. 56.

Washington, B. T. (1901). *The story of my life and work*. Toronto, Naperville, Atlanta: J. L. Nichols & Co. Quoted from Scottsville, CA: CreateSpace Independent Publishing reprint (2015), p. 118.

Winfrey, O. (no date). Quoted in Egan, J. (2015). *3000 astounding quotations*. Morrisville, NC: Lulu Publishing, p. 75.

Winfrey, O. (2007, January). *O magazine*, pp. 160 & 217.

References – General

Anderson, J. (2005). *Mechanically inclined*. Portland, ME: Stenhouse.

Bakhtin, M. M. (1996). *Speech genres and other late essays*. (eds. C. Emerson & M. Holquist, trans. V. W. McGee). Austin: University of Texas.

Bakhtin, M. M. (2002/1934). *The dialogic imagination by M. M. Bakhtin: Four essays*. (ed. M. Holquist, trans. C. Emerson & M. Holquist). Austin: University of Texas.

Bartholomae, D. (2005). *Writing on the margins: Essays on composition and teaching*. Boston: Bedford/St. Martin's.

Bean, J. C. (2011). *Engaging ideas: The professor's guide to integrating writing, critical thinking, and active learning in the classroom*. 2nd edition. San Francisco: Jossey-Bass.

Berlin, J. A. (1987). *Rhetoric and reality: Writing instruction in American colleges, 1900–1985*. Carbondale Southern Illinois Press.

Bizzell, P. (1992). *Academic discourse and critical consciousness*. Pittsburgh series in composition, literacy, and culture. Pittsburgh: University of Pittsburgh.

Bruffee, K. A. (1999). *Collaborative learning: Higher education, interdependence, and the authority of knowledge*. 2nd edition. Baltimore: Johns Hopkins University Press.

Carroll, L. A. (2002). *Rehearsing new roles: How college students develop as writers*. Studies in writing and rhetoric series. Carbondale and Edwardsville: Southern Illinois University Press.

Carter, G. M., & Thelin, W. H. (2017). *Class in the composition classroom: Pedagogy and the working class*. Logan; Utah State University Press.

Christensen, F. & Christensen, B. (2007). *Notes toward a new rhetoric: 9 essays for teachers*. 3rd edition. Booklocker.com.

Delpit, L. (2006). *Other people's children: Cultural conflict in the classroom*. New York: New Press.

Dewey, J. (1967). *Democracy and education*. New York: Free Press.

Dewey, J. (1963). *Experience and education*. New York: Collier.

Doe, S., & Langstraat, L. (eds.). (2014). *Generation vet: Composition, student-veterans, and the post-9/11 university*. Logan, UT: Utah State University Press.

Drago-Severson, E. (2004). *Becoming adult learners: Principles and practices for effective development*. New York: Teachers College Press.

Elbow, P. (1986). *Embracing contraries: Explorations in learning and teaching*. New York: Oxford University Press.

Eodice, M., Geller, A. E., & Lerner, N. (2016). *The meaningful writing project: Learning, teaching and writing in higher education*. Logan: Utah State University Press.

Farmer, F. (2001). *Saying and silence: Listening to composition with Bakhtin*. Logan, UT: Utah State University Press.

Farrell, T. S. C. (2013). *Reflective writing for language teachers*. Sheffield, UK: Equinox.

Fecho, B. (2011). *Writing in the dialogical classroom: Students and teachers responding to the texts of their lives*. Urbana: National Council of Teachers of English.

Fesmire, S. (2003). *John Dewey and moral imagination: Pragmatism in ethics*. Bloomington: Indiana University.

Fishman, S. M. & McCarthy, L. (1998). *John Dewey and the challenge of classroom practice*. New York: Teachers College and Urbana: National Council of Teachers of English.

Flower, L. (1994). *The construction of negotiated meaning: A social cognitive theory of writing*. Carbondale and Edwardsville: Southern Illinois University Press.

Gamel, A. L. (2019). *Compassionate teaching: Unlocking the potential of first-genertaion marginalized students*. Middletown, DE: Equitable Edu.

Gee, J. P. (2004). *Situated language and learning: A critique of traditional schooling*. London: Routledge.

Gere, A. R. (1987). *Writing groups: History, theory, and implications*. Carbondale: Southern Illinois University Press.

Graff, G., & Birkenstein, C. (2012). *They say, I say: The moves that matter in academic writing*. 2nd edition. New York: W.W. Norton.

Graves, R. L. (ed.). (1984). *Rhetoric and composition: A sourcebook for teachers and writers*. Upper Montclair, NJ: Boynton/Cook.

Halasek, K. (1999). *A pedagogy of possibility: Bakhtinian perspectives on composition studies*. Carbondale: Southern Illinois University Press.

Harbour, C. P., & Ebie, G. (2011). Deweyan democratic learning communities and student marginalization. In E. M. Cox & J. S. Watson (eds.), *Marginalized students: New directions for community colleges* (pp. 5–14). San Francisco: Jossey-Bass.

Hunzer, K. M. (ed.). (2012). *Collaborative learning and writing: Essays on using small groups in teaching English and composition*. Jefferson, NC: McFarland.

Huot, B. (2002). *(Re) articulating writing assessment for teaching and learning*. Logan, UT: Utah State University Press.

Huot, B., & O'Neill, P. (eds.). (2009). *Assessing writing: A critical sourcebook*. Boston: Bedford/St. Martin's and Urbana: National Council of Teachers of English.

Inoue, A. B. & Poe, M. (eds.). (2012). *Race and writing assessment*. New York: Peter Lang.

Kezar, A. & Maxey, D. (eds.). (2016). *Envisioning the faculty for the twenty-first century: Moving to a mission-oriented and learner-centered model*. New Brunswick, NJ: Rutgers University Press.

Lutzke, J., & Henggeler, M. F. (2009, November). The rhetorical triangle: Understanding and using logos, ethos, and pathos. Indiana University of Pennsylvania Writing Center. Retrieved from www.iupui.edu/~uwc The Rhetorical Triangle: Understanding and Using Logos, Ethos, and Pathos. https://liberalarts.iupui.edu/uwc/files/documents/Rhetorical_Triangle.pdf

Lynne, P. (2004). *Coming to terms: A theory of writing assessment*. Logan, UT: Utah State University Press.

Macrorie, K. (1988). *The I-Search Paper*. Revised edition of *Search Writing*. Portsmouth, NH: Heinemann.

Michigan State University School of Journalism. (2016). *To my professor: Student voices for great college teaching – What college students really say about their instructors, with advice from master educators and teacher trainers*. Canton, MI: Read the Spirit Books.

Oslund, C. (2014). *Supporting college and university students with invisible disabilities: A guide for faculty and staff working with students with autism, AD/HD, language processing disorders, anxiety, and mental illness*. Philadelphia: Jessica Kingsley.

Palmer, P. J. & Zajonc, A. (2010). *The heart of higher education: A call to renewal – transforming the academy through collegial conversations*. San Francisco: Jossey-Bass.

Pappas, G. F. (2008). *John Dewey's ethics: Democracy as experience*. Bloomington: Indiana University Press.

Piaget, J. (1977). *The essential Piaget*. (eds. H. E. Gruber & J. J. Voneche). New York: Basic Books.

Powell, P. R. (2013). *Retention and resistance: Writing instruction and students who leave*. Logan: Utah State University Press.

Scheuermann, J. A. (2018, February 5). Group vs. collaborative learning: Knowing the difference makes the difference. *Faculty focus: Higher ed teaching strategies*. Madison, WI: Magna.

Severino, C., Guerra, J. C., & Butler, J. E. (eds.). (1997). *Writing in multicultural settings*. New York: Modern Language Association of America.

Skinner, B. F. (1953). *Science and human behavior*. New York Simon and Schuster.

Sommers, N. (2013). *Responding to student writers*. Boston: Bedford/St. Martin's.

Suskie, L. (2009). *Assessing student learning: A common sense guide*. 2nd edition. San Francisco: Jossey-Bass.

Tatum, B. D. (2007). *Can we talk about race? And other conversations in an era of school resegregation*. Boston: Beacon.

Tomlinson, C. A. (1999). *The differentiated classroom: Responding to the needs of all learners*. Alexandria: Association for Supervision and Curriculum Development.

Villanueva, V., & Arola, K. L. (eds.). (2011). *Cross-talk in comp theory: A reader*. 3rd edition. Urbana: National Council of Teachers of English.

Vygotsky, L. (2012/1934). *Thought and language*. (eds. and trans. E. Hanfmann, G. Vakar, & A. Kozulin). Cambridge: Massachusetts Institute of Technology. Available as *Thinking and speech. The collected works of Lev Vygotsky* (Vol. 1). New York, NY: Plenum Press, 1987. Retrieved from https://www.marxists.org/archive/vygotsky/works/words/Thinking-and-Speech.pdf

Ward, I. (1994). *Literacy, ideology, and dialogue: Towards a dialogic pedagogy*. Albany: State University of New York.

Wiggins, G. & McTighe, J. (1998). *Understanding by design*. Alexandria: Association for Supervision and Curriculum Development.

Zebroski, J. T. (1989). A hero in the classroom. *Encountering student texts: Interpretive issues in reading student writing* (pp. 35–47). Urbana: National Council of Teachers of English.

Zebroski, J. T. (1994). *Thinking through theory: Vygotskian perspectives on the teaching of writing*. Portsmouth, NH: Boynton/Cook.

Figure A.7. Ticket Out

Index

$10 word 63, 139, 162–163, 165–166, 168–169, 172–173, 175–176

action verb 68, 83, 108, 117, 126, 184, 191
adjunction 3–4, 14, 148–149
adverbial conjunction 108, 111, 114, 125, 172, 174–175, 210, 211, 224–228
American Psychological Association (APA) 8, 60, 68, 77, 132, 168, 170, 172–173, 175–176
Anderson, Jeff 104, 210, 229
Arola, Kristin L. 80
attitude 11, 19, 21, 23, 56, 75, 180

Baker, Dusty 24
Bakhtin, Mikhail M. 73, 76, 78
Bale, Christian 192, 208
Barth, Roland S. 1, 161–162, 164–165, 167–168, 171–172, 175, 177, 180–182, 186–189, 214–228
Bartholomae, David 80
Batman 192, 208
Bean, John C. 3
Beard, Charles A. 192, 199
being verb 68, 83, 108, 117, 126, 184, 191
Berlin, James A. 80
Birkenstein, Cathy 3
Bizzell, Patricia 80
Bruffee, Kenneth A. 40
Burnham, Daniel 192, 197
Burton, Patricia 18
Butler, Johnella E. 5

Carroll, Lee Ann 3
Carter, Genesea M. 6
Chicago Cubs 24, 101
Christensen, Bonniejean 80
Christensen, Francis 80
citation 61, 67, 176
Clifty Falls State Park, Indiana 14, 129, 131
coach 10, 13, 17–19, 28–30, 54
Coffee Klatsch Collegial Conversation 10–11, 19, 37, 46, 48, 54, 61, 73, 87, 105, 130, 146, 153
college success 6, 10, 14, 147, 152
Collins, Marva 192, 198–199
Colorado fourteeners 1–2, 9, 14, 20, 22–23
complex (cx) sentence 23, 25, 69, 77, 83, 110, 112, 114, 117, 125, 127, 139, 144, 168, 172, 175–177, 181, 190, 210–212, 214–216, 229

compound (cd) sentence 23, 43, 77, 110, 112, 114, 117, 123–127, 139, 162, 168, 171–172, 175–177, 181, 190, 210–212, 214–216, 229
compound-complex (cd-cx) sentence 67, 109–110, 112–114, 125–127, 139, 144, 162, 165, 168, 171–172, 174–177, 181, 190, 210–212, 214–216, 229
conferencing 66–67
conjunction 69, 83, 97, 106–115, 117, 123, 125, 127, 142, 162, 165, 168, 172, 174–175, 191, 210–212, 216–229
constructive collusion 10, 13, 46–48, 51, 65
coordinating conjunction 23, 43, 110–114, 117, 123, 125, 127, 162, 168, 172, 175, 210–211, 216–218, 229

Davey Dogwoods Park, Texas 14, 104–106
Deadman's Hill, Michigan 14, 45–47
Dean, Deborah 104, 210
Delpit, Lisa 5
democratic classroom 40, 75–77, 80, 90–91, 94, 97, 99, 106, 132, 134, 140
dependent clause 43, 69, 83, 108–111, 125–126
developmental course 4, 6, 8, 11, 34, 37, 212
DeVries, Peter 128, 190
Dewey, John 72–73, 75–76, 78, 192, 196
dialogical classroom 79–80
dialogical interaction 60, 82, 91, 119, 212
dialogical process 5, 13, 76, 78, 80, 131, 163, 165, 176
Dickens, Charles 192, 208
Disney, Walt 102, 192, 205–206
diversity 6, 14, 33, 64, 75, 78, 87–88, 90, 92, 94–97, 119, 140, 150, 192, 202, 207
Doctorow, E. L. 143, 192, 207
Doe, Sue 6
drafting 58, 77, 139, 141
Drago-Severson, Eleanor 6
Dyson, Freeman 192, 202

Ebie, Gwyn 72, 75
editing 58, 136–137, 139, 142, 163, 166, 177
Egan, James 232
Elbow, Peter 45, 106
Empire Bluff Trail 18, 20
Eodice, Michele 106
essay draft 52, 59, 77
essay evaluation form 133, 140, 157–158, 159, 162–163, 165–166, 168, 170, 172–173, 175–177

Figure A.8. Calaveras Big Trees State Park in the Sierra Nevada, California.
Credit: Cathy Mulder

CPSIA information can be obtained
at www.ICGtesting.com
Printed in the USA
BVHW022243030720
582573BV00003B/49